AGING WELL IN ASIA
ASIAN DEVELOPMENT POLICY REPORT

MAY 2024

ASIAN DEVELOPMENT BANK

ADB

© 2024 Asian Development Bank
6 ADB Avenue, Mandaluyong City, 1550 Metro Manila, Philippines
Tel +63 2 8632 4444; Fax +63 2 8636 2444
www.adb.org

Some rights reserved. Published in 2024.

ISBN 978-92-9270-692-0 (print); 978-92-9270-693-7 (PDF); 978-92-9270-694-4 (e-book)
Publication Stock No. SGP240253-3
DOI: http://dx.doi.org/10.22617/SGP240253-3

The views expressed in this publication are those of the authors and do not necessarily reflect the views and policies of the Asian Development Bank (ADB) or its Board of Governors or the governments they represent.

ADB does not guarantee the accuracy of the data included in this publication and accepts no responsibility for any consequence of their use. The mention of specific companies or products of manufacturers does not imply that they are endorsed or recommended by ADB in preference to others of a similar nature that are not mentioned.

By making any designation of or reference to a particular territory or geographic area in this document, ADB does not intend to make any judgments as to the legal or other status of any territory or area.

Please contact pubsmarketing@adb.org if you have questions or comments with respect to content, or if you wish to obtain copyright permission for your intended use that does not fall within these terms, or for permission to use the ADB logo.

Corrigenda to ADB publications may be found at http://www.adb.org/publications/corrigenda.

Notes:
In this publication, "$" refers to United States dollars.
ADB recognizes "China" as the People's Republic of China, "Korea" as the Republic of Korea, "United States of America" as the "United States", and "Vietnam" as Viet Nam.

Cover design by Cleone Baradas.

Contents

Tables, Figures, and Boxes

TABLES

FIGURES

BOXES

Foreword

Population aging is a megatrend that will reshape the economic and social landscape of Asia and the Pacific in the decades to come. Across the diverse region, economies are experiencing demographic shifts at unprecedented speed, accompanied by increased longevity, changing epidemiological patterns, and evolving family structures. These are urgent challenges that no economy, regardless of its demographic stage, can afford to ignore.

Aging Well in Asia, an Asian Development Policy Report, explores how policymakers can strengthen the well-being of the region's older citizens. Despite considerable economic and social progress in reducing poverty among older people, the rapid expansion of this demographic demands proactive and tailored policies to ensure they age well.

There is ample scope for governments in Asia and the Pacific to promote old-age well-being. As detailed in the report, the Asian Development Bank (ADB) stands ready to support our members, helping them to achieve universal health coverage, invest in quality infrastructure, foster age-friendly urban development, reform pensions and social security, and build robust community-based long-term care systems. Further, ADB is ready to equip policymakers with the data and analysis needed for informed decision-making.

Through greater collaboration, I am confident that we can forge a future that respects and uplifts the dignity of every aging individual in Asia and the Pacific.

Masatsugu Asakawa
President
Asian Development Bank

Acknowledgments

I am pleased to present the inaugural *Asian Development Policy Report (ADPR)*. Examining regional progress toward achieving the timely goal of aging well, the report provides new data, analysis, and insights to better inform policy debate about population aging in developing Asia.

The *ADPR* is a new annual flagship publication launched to address major development challenges confronting Asia and the Pacific. We are confident that it will provide high-quality data and analysis to support evidence-based policy making that contributes to a prosperous, inclusive, resilient, and sustainable developing Asia.

The 2024 report, *Aging Well in Asia*, was prepared by staff of the Economic Research and Development Impact Department (ERDI) of the Asian Development Bank (ADB). ADB's Human and Social Development Sector Group and five regional departments provided background material and suggestions toward ensuring that the report spoke to the needs of policymakers in Asia and the Pacific.

This report was authored by an ADB team of ERDI economists: Aiko Kikkawa (lead), Donghyun Park (co-lead), Gemma Estrada, Minhaj Mahmud, Silvia Garcia Mandico, Arturo Martinez Jr., Martino Pelli, Lennart Reiners, and Paul Vandenberg. Data harmonization and visualization was provided by Filipinas Bundoc, Jade Laranjo, and Lilibeth Poot. Raymond Gaspar and Vasoontara Yiengprugsawan contributed box articles.

Guidance and support came from ERDI management: Deputy Director General Chia-Hsin Hu, Director Lei Lei Song, Deputy Chief Economist Joseph E. Zveglich Jr., and me. The report was refined through reviews and comments from Jinkook Lee, Sang-Hyop Lee, Philip O' Keefe, Yasuyuki Sawada, and Yaohui Zhao, who served as external expert reviewers; further comments and suggestions provided by Oleksiy Ivaschenko, Meredith Wyse, and Vasoontara Yiengprugsawan, who were ADB internal reviewers; and additional inputs from Rafal Chomik and John Piggott. Comments and suggestions from participants in the ADPR 2024 Background Papers' Workshop held on 2–3 October 2023 and the ADPR 2024 Review Workshop held on 6 March 2024 enhanced the first draft, as did review by Thanh Long Giang and Norma Mansor. The report benefited from technical support and comments from the ADB Office of the President and Board of Directors.

Background papers written for this report were authored by Jose Ramon G. Albert, Khadija Ali, Halimah Awang, Jose Albert Nino Bulan, Zeyuan Chen, Rafal Chomik, Lakshman Dissanayake, Gretchen Donehower, Isaac Ehrlich, Raymond Gaspar, Long Thanh Giang, Muqi Guo, Thanh Hoang, Aiko Kikkawa, Hyun Kyung Kim, Chi Kin Law, Sang-Hyop Lee, Zhiqiang Liu, Paul Kowal, Norma Mansor, Arturo Martinez Jr., Andrew Mason, Maki Nakajima, Nawi Ng, Philip O'Keefe, Naohiro Ogawa, Dwi Oktarina, Takashi Oshio, Cheol-Kon Park, Donghyun Park, Martino Pelli, John Piggott, Douglas Rhein, Lennart O. Reiners, Yana van der Meulen Rodgers, Yasuyuki Sawada, Iva Sebastian-Samaniego, Satoshi Shimizutani, Tetsushi Sonobe, Ni Wayan Suriastini, Mar Andriel Umali, Zhenglian Wang, Ika Yulia Wijayanti, Hanna Xue, Vasoontara Sbirakos Yiengprugsawan, Jiaying Zhao, Yi Zeng, Joseph E. Zveglich Jr., and me. The papers were edited by Ricardo Chan and are listed at the end of the report.

ADB technical assistance under the Japan Fund for Prosperous and Resilient Asia and the Pacific funded the research behind many of the background papers that informed this report, as well as the collection of microdata on older people in selected regional economies. Special thanks go to a team of regional scholars who joined the first regional comparative research program led by ADB, which examined the health capacity to work of older people in the region. Peter Fredenburg carefully edited the entire report. Joseph Manglicmot typeset and laid out the report, assisted by Alvin Tubio, and Tuesday Soriano proofread it. Cleone Baradas created the cover design and header graphics with input from Anthony H. Victoria. Aileen Gatson, Ana Kristel Lapid, Editha Lavina, Elenita Pura, and Priscille Villanueva provided administrative support. A team from the Department of Communications and Knowledge Management, led by David Kruger and Terje Langeland, coordinated report dissemination, with support from Lean Alfred Santos. Kevin Nellies and Ralph Romero designed the landing webpage.

Albert F. Park
Chief Economist and Director General
Economic Research and Development Impact Department
Asian Development Bank

Abbreviations

AAM	automatic adjustment mechanisms
ADL	activity of daily living
ADPR	Asian Development Policy Report
CHARLS	China Health and Retirement Longitudinal Study
COFACE	Confederation of Family Organisations in the European Union
COVID-19	coronavirus disease
DALY	disability-adjusted life year
FSM	Federated States of Micronesia
GDP	gross domestic product
HART	Health, Aging, and Retirement in Thailand
HALE	health adjusted life expectancy
IADL	instrumental activity of daily living
ILAS	Indonesia Longitudinal Aging Survey
ILO	International Labour Organization
ISSA	International Social Security Association
IOPS	International Organization of Pension Supervisors
KLoSA	Korean Longitudinal Study of Aging
Lao PDR	Lao People's Democratic Republic
LASI	Longitudinal Ageing Study in India
LE	life expectancy
LSAHP	Longitudinal Study of Ageing and Health in the Philippines
LTC	long-term care
MARS	Malaysia Ageing and Retirement Survey
NAP	National Academies Press
NCD	noncommunicable disease
OECD	Organisation for Economic Co-operation and Development

PRC	People's Republic of China
ROK	Republic of Korea
SDR	self-dependency ratio
SHRC	Silver Human Resources Center
UCW	unpaid care work
UHC	universal health coverage
UNESCAP	United Nations Economic and Social Commission for Asia and the Pacific
VNAS	Vietnam Aging Survey
WHO	World Health Organization

Definitions and Assumptions

The economies discussed in Asian Development Policy Report 2024 are classified by major analytic or geographic group. For the purposes of this report, the following apply:

- Association of Southeast Asian Nations (ASEAN) comprises Brunei Darussalam, Cambodia, Indonesia, the Lao People's Democratic Republic, Malaysia, Myanmar, the Philippines, Singapore, Thailand, and Viet Nam. ASEAN 4 are Indonesia, Malaysia, the Philippines, and Thailand.

- Developing Asia comprises 46 regional members of the Asian Development Bank listed below by geographic group.

- Caucasus and Central Asia comprises Armenia, Azerbaijan, Georgia, Kazakhstan, the Kyrgyz Republic, Tajikistan, Turkmenistan, and Uzbekistan.

- East Asia comprises Hong Kong, China; Mongolia; the People's Republic of China; the Republic of Korea; and Taipei,China.

- South Asia comprises Afghanistan, Bangladesh, Bhutan, India, Maldives, Nepal, Pakistan, and Sri Lanka.

- Southeast Asia comprises Brunei Darussalam, Cambodia, Indonesia, the Lao People's Democratic Republic, Malaysia, Myanmar, the Philippines, Singapore, Thailand, Timor-Leste, and Viet Nam.

- The Pacific comprises the Cook Islands, the Federated States of Micronesia, Fiji, Kiribati, the Marshall Islands, Nauru, Niue, Palau, Papua New Guinea, Samoa, Solomon Islands, Tonga, Tuvalu, and Vanuatu.

- Asia and the Pacific comprises the 49 regional members of the Asian Development Bank.

Unless otherwise specified, the symbol "$" and the word "dollar" refer to US dollars.

Highlights

1. The Well-Being of Older Asians to the Fore

- **Developing Asia is aging rapidly, with the pace accelerating in some economies.** Greater longevity is an achievement of long-term socioeconomic development in the Asia and Pacific region, but it also poses new challenges. While older people, those aged 60 and above, accounted for 13.5% of the regional population in 2022, that figure is expected to nearly double to 25.2% by 2050. While aging is more advanced in some economies, even relatively younger ones are facing rapid demographic transition. The unprecedented speed of population aging in Asia and the Pacific stands out, with the onset happening at lower incomes than when advanced economies faced this change. The speed of change in economies like the Republic of Korea (ROK) and the People's Republic of China (PRC) even outpaced earlier projections as birth rates plunged. A concern across the region is the risk that societies will grow old before they amass sufficient resources to adequately support their aging populations.

- **Absolute poverty for older people has declined, but relative poverty remains substantial.** Available data from 22 economies in developing Asia indicate that the incidence of extreme poverty among those aged 65+ declined from 13.1% in 2010–2015 to 3.2% in 2016–2022. This improvement mirrored a reduction in poverty across all age groups in the region. However, in many regional economies, relative poverty rates for older people exceed those of the entire population. Further, conventional poverty data may not capture some complexities of poverty for older people, such as being disadvantaged in resource allocation within households. Population aging may exacerbate inequality by widening income gaps between older people and between them and younger people.

- **Physical and mental health challenges become more acute with age.** Older persons face persistent burdens of lifestyle disease and heightened incidence of loneliness and social isolation, which is exacerbated by insufficient access to essential services such as health and long-term care. A new harmonized dataset on older people in nine economies in developing Asia found that on average 57% of older people have at least one diagnosed noncommunicable disease (NCD), but only 40% receive regular health checks and 43% of older people with functional limitation lack long-term care. Depression is widespread with 31% of older persons reporting elevated depressive symptoms, owing to illness, social isolation, and economic insecurity.

- **Pervasive informal employment and stark gender inequality further impede well-being in old age.** Up to 94% of workers aged 65+ in the region are employed in the informal sector. Informal workers enjoy little or no paid leave, disability allowance, or access to pensions. Many have little choice but to work as long as their health permits. Women can expect to live longer than men but are more prone to disease and therefore face insecurity in old age. Time spent on housework and family care constrains women's economic opportunity and leaves them more vulnerable in old age.

■ **A life-cycle and lifelong approach to policy will help to ensure the well-being of older people.** The sheer speed and scale of aging, coupled with the heightened vulnerability of older persons, underscores the urgency for the region to tackle the aging challenge. Four key dimensions of older persons' well-being are health, productive work, economic security, and social engagement. Among these dimensions, health—both physical and mental —is central to overall well-being as it keeps older people productive, economically secure, and socially engaged. Yet health in old age depends on choices individuals make over a lifetime, not just in old age. Thus, for younger and older alike, governments in the region can adopt policies and programs that encourage and enable choices that promote well-being in later years.

2. Health of Older People

■ **Extended life years are not necessarily all healthy ones.** Over the past 2 decades, life expectancy at age 60 in the region increased by more than 5 years. But the expected number of years lived in less than full health also rose in most economies. Meanwhile, the share of NCD in overall burden, mainly from coronary heart disease, stroke and diabetes remains high and exceeds 80% in all subregions. Over the past two decades, the disease burden from Alzheimer's and other forms of dementia increased by 7.8% in developing Asia, making dementia the seventh most prevalent health condition afflicting older people. The coronavirus disease (COVID-19) pandemic made it evident that older people with NCDs are more vulnerable to infectious disease, and they also are more affected by extreme weather events which are becoming more frequent with climate change.

■ **Older people, especially women, face high rates of noncommunicable diseases and depression.** The share of older people reporting at least one diagnosed NCD ranges from 35% to 68% across nine economies in the region. Diabetes and hypertension are universally higher in older women than men in these economies. For example, in Indonesia the share of older persons with hypertension is 12 percentage points higher for women and in Bangladesh the share with diabetes is 11 points higher. Women also are more likely to report elevated depressive symptoms. In the PRC where older people have the highest prevalence of elevated depressive symptoms, the shares are 43% of older women compared to 31% of older men.

■ **Universal health coverage must meet diverse health needs of older people.** While the ROK and Thailand have achieved universal health coverage, others lag behind with India having the lowest health insurance coverage among older people at 21%. Unequal access to health insurance is evident in other parts of the region. The Philippines and the PRC stand out for having relatively low coverage of poor older people. Those in the poorest quintile constitute 47% of all uninsured people in the Philippines and 35% in the PRC. In Bangladesh, Indonesia, and India, more than half of those without access to health care are in the bottom two wealth quintiles. In addition to making progress achieving universal health coverage, it also is critical to extend essential services and interventions that optimize older people's physical and functional capacity.

■ **Good health in old age can be ensured through promoting investments over a lifetime.** Healthy aging therefore requires consistent promotion of healthy diets and investment in primary care and health-care infrastructure, and the creation of an integrated system of health-care delivery to serve the needs of people of all ages. Free annual health checkups and lifestyle evaluations should be available to people of all ages. Comprehensive health awareness campaigns should be conducted regularly to promote healthy behavior including exercise, eating habits and nutrition. To reduce the consumption of unhealthy food products, sin taxes can be levied and enforced.

■ **Cost-effective mental health care is urgently needed in primary health-care systems.** Mental health services can be made accessible to older people by integrating them with NCD care in primary health-care systems, for example by facilitating use of digital mental health apps and platforms for remote consultations with specialists. Mental health also can be improved by addressing functional limitations. Simply providing eyeglasses, a hearing aid, or a walker can greatly improve their mental health, reduce their sense of isolation, and improve autonomy and self-esteem.

3.   Work and Retirement of Older Persons

■ **The labor force participation of people aged 65 and above was 32.0% for men and 15.2% for women on average in 2021, both of which exceeded those in advanced economies.** The rate has trended down for men since 2000, while rising for women in that period. Actual retirement age varies across the region from 51 to 63 years on average, with further variation within economies. Work and retirement patterns are notably different for workers in formal versus informal employment, and in rural versus urban areas.

■ **A large share of older people work in agriculture, which is mostly informal work.** The share of informal workers among older workers ranges from 64% to 99% in the region. Older women and people with less formal education are disproportionately employed in informal jobs. Workers who did not complete elementary school retire much later than those with higher education. Many of these workers work without basic labor protections in physically taxing jobs that put their health and well-being at risk as they age.

■ **At the same time, older people's capacity to work is a sizable untapped resource in the region.** Formal workers typically retire as soon as they become eligible for a pension, or even before, despite a substantial increase in healthy longevity. For men aged 55–69, the health-determined additional capacity to work is estimated to be between 0.3 and 2.2 years (or 4–26 months) in seven out of eight Asian economies studied. More than 80% of men aged 60–64 are healthy enough to work, but among this potential workforce, across different economies, 10%–23% are not employed. The silver dividend or additional productivity that could be gained from untapped work capacity among older persons is substantial and could equal up to 1.5% of gross domestic product in the economies studied.

■ **Policy action must address the vulnerability of older workers in the informal economy.** More targeted policies are needed across the region to improve the jobs available to older informal workers. In the short run, governments with large informal economies can take policy action that helps transition older informal workers, including those in agriculture, into jobs that are less physically demanding and more flexible. Such policies could promote automation or other technological solutions, upgrade workers' skills, and provide access to credit. Expanded basic labor protection should include accident and illness insurance, disability allowances, pensions, and programs that facilitate saving for retirement, which smooths the transition from work.

■ **Lifelong learning and other proactive labor policies can keep older people productive and employable.** Formal and informal workers alike benefit from lifelong learning that imparts employable skills and digital literacy. Governments can offer incentives for employers to hire and retain older workers. However, the low employment rates of older women are likely to continue until the gender imbalance in informal care burden is addressed. Policies that promote employment for older workers can mitigate some of the negative macroeconomic effects of population aging, notably declining workforce and rising expenditure on social security.

■ **Transitions from work to retirement should be more flexible.** Economies with an outdated statutory retirement age need to move it later or introduce more flexibility, while ensuring stronger social protection for those who lose their job before being able to access a pension. Flexible work arrangements, such as the option to work part-time, help older workers transition to retirement while ensuring that tax and pension systems do not unduly penalize those who work longer. Remuneration based on seniority, as is prevalent in many Asian economies, must be reformed to make the retention and hiring of older workers more affordable. Widespread ageism in Asian labor markets calls for legislation, improved monitoring and public awareness to change attitudes and perceptions.

4.   Economic Security in Old Age and Pensions

■ **Family transfers are still the main income support for many older people.** Despite a gradual shift toward more independent living arrangements, older people in the region still rely heavily on transfers and other forms of support from their families. These transfers account for at least a third of older people's income in most Asian economies, and often more than two-thirds. Changing social norms may alter these arrangements in the future, making financial preparedness increasingly critical to keep older persons out of poverty.

■ **Financial preparedness for retirement varies across the region.** An individual is considered financially prepared for old age if income, including from assets available for liquidation, meets consumption needs for the expected duration of retirement. A newly developed financial preparedness index shows the share of financially prepared near-old people—those within 5 years or so of retirement—to be as high as 86% in Japan and 73% in India, but somewhat lower at 64% in the PRC and 58% in the ROK. There is a wide rural–urban preparedness gap in the PRC with only 44% of rural residents prepared, barely half of the 82% of urban residents who are prepared. In India, the PRC, and the ROK, 80%–90% of financial resources for retirement come from private income and assets, not public pensions or social assistance.

■ **Contributory pensions have low coverage but social pensions help fill the gap.** Contributory pension coverage is generally low among older people at 19% on average in the region based on surveys. In many economies, coverage is substantially lower for women and rural residents, and even working-age enrollment languishes below 10% for some. Low coverage largely reflects the prevalence of informality. Noncontributory social pensions are a widespread response to low formal pension coverage. No fewer than 28 of 35 economies surveyed in developing Asia now have noncontributory social pensions. Coverage of social pensions is significantly higher than that of contributory pensions, reaching 46% of older persons, on average. These pensions include some income redistribution as coverage is highest in the poorest wealth quintiles, exceeding 30% in economies with available survey data. At the same time, the social pension coverage in the wealthiest quintile also exceeds 15% in almost all of these economies. Even where social pension coverage is high, low benefits mean modest impact on improving elder well-being.

■ **Governments must foster greater financial literacy, inclusion, and preparedness for retirement.** Financial literacy campaigns raise awareness and understanding of simple financial concepts such as compound interest. To help individuals make better financial decisions and become long-term savers, governments and financial institutions can leverage new behavioral insights that favor, for example, a narrow set of high-quality financial products over a bewildering array of options. Financial literacy brings the most benefits if achieved at an early age or introduced at the point of decision.

■ **Pensions will play greater roles in economic security as Asia ages.** The governments should expand contributory pension coverage to informal workers and increase coverage of social pensions among poorer old people. For contributory pensions, top policy priorities are to introduce schemes in which public funds are matched with the voluntary contributions of informal workers including women, expand coverage in the formal sector, and increase benefits for lower-income contributors through redistribution within programs. Reform should pay close attention to gender aspects of program design. Economies that lack social pensions should consider introducing them. Finally, pension systems can be made more efficient and effective by adopting innovative pension design and administrative tools such as the automatic adjustment of benefits based on demographic and economic indicators, introducing digital payment and auto-enrollment, and leveraging technology and behavioral insights.

5.   Family, Care, and Social Engagement

■ **As more older people in the region live alone, some of them will face greater vulnerability.** The share of older people living alone has increased by 17% since the turn of the millennia as fertility has fallen and longevity risen. A preference for independent living is expected to strengthen as living standards improve. However, some live alone involuntarily and are more vulnerable. Women's relative longevity and economic insecurity leaves more older women than men living alone, often in precarious circumstances.

■ **Older women and the poor have many unmet needs for long-term care, which are likely to increase as populations age.** Families will continue to play a pivotal role in old-age care, despite evolving social norms. Yet the current model of long-term care leaves large care gaps. Care needs are unmet for an average of 43% of older people with physical limitations, jeopardizing their well-being, with women and the poor being disproportionately affected. Without policy intervention, gaps in long-term care threaten to widen further with population aging, family shrinkage, and changing cultural norms.

■ **Social isolation is an emerging issue that requires more attention.** In the region, 16% of older people surveyed say they feel lonely most of the time, a condition often associated with depression. People who live alone tend to feel isolated. In different Asian economies, 10%–30% of older individuals report not having weekly contact with even one of their children, with older women having less social engagement than men.

■ **Support for family caregivers is essential to older people's well-being.** Long-term care systems should support aging in place. Many economies in the region have implemented low-cost community-driven interventions that provide community caregivers with information, counseling, and training. Such support should be extended to family caregivers, including older caregivers who are often excluded from these programs. Further, governments should provide respite care, which has proved very effective at alleviating the burden on family caregivers and thus improving the quality of care.

■ **Integrated care systems tap families, markets, and governments to provide seamless long-term care.** The provision of long-term care requires ensuring adequate human resources, by upskilling and formalizing informal caregivers and engaging youth and volunteers. Also critical is to integrate regional labor markets and facilitate well-regulated migration of caregivers across borders. A smooth transition requires that integrated care systems be financially viable. Sustained public contributions are required to earn public support and trust and to ensure system sustainability. Governments should develop national and community coordinating mechanisms to facilitate collaboration by the government, community stakeholders, and families. More evidence should be collected on how various policies can improve care system design and implementation.

■ **Social engagement in the community can prevent isolation.** Community health workers and social workers can be trained to identify vulnerable people, conduct needs assessments, and direct older people to appropriate community initiatives to promote their social engagement. Effective community-based initiatives include clubs for older people, volunteer and intergenerational activities, and cohousing solutions. Efforts should be made as well to remove barriers to social connectivity by developing age-friendly cities, investing in public transport, and reducing the digital divide that excludes older people.

6.   Living Well and Aging Well

■ **As Asia ages, it needs to step up efforts to help people age well.** Economic and social progress in the region has sharply reduced poverty, tangibly improved the quality of life, and significantly extended longevity. Yet the well-being of current and future cohorts of older people in the region remain at risk from multiple threats. Yawning inequality separates older citizens across all four dimensions of well-being: health, productive work, economic security, and social engagement. A key policy agenda across the region is to ensure the well-being of older people by helping them to age well. Well-being in old age can be enhanced by individuals' lifetime investment in their own health, education, skills, financial preparedness for retirement, and family and social ties. Policies for aging well should promote in particular healthy lifestyles, lifelong learning to update skills and learn new ones, and long-term financial planning for retirement.

■ **The four dimensions of well-being in old age are closely interconnected.** Some are inherently mutually reinforcing such as health and social engagement while others can create unintended consequences such as the work disincentives of pension benefits. Among the four dimensions of well-being, healthy aging is the overarching goal, critically influencing the other three. It is thus essential for governments to design and implement well-aligned and coordinated policy actions. The private sector can play an important role by creating age-friendly jobs, offering suitable financial products for retirement, and developing the care economy. Because an extensive knowledge gap bedevils aging issues across the region, policymaking would benefit from generating microdata on older people, collating administrative data, and rigorously evaluating programs and policies to better understand the costs and benefits of various policy options and interventions.

■ **A lifelong, life-cycle, population-wide approach is needed to meet the aging challenge.** This three-pronged strategy can help the region raise the well-being of its older citizens. A lifelong approach encourages continuous investment in human capital throughout people's lives. A life-cycle approach provides adequate interventions in accordance with age-specific needs. And population-wide outreach targets people of all ages. Comprehensive aging policies can ensure a healthy and productive older population offering a large silver dividend and other economic and social contributions.

■ **Governments can do more to empower their citizens to plan and prepare for old age.** They can disseminate information and raise awareness that helps workers of all ages set realistic expectations about future retirement needs, taking into account that future policies may change the retirement age and pension terms. They can also support initiatives that help firms and workers develop career plans and retirement paths in anticipation of longer working lives.

■ **Promoting well-being in old age has fiscal costs, but countermeasures can help contain them.** The expansion of health and long-term care services, and enhancement of pension coverage and adequacy, will entail substantial fiscal costs. Experience in advanced economies shows that expanded fiscal space is indispensable. Fiscal space can be augmented by strengthening tax revenue mobilization and promoting growth-oriented fiscal spending. Public and private investment in human capital—beginning in the cradle with preventative and curative health care, followed by lifelong education—can generate over time bigger silver dividends as healthy and educated older people become more productive. Retirement savings can be significant new sources of capital for productive investment that generates more economic growth and tax revenue.

- **Early investment is key for Asia to harness its silver dividend.** Future generations of older people will live healthier and longer lives and be more educated. To leverage their full potential to the benefit of their own well-being and the broader society, the time is now for Asian governments to take action to improve all four dimensions of well-being in old age. If they do this, people throughout Asia and the Pacific can aspire to live well and age well.

1 The Well-Being of Older Asians to the Fore

The well-being of older Asians comes to the fore. Rapid socioeconomic progress in developing Asia has enhanced the quality of life, lengthened lifespans, and lowered fertility rates, consequently aging the population. A key policy challenge facing the region now is to ensure the well-being of older Asians.[1] Well-being is a state in which various human needs are met in a holistic and multidimensional way. For older people, four interconnected dimensions of well-being are especially important: health, productive work, economic security, and social engagement.

This report examines the progress made in Asia and the Pacific toward achieving the goal of aging well and the challenges ahead. It proposes policy directions to improve the four major facets of well-being of older Asians. A person's well-being in old age reflects human capital investment and the various life choices one makes over a lifetime. Policy that promotes well-being in old age therefore needs to be directed toward people of all ages and throughout their lifetimes. Although the focus of this report is not the macroeconomic consequences of population aging, improving the well-being of older persons is key to maximizing their economic productivity and reducing social and economics costs of caring for older persons who have poor physical and mental health.

Absolute poverty has declined among older people, but relative poverty remains high in some economies. Data from 22 economies in developing Asia indicate that the incidence of absolute poverty among older Asians aged 65+ declined from 13.1% in 2010–2015 to 3.2% in 2016–2022, mirroring a reduction in absolute poverty overall across the region. However, the data also show relative poverty rates among older people often exceeding those of the whole population in a number of regional economies.[2] Further, conventional poverty data fail to capture fully the complexities of poverty affecting older people, who may be disadvantaged in, for example, accessing resources within a household. The analysis indicates that freedom from poverty is necessary for well-being, but not a guarantee.

Well-being in old age is at risk in many ways, not least from a lack of preparedness in the region. On average, 57% of older people in the region are reported to have at least one diagnosed noncommunicable disease, but only 40% attend regular health checkups, according to a new harmonized dataset on older Asians in nine economies in developing Asia (Box 1.1). In different regional economies, 94% of workers aged 65+ work in the informal sector, and 40% of older people have no access to either social or contributory pensions, while 43% of those with physical function impairments lack long-term care. Up to 31% of older people exhibit elevated symptoms of depression owing largely to illness, social isolation, and financial insecurity. Meanwhile, the region is unprepared for a rapidly unfolding demographic transition. Asian policymakers must address the aging challenge with urgency.

Two major regional challenges to well-being in old age are pervasive work informality and gender inequality. Few informal workers in the region have paid leave, insurance or other protection against illness and injury, disability allowance, or a pension or other savings option. Many have little choice but to work

---

1   In this report, older people are defined as those aged 60 years and over (UNESCAP 2022a), unless otherwise specified, usually as people aged 65 years and over, as dictated by the data source.

2   The relative poverty rate is defined as the share of the group living on less than half the economy's median disposable income.

Box 1.1: Harmonizing Aging, Health, and Retirement Surveys across Asia and the Pacific

To generate comparable descriptive data and analysis on the state of older people's well-being in the region, the Asian Development Policy Report (ADPR) compiled, harmonized, and merged surveys on population aging, health, and retirement in nine economies in East, Southeast, and South Asia: Bangladesh, India, Indonesia, Malaysia, the People's Republic of China, the Philippines, the Republic of Korea, Thailand, and Viet Nam. Building on an existing harmonization effort by the Gateway to Global Aging Data Project (g2aging.org),[a] ADPR data harmonization added more economies and included variables specific to Asia and developing economies. The surveys are nationally or regionally representative,[b] cover the most recent data available at the time of writing this report, and include respondent characteristics specific to aging. The nine economies in the dataset comprise 84% of all older people aged 60+ in Asia and the Pacific. The survey years range from 2017 to 2023 and some are more up-to-date than others.

For some economies, their data may not reflect the effect of recent policy reforms in areas such as health, labor, pension and long-term care.

The variables in the harmonized data range from basic demographic characteristics to social inclusion and expenditure, further covering issues specific to older people: family and living arrangements; physical, mental, and cognitive health; access to health and old-age care; ability to perform personal activities of daily living and household instrumental activities of daily living; pensions and retirement; family relationships; and participation in social activities. Some 200 harmonized variables are thus available to analyze a diverse set of issues related to aging. They are accompanied by technical information on sample weights, household structure, and currency conversion.

Overview of Harmonized Aging Data

Economy	Data Source	Survey Year	Sample Size	Data Owner/Custodian
Bangladesh	Mahbub Hossain Panel Data	2023	5,522	Ministry of Health and Family Welfare; and ADB
India	Longitudinal Ageing Study in India (LASI)	2017–2019	72,269	Ministry of Health and Family Welfare, National Programme for Health Care of Elderly; International Institute for Population Sciences; Harvard T. H. Chan School of Public Health; and the University of Southern California
Indonesia	Indonesia Longitudinal Aging Survey (ILAS)	2023	4,177	National Development Planning Agency; SurveyMeter, Lembaga Demografi; and ADB
Malaysia	Malaysia Ageing and Retirement Survey (MARS)	2021–2022	4,821	Employees Provident Fund, the Social Security Organisation; ADB; and Social Wellbeing Research Center
People's Republic of China	China Health and Retirement Longitudinal Study (CHARLS)	2018	19,816	National School of Development, Peking University
Philippines	Longitudinal Study of Ageing and Health in the Philippines (LSAHP)	2018	5,985	Demographic Research and Development Foundation, Inc.; and Economic Research Institute for ASEAN and East Asia
Republic of Korea	Korean Longitudinal Study of Aging (KLoSA)	2018	6,940	Korea Employment Information Service, Ministry of Health and Welfare

continued on next page

Table *continued*

Economy	Data Source	Survey Year	Sample Size	Data Owner/Custodian
Thailand	Health, Aging, and Retirement in Thailand (HART)	2020	2,863	National Institute of Development Administration
Viet Nam	The Survey on Older Persons and Social Health Insurance	2019	4,333	Ministry of Health; ADB; and Institute of Social and Medical Studies
	Vietnam Aging Survey (VNAS)	2022	3,183	

ADB = Asian Development Bank, ASEAN = Association of Southeast Asian Nations.

Source: ADB.

To make the analysis comparable across economies, data harmonization followed three steps. First, a set of harmonized variables was identified in a survey harmonization matrix according to the broad themes of the report. Second, each individual questionnaire was reviewed and mapped to the matrix. Compatibility between questions and answer choices was examined across the nine economies and then standardized, mostly at the lowest denominators of disaggregation. Finally, the survey variables were recoded according to the chosen harmonized variable definitions before being merged into a single data file. The resulting dataset thus consists of variables that are comparable across economies and includes about 130,000 respondents aged 40 and over. While not every variable is available for every economy, most of the information is consistently coded and readily available. A harmonized micro-dataset of older people enables the well-being and characteristics of various groups of older people to be evaluated, with comparisons across economies of various indicators of well-being. The dataset does not, however, allow detailed comparisons of older people against populations younger than age 40. It excludes as well older people in residential care or hospitals, as well as those constrained from expressing themselves due to impaired physical or cognitive function.

[a] This initiative harmonized and combined 11 datasets on aging from around the world to facilitate cross-country, longitudinal analyses.

[b] All datasets except that of Indonesia are nationally representative. The Indonesia dataset is regionally representative covering West Sumatera, Lampung, Special Region of Yogyakarta, East Java, Bali and South Sulawesi, West Java, South Kalimantan, and Mollucas.

Source: Asian Development Bank.

as long as their health permits. Workers who did not complete elementary school, for example, retire on average 2 years later than those with upper secondary and tertiary education. Older women can expect to live longer than men, but they are more prone to disease. Gender inequality has narrowed in some areas, but persists institutionally in pensions, which are tied to the contribution periods of formal employees, and in cultural norms that impose informal household and care burdens on women in particular, limiting their economic opportunities and leaving them vulnerable in old age.

A key challenge facing the region is how to ensure the well-being of older Asians. Income alone falls short as a measure of well-being. The governments in the region must create an environment conducive to furthering all four aspects of well-being: physical and mental health, productive work, economic security, and social engagement. In particular, healthy aging is central to well-being in old age. Good health drives productivity and economic security while promoting older people's active social engagement and reducing their need for long-term care. Comprehensive aging policies should foster healthy and productive cohorts of older people to maximize their contribution to the economy and society.

1.1 | Asia's Aging Population

Developing Asia is transitioning toward a much older demographic structure. The region's share of older people in the whole population rose from 5.9% in 1960 to 8.2% in 2000 and 13.5% in 2022. The population aged 60 and above is forecast to double from 567.7 million in 2022 to 1.2 billion in 2050, when it will account for 25.2% of the regional population (Figure 1.1). Further, 55.6% of the world's older population will live in developing Asia by 2050. Asia's aging will affect a wide range of economic and social indicators, including economic growth (see Annex) and fiscal balances.[3]

Some economies in developing Asia are aging rapidly, while others are undergoing a more gradual transition. In 2022, older people's share of the population exceeded 20% in 8 of 46 regional economies: Hong Kong, China; the Republic of Korea (ROK); Taipei,China; Georgia; Niue; Singapore;

Thailand; and Armenia (Figure 1.2). The speed of aging, measured by the number of years required for the share of older people to double from 10% to 20%, has been rapid in Singapore at 17 years, Thailand 18 years, and the ROK 19 years. Of the 38 economies that have not yet reached the 20% threshold, 13 will do so by 2050. Among them, the transition is expected to take 13 years in Maldives; 16 years in Brunei Darussalam; and 21 years in Azerbaijan, Bhutan, and Palau. By 2050, 20 economies in developing Asia will have 20% shares, 22 economies will have shares above 10%, and 4 economies—Afghanistan, Pakistan, Solomon Islands, and Vanuatu—will still have shares lower than 10%.[4] In some areas, the speed of demographic transition is outpacing earlier projections. Differences between transition duration projections made in 2000 and actual transitions are 4 years for Hong Kong, China, with 36 years projected against 32 years actual; 3 years for the ROK and Thailand; and 2 years for the People's Republic of China (PRC).

Figure 1.1: Population Shares by Age Group, Developing Asia

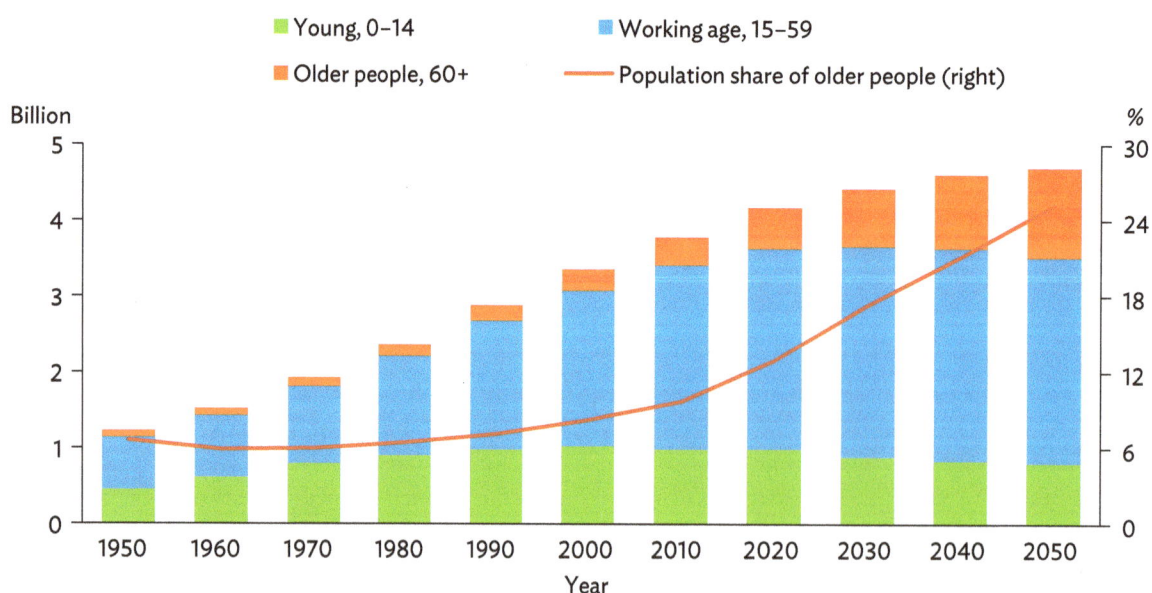

Note: Projections assume a medium-fertility scenario.

Source: Asian Development Bank estimates using data from the United Nations, Department of Economic and Social Affairs, Population Division. 2022. World Population Prospects 2022 Online Edition (accessed 2 August 2023).

---

[3]   Lee, Kim, and Park (2017) forecast that demographic change will have a significant impact on fiscal sustainability in Asian economies.

[4]   ADB placed on hold its regular assistance to Afghanistan effective 15 August 2021. This report was prepared based on information available for Afghanistan as of 31 July 2021 or obtained from external sources.

Figure 1.2: Population Share of Older People in Developing Asia

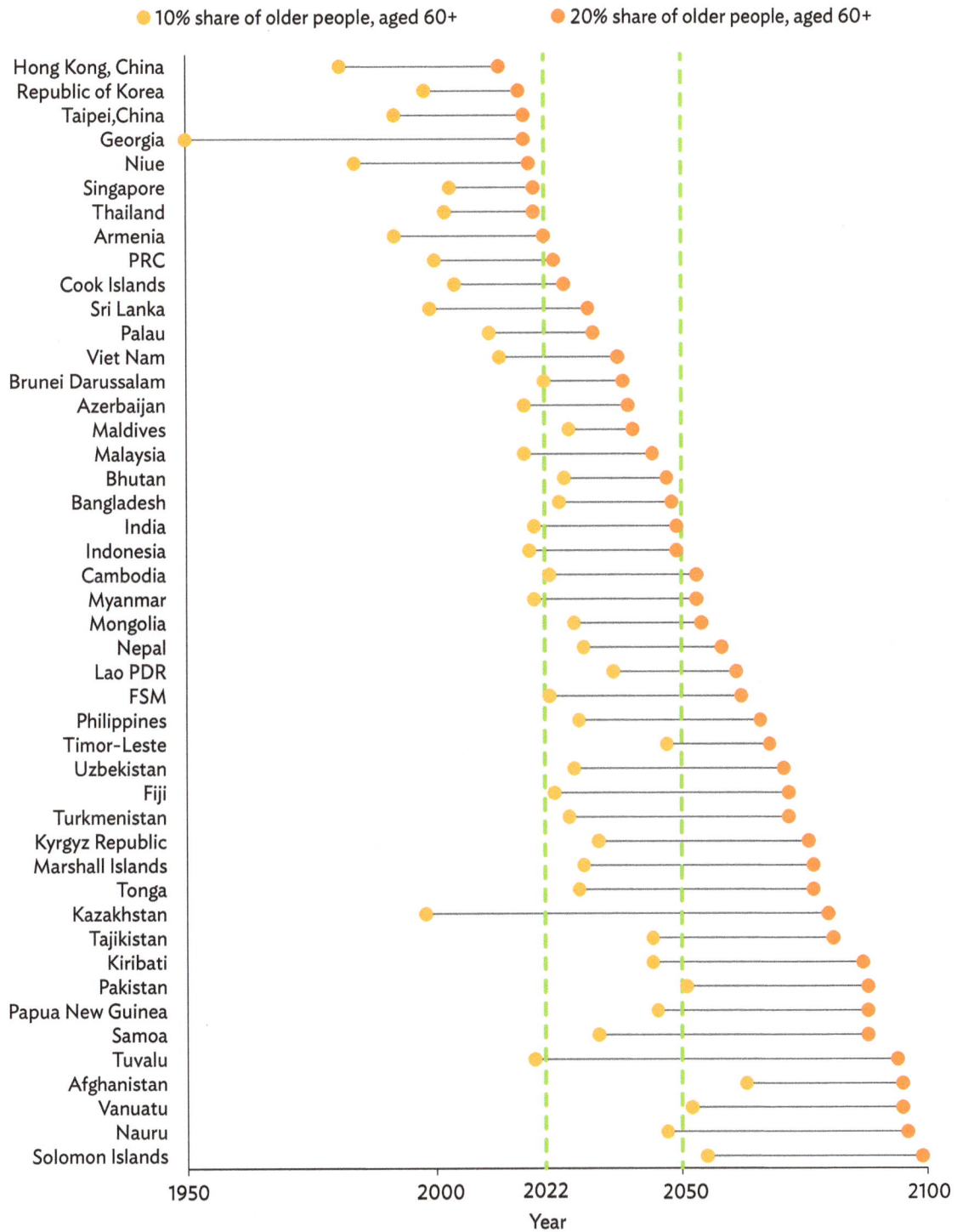

FSM = Federated States of Micronesia, Lao PDR = Lao People's Democratic Republic, PRC = People's Republic of China.

Note: Developing Asia reached the threshold of 10% older people aged 60+ in 2013 or 2014, which coincided with it becoming an "aging society," defined as one with 7%–14% of the population aged 65+ (UNESCAP 2022).

Source: Asian Development Bank estimates using data from United Nations, Department of Economic and Social Affairs, Population Division. 2022. World Population Prospects 2022, Online Edition (accessed 2 August 2023).

Over the next few decades, even regional economies with younger populations are expected to transition to much older demographic profiles. Old-age dependency ratios are projected to double in several economies by 2050, which means a huge decline in the number of working age adults to support older populations (Figure 1.3). Asian economies in the middle range will experience dramatic shifts in population age structure as fertility rates decline and longevity lengthens. In Cambodia, the Philippines, and Uzbekistan, fertility rates are currently high at 2.3–2.8 live births per woman, but will fall by 2050 (Figure 1.4). Across the region, projections to 2050 are for fertility rates to either decline or remain low.

Figure 1.3: Old-Age Dependency Ratio, Selected Asian Economies with Younger Populations

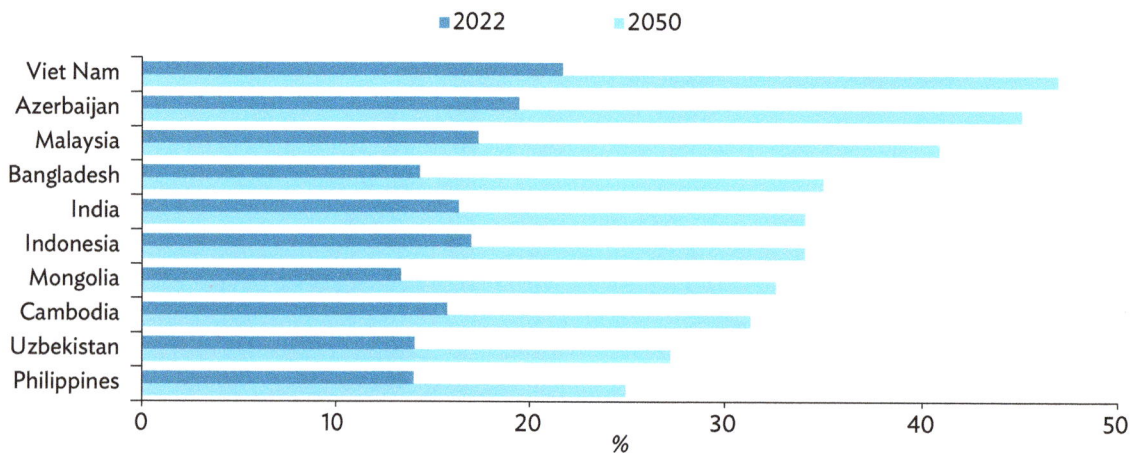

Note: The old-age dependency ratio is the population in the old-age group, defined as 60+, over the population aged 15–59.

Source: Asian Development Bank estimates using data from United Nations, Department of Economic and Social Affairs, Population Division. 2022. World Population Prospects 2022, Online Edition (accessed 2 August 2023).

Figure 1.4: Fertility Rates in Developing Asia and Selected Younger Economies

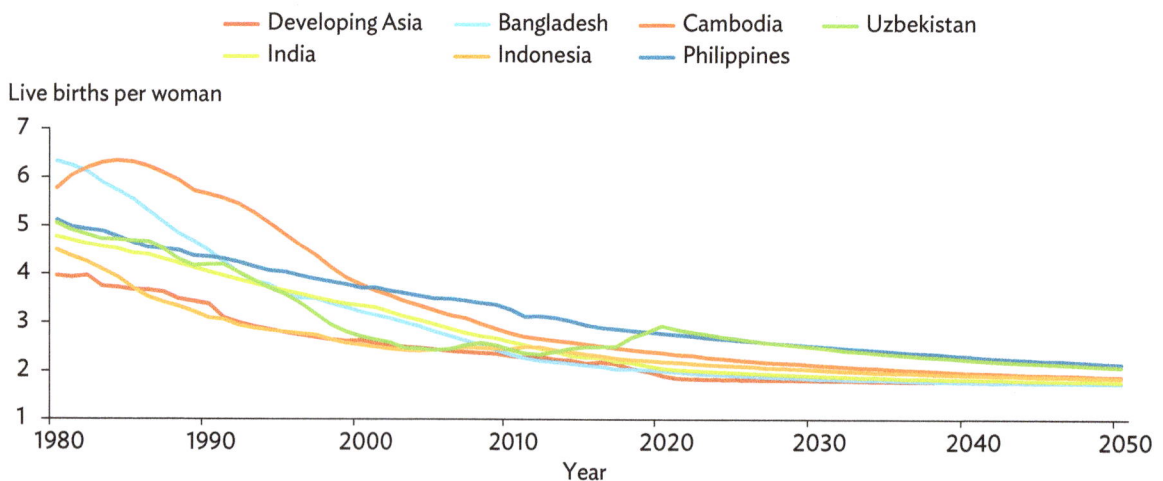

Note: Projections assume a medium-fertility scenario.

Source: United Nations, Department of Economic and Social Affairs, Population Division. 2022. World Population Prospects 2022, Online Edition (accessed 2 August 2023).

Life expectancy at age 60 in the region is expected to rise by 3.7 years for women and 4.1 years for men from 2022 to 2050. This will raise the average regional life expectancy at age 60 from 21.6 to 25.3 years for women and from 18.2 to 22.3 years for men. Older women in India will see the greatest increase in life expectancy at 6.4 years, followed by Kazakhstan; Georgia; and Hong Kong, China at 4.6 years (Figure 1.5). For older men, Armenia will have the highest increase in life expectancy at 6.1 years, followed by India at 5.7 years and Georgia at 5.2 years. In 33 of 46 regional economies, increases in life expectancy to 2050 will be greater for older women than for older men.

Figure 1.5: Life Expectancy at Age 60

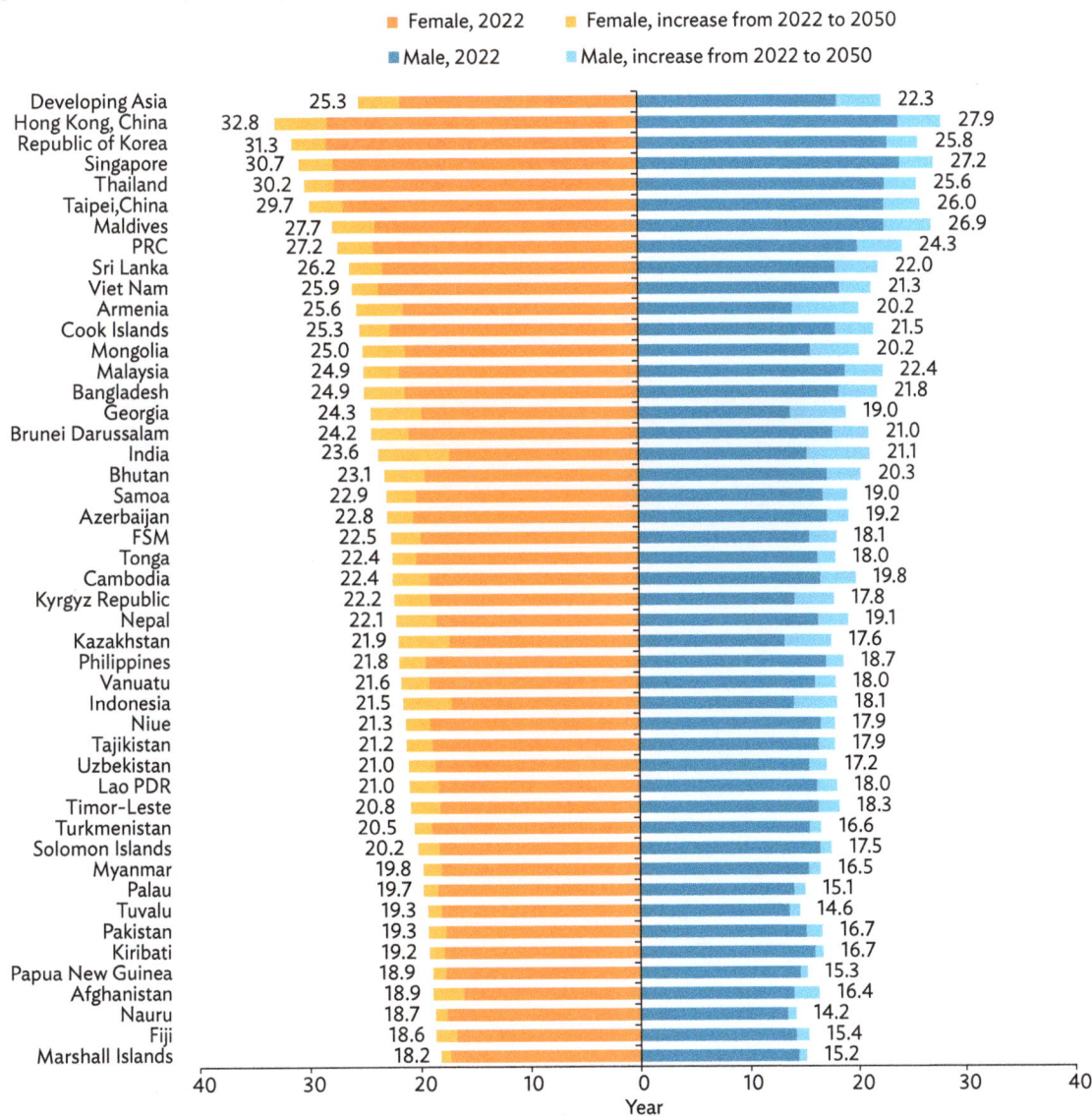

FSM = Federated States of Micronesia, Lao PDR = Lao People's Democratic Republic, PRC = People's Republic of China.

Note: The data use a medium-scenario projection and the average number of years expected by a hypothetical cohort of individuals alive at age 60, who are subject during the remaining of their lives to the mortality rates of a given year. The number beside each bar refers to the life expectancy at age 60 in 2050.

Source: Asian Development Bank estimates using data from United Nations, Department of Economic and Social Affairs, Population Division. 2022. World Population Prospects 2022, Online Edition (accessed 2 August 2023).

1.2 Changing Profile of Older People

The profile of older people in the region is undergoing profound change, as older people today differ from those of the past. One clear positive development is improved human capital among older Asians, evidenced by their improved educational attainment and literacy. Life expectancy is increasing, especially for women, and pushing up the share of the oldest old and the share of women in the cohort of old people. Meanwhile, challenges are arising for older people as living arrangements shift from extended families toward more diverse patterns, including one-person households and couples. Those who live alone are at a greater risk of poverty than those who live with family members. This study considers how these and other trends affect older Asians.

1.2.1 Age and Gender Composition

Skewed gender distribution in the older group will moderate somewhat toward greater representation of older men. From 1980 to 2022, life expectancy at

age 60 rose by 4.7 years for women and by 3.5 years for men. Older women consequently outnumber older men, with the gap widening for the very old. Going forward, however, skewed sex ratios at birth favoring boys in some areas will raise the share of males in middle age and older cohorts (Figure 1.6). Even then, older women will outnumber older men in all cohorts, but especially among the older old.

A marked change in older populations is an increasing share of the oldest old. The share of those aged 80 and above, the oldest old, in the older population reached 11.6% in 2022, or 65.7 million individuals. This share will climb further to 21.0% in 2050, reaching nearly 250 million (Figure 1.7). The region will require greater resources to provide health and long-term care for the oldest old.

By subregion, East Asia will have the highest share of the oldest old in 2050. Economies in Southeast Asia and the Pacific will also see large increases in the oldest old by 2050. Ten economies in Figure 1.7 will see their share of the oldest old in the top 20%. Such rapid aging is a sign of development and success, but it also creates greater challenges ahead to address the needs of older populations.

Figure 1.6: Age Distribution, by Gender in Developing Asia

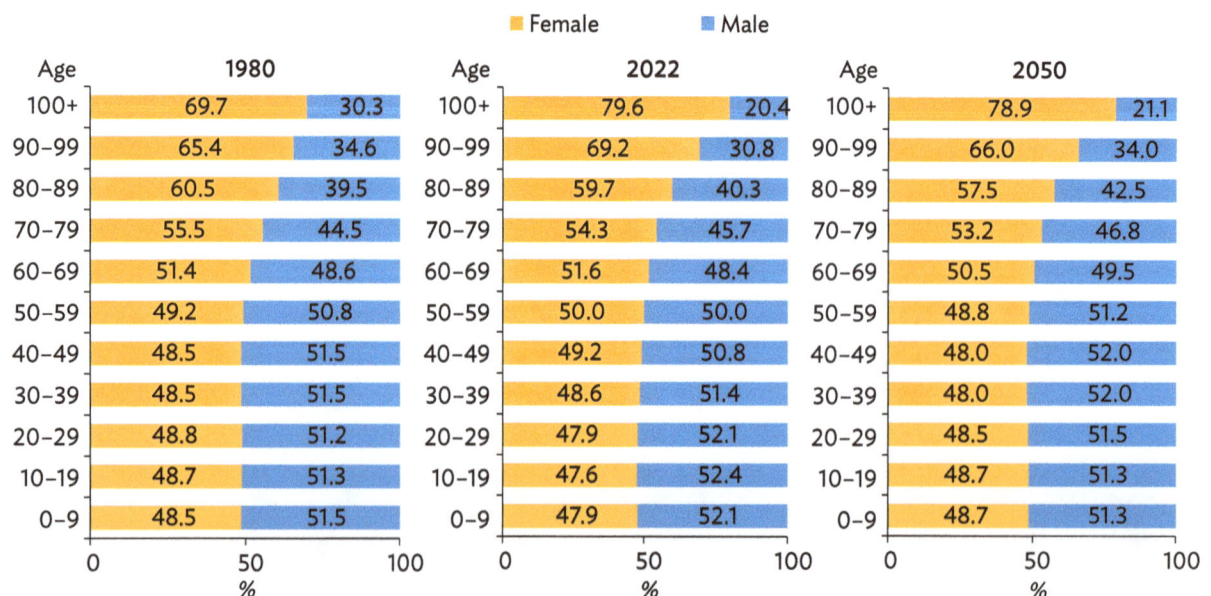

Source: Asian Development Bank estimates using data from United Nations, Department of Economic and Social Affairs, Population Division. 2022. World Population Prospects 2022, Online Edition (accessed 2 August 2023).

Figure 1.7: Share of the Oldest Old in Older Populations

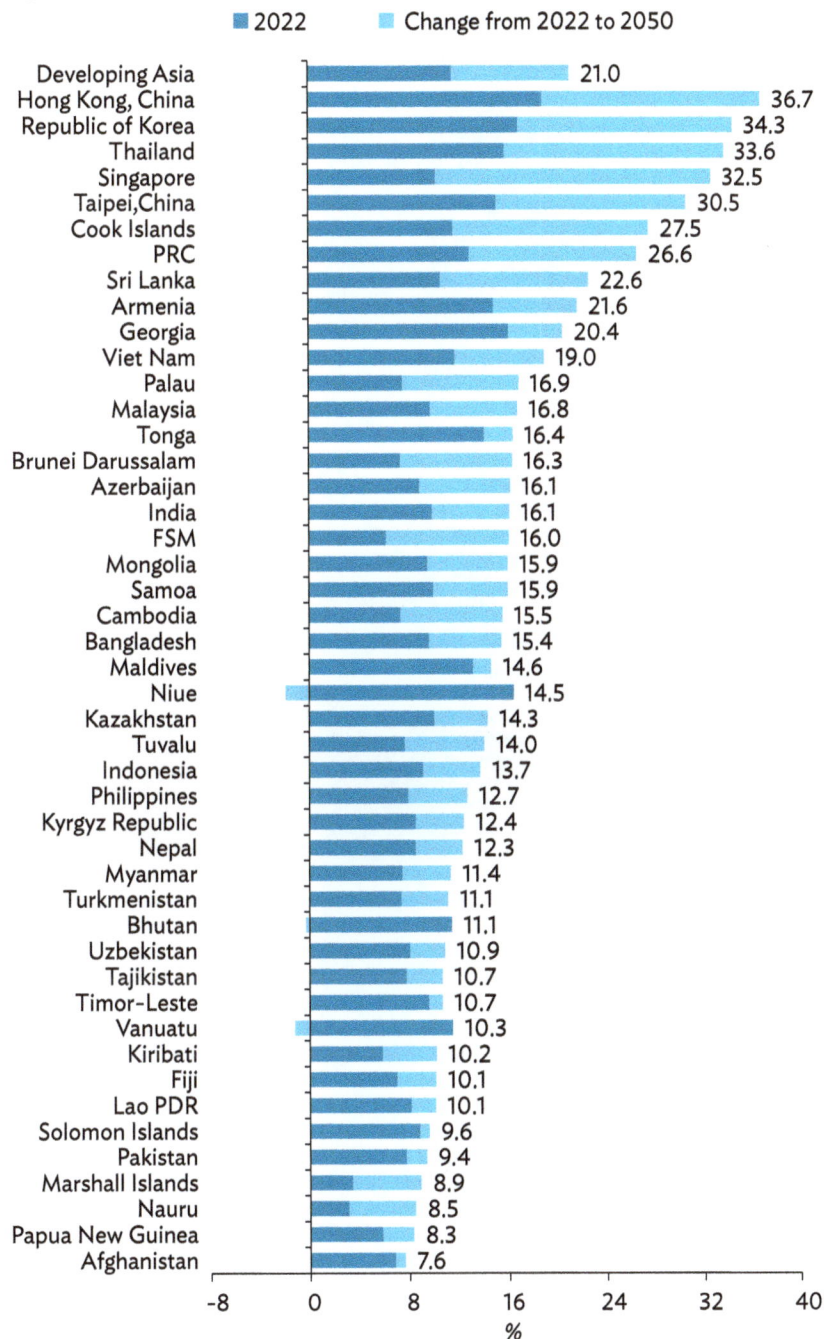

■ 2022   ■ Change from 2022 to 2050

Country	Value (2050)
Developing Asia	21.0
Hong Kong, China	36.7
Republic of Korea	34.3
Thailand	33.6
Singapore	32.5
Taipei,China	30.5
Cook Islands	27.5
PRC	26.6
Sri Lanka	22.6
Armenia	21.6
Georgia	20.4
Viet Nam	19.0
Palau	16.9
Malaysia	16.8
Tonga	16.4
Brunei Darussalam	16.3
Azerbaijan	16.1
India	16.1
FSM	16.0
Mongolia	15.9
Samoa	15.9
Cambodia	15.5
Bangladesh	15.4
Maldives	14.6
Niue	14.5
Kazakhstan	14.3
Tuvalu	14.0
Indonesia	13.7
Philippines	12.7
Kyrgyz Republic	12.4
Nepal	12.3
Myanmar	11.4
Turkmenistan	11.1
Bhutan	11.1
Uzbekistan	10.9
Tajikistan	10.7
Timor-Leste	10.7
Vanuatu	10.3
Kiribati	10.2
Fiji	10.1
Lao PDR	10.1
Solomon Islands	9.6
Pakistan	9.4
Marshall Islands	8.9
Nauru	8.5
Papua New Guinea	8.3
Afghanistan	7.6

%

FSM = Federated States of Micronesia, Lao PDR = Lao People's Democratic Republic, PRC = People's Republic of China.

Notes: Older populations are aged 60+, and the oldest old aged 80+. The number at the end of each bar refers to share of the oldest old in 2050.

Source: Asian Development Bank estimates using data from United Nations, Department of Economic and Social Affairs, Population Division. 2022. World Population Prospects 2022, Online Edition (accessed 2 August 2023).

1.2.2 Education and Literacy

The current generation of older adults are more educated than same-age cohorts 4 decades ago. The average years of schooling for older Asians increased from 1.5 years in 1980 to 5.7 years in 2020 (Figure 1.8).[5] By subregion, average schooling rose rapidly in the Caucasus and Central Asia—especially in Armenia, Georgia, and Tajikistan—to reach 10–12

years in 2020. In East Asia, Mongolia, the ROK, and Taipei,China also experienced remarkable progress in schooling, adding 6.5–7.7 years to achieve an average of 9–10 years of schooling in 2020. In Southeast Asia, additional years of schooling varied from a low of 0.9 years in Timor-Leste to a high of 7.7 years in Singapore. In the Pacific, the Federated States of Micronesia was a standout performer, with years of schooling rising from less than 1 year in 1980 to 8.6 years by 2020.

Figure 1.8: Average Schooling Years for Older People Aged 60+

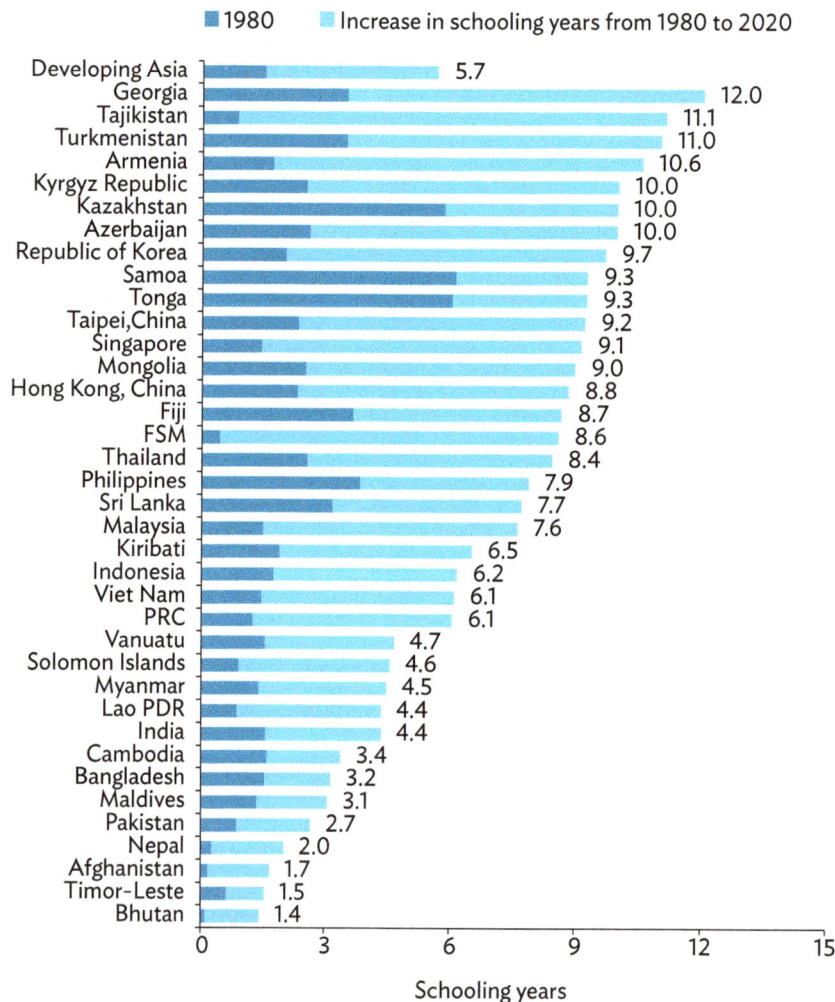

Legend: ■ 1980   ■ Increase in schooling years from 1980 to 2020

Country	2020
Developing Asia	5.7
Georgia	12.0
Tajikistan	11.1
Turkmenistan	11.0
Armenia	10.6
Kyrgyz Republic	10.0
Kazakhstan	10.0
Azerbaijan	10.0
Republic of Korea	9.7
Samoa	9.3
Tonga	9.3
Taipei,China	9.2
Singapore	9.1
Mongolia	9.0
Hong Kong, China	8.8
Fiji	8.7
FSM	8.6
Thailand	8.4
Philippines	7.9
Sri Lanka	7.7
Malaysia	7.6
Kiribati	6.5
Indonesia	6.2
Viet Nam	6.1
PRC	6.1
Vanuatu	4.7
Solomon Islands	4.6
Myanmar	4.5
Lao PDR	4.4
India	4.4
Cambodia	3.4
Bangladesh	3.2
Maldives	3.1
Pakistan	2.7
Nepal	2.0
Afghanistan	1.7
Timor-Leste	1.5
Bhutan	1.4

Schooling years

FSM = Federated States of Micronesia, Lao PDR = Lao People's Democratic Republic, PRC = People's Republic of China.

Note: The number at the end of each bar refers to the schooling year in 2020.

Source: Asian Development Bank calculations based on data from Wittgenstein Centre for Demography and Global Human Capital. Wittgenstein Centre Human Capital Data Explorer (accessed 19 November 2023).

---

[5]   This was calculated from data on 37 economies in developing Asia from Wittgenstein Centre for Demography and Global Human Capital. Wittgenstein Centre Human Capital Data Explorer (accessed 19 November 2023).

Years of schooling for older people will further rise by 2.9 years from 2020 to 2050 to reach 8.6 years. Improved literacy among older people reflects expanded access to schooling. The average literacy rate for those aged 65 and over in the region improved from 61.3% in 2010–2014 to 71.3% in 2019–2022 (Figure 1.9). More education means more economic opportunity in old age. This comes from better access to decent jobs and enhanced capacity for training and reskilling. Further, education diversifies choice and offers a greater sense of purpose in life, supports social relationships, and enhances social and economic rights.

1.2.3 Living Arrangements and Family Ties

Family and living arrangements for older people are becoming more diverse, with more solitary households and couples. The extended family household with multiple generations has traditionally been the common living arrangement for older individuals. The share of extended-family households in the region is still high but declining. Not surprisingly, some studies find that living with one's children and grandchildren helps sustain older people's physical and mental health and well-being (Rodgers et al. 2024). Overall, findings are inconclusive, however, as

Figure 1.9: Literacy Rates for Older People Aged 65+

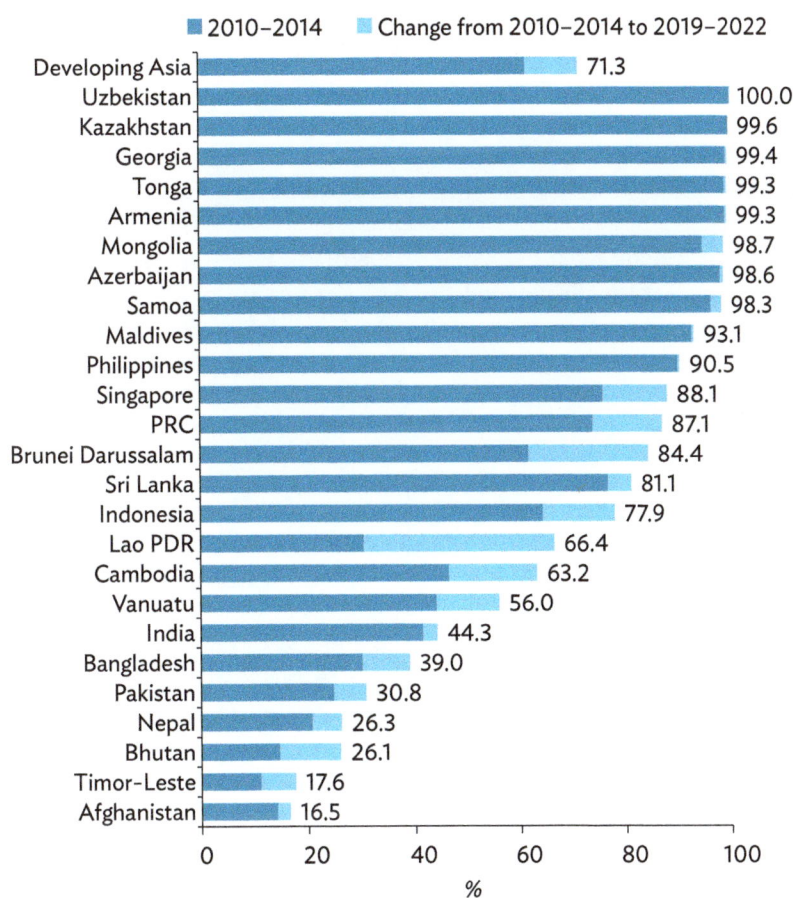

	2010–2014	Change from 2010–2014 to 2019–2022
Developing Asia		71.3
Uzbekistan		100.0
Kazakhstan		99.6
Georgia		99.4
Tonga		99.3
Armenia		99.3
Mongolia		98.7
Azerbaijan		98.6
Samoa		98.3
Maldives		93.1
Philippines		90.5
Singapore		88.1
PRC		87.1
Brunei Darussalam		84.4
Sri Lanka		81.1
Indonesia		77.9
Lao PDR		66.4
Cambodia		63.2
Vanuatu		56.0
India		44.3
Bangladesh		39.0
Pakistan		30.8
Nepal		26.3
Bhutan		26.1
Timor-Leste		17.6
Afghanistan		16.5

Lao PDR = Lao People's Democratic Republic, PRC = People's Republic of China.

Note: The number at the end of each bar refers to literacy rate in 2019–2022.

Source: Asian Development Bank calculations based on data from United Nations Educational, Scientific and Cultural Organization. Sustainable Development Goal 4 (accessed February 2023 and November 2023).

significant variation exists across the region (Ichimura et al. 2017; Nakajima et al. 2024). One factor that explains this variation is that richer, more educated older Asians often prefer to live with their spouse, separate from but near their children. Chapter 5 discusses in detail the changing family structures and living arrangements for older people and their effect on well-being.

1.3 Aging and Poverty

Poverty undermines the well-being of older people in several ways. Poverty may mean eating less food and/or food of lower nutritional quality. It can mean not being able to pay for health care. As poverty and financial insecurity can trigger anxiety and depression (Ridley et al. 2020), not being poor is prerequisite to aging well. Inequality between the old and the rest of the population, and among the old generally, grows as a consequence of population aging, and this can diminish the well-being of older Asians.

Absolute poverty has declined among older people in developing Asia, mirroring poverty decline overall in the region. Data from 22 economies in developing Asia indicate that absolute (extreme) poverty among Asians aged 65 and over declined from 13.1% in 2010–2015 to 3.2% in 2016–2022 (Albert et al. 2024).[6] Rapid economic growth in developing Asia dramatically reduced rates of extreme poverty from 58.1% in 1990 to 15.6% in 2011 and 5.7% in 2019. Further, the percentage of people living in moderate poverty in developing Asia fell from 84.4% in 1990 to 44.1% in 2011 and 24.7% in 2019. However, the crises caused by COVID-19 and the subsequent inflation have set back poverty reduction. In 2020, the percentage of people living in extreme poverty in developing Asia increased to 6.9%, and in moderate poverty to 26.2% (Figure 1.10).[7]

Absolute poverty affecting older people is in decline in most Asian economies. Figure 1.11 shows age-disaggregated rates of extreme poverty among older people and the general population across economies in developing Asia. The decline in extreme poverty among older people reflects poverty reduction in the region as a whole, with notably steep declines in Indonesia and the Lao People's Democratic Republic, but rates still high in Bangladesh, the Federated States of Micronesia, Solomon Islands, and Timor-Leste. Poverty rates for older people are generally lower than for the population as a whole.

Poverty statistics may fail to capture important aspects of the poverty status of older persons. While conventional poverty data can shed light on trends, they may not consider some factors that are important for older people, in particular differences in intra-household resource allocation, individuals' varying needs and costs, and household economies of scale (Deaton and Paxson 1995, 1997).

Absolute poverty has declined for older people in developing Asia, but relative poverty is high. Relative poverty rates for older people tend to be higher than for other demographic groups (see footnote 2). Recent data show relative poverty rates for older people higher than for children or for the population as a whole in the PRC, the ROK, Viet Nam, and Taipei,China (Figure 1.12). Relative poverty is a manifestation of income inequality. In Asia, overall inequality has increased (Huang, Morgan, and Yoshino 2019), and rising inequality is partly driven by population aging (Deaton and Paxson 1994; Ohtake and Saito 1998). Inequality among older people could worsen as more educated and skilled people accumulate more wealth and earn higher returns than those with less education and skills. Population aging may worsen inequality by increasing the relative poverty rate of older people in the whole population and within the older group.

---

[6]   Those in extreme poverty live on less than $2.15 a day (expressed in 2017 dollars at purchasing power parity), and those in moderate poverty on less than $3.65.

[7]   Compared with pre-pandemic numbers, or projections of what would have transpired if these crises have not occurred, at least 67.8 million more people lived in extreme poverty in developing Asia in 2022 (ADB 2023a).

Figure 1.10: Absolute Poverty Incidence, Developing Asia versus Other Regions

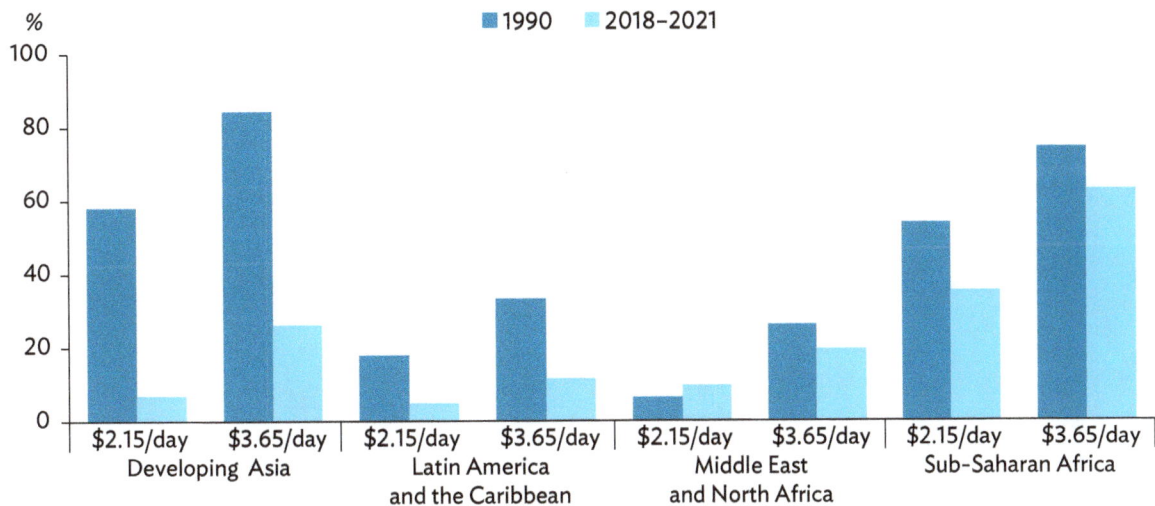

Note: The later year is 2018 for the Middle East and North Africa, 2019 for Sub-Saharan Africa, 2020 for Developing Asia, and 2021 for Latin America and the Caribbean.

Sources: Asian Development Bank. Key Indicators Database and World Bank. Poverty and Inequality Platform (both accessed 13 March 2024).

Figure 1.11: Incidence of Absolute Extreme Poverty among Older People and in the General Population in Developing Asia

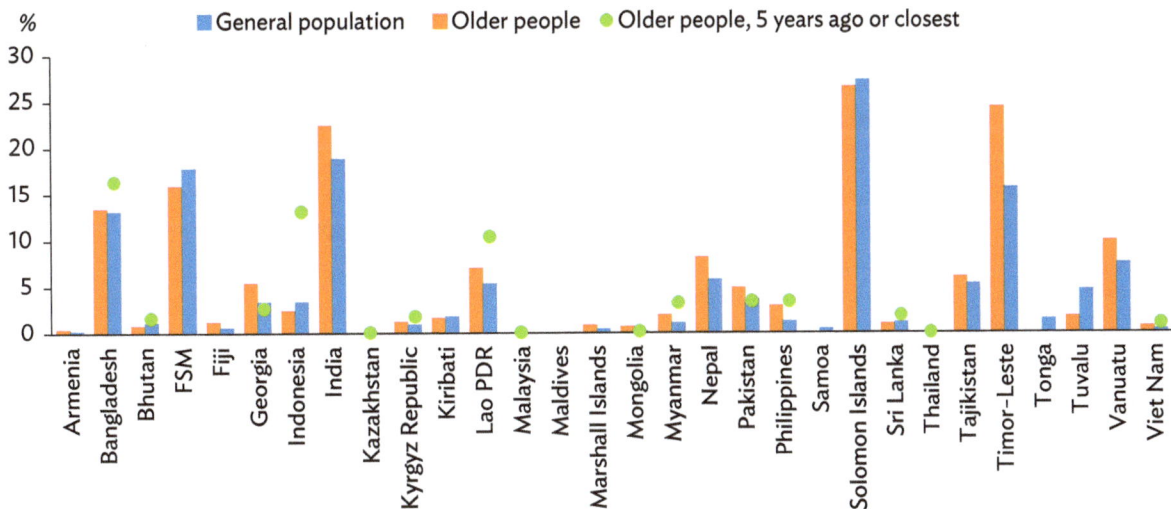

FSM = Federated States of Micronesia, Lao PDR = Lao People's Democratic Republic.

Note: Reference years range from 2010 to 2022. They are 2021 for Armenia, 2016 and 2010 for Bangladesh, 2017 and 2012 for Bhutan, 2013 for the FSM, 2019 for Fiji, 2021 and 2015 for Georgia, 2022 and 2015 for Indonesia, 2011 for India, 2018 and 2015 for Kazakhstan, 2020 and 2015 for the Kyrgyz Republic, 2019 for Kiribati, 2018 and 2012 for the Lao PDR, 2018 and 2015 for Malaysia, 2019 for Maldives, 2019 for the Marshall Islands, 2018 and 2014 for Mongolia, 2017 and 2015 for Myanmar, 2010 for Nepal, 2018 and 2015 for Pakistan, 2018 and 2015 for the Philippines, 2013 for Samoa, 2012 for Solomon Islands, 2019 and 2012 for Sri Lanka, 2021 and 2015 for Thailand, 2015 for Tajikistan, 2014 for Timor-Leste, 2015 for Tonga, 2010 for Tuvalu, 2019 for Vanuatu, and 2020 and 2014 for Viet Nam.

Sources: United Nations, Department of Economic and Social Affairs. SDG Indicators Database (accessed 8 May 2023).

Figure 1.12: Relative Poverty Rates in Some Asian Economies, Latest Available Year

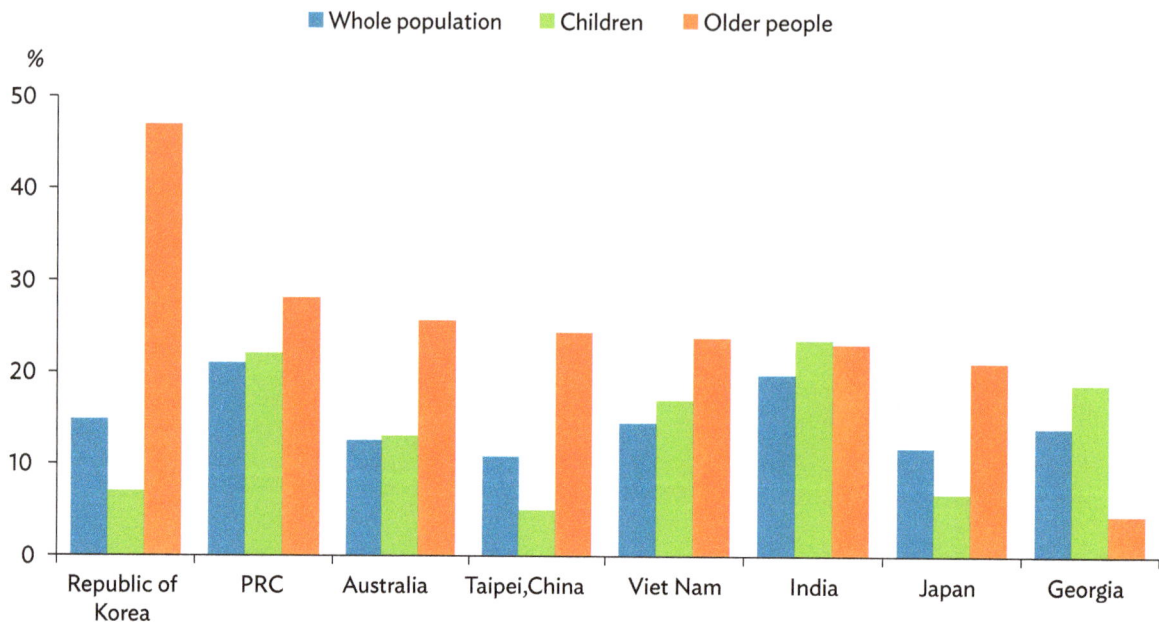

PRC = People's Republic of China.

Notes: The relative poverty rate is the share of the group living on less than half of the median disposable income in the economy (definition adopted from the Organisation for Economic Co-operation and Development iLibrary). Reference years range from 2011 to 2021. They are 2011 for Viet Nam; 2013 for India; 2016 for Japan; 2018 for the PRC and the Republic of Korea; 2019 for Australia; and 2021 for Georgia and Taipei,China.

Source: LIS Cross-National Data Center in Luxembourg. LIS Inequality and Poverty Key Figures (accessed 12 September 2023).

Old-age poverty may be underestimated because research ignores intra-household resource allocation. A number of empirical studies in Asia find that intra-household resource allocation decisions tend to disfavor older household members, especially women. Using household data from Bangladesh to quantify the extent of consumption inequality within families, Brown, Calvi, and Penglase (2021) found that older women faced a significantly higher probability of living in poverty even in households with expenditure per capita above the poverty line. Even worse, Paudel (2021) found a large increase in allowances under a nationwide senior citizen program in Nepal associated with reduced food consumption by women, even though it increased the likelihood of financial assistance by 64.4%. Strikingly, eligible female beneficiaries were 8.8% more likely to eat fewer meals and 5.3% more likely to go to bed hungry. This unforeseen consequence was partly explained by higher allowances attracting would-be beneficiaries and thus generating larger households, which reduced the resources available to older women. In neighboring

India, Calvi (2020) used a natural experiment to show that a prime cause of the high and excess poverty and mortality rates among older women was their declining bargaining power within the household as they aged, and their consequently reduced share of household resources.

1.4 Well-Being of Older People

Well-being encompasses quality of life and its potential, which depend on factors beyond the traditional notion of poverty. Well-being is achieved when various human needs are met in a holistic and multidimensional way. It is strongly linked to happiness and life satisfaction as well as to functioning effectively and, in particular, to having the capacity to develop one's potential, gain some control over one's life, find purpose in life, and experience positive relationships (Huppert 2009).[8]

Well-being cannot be measured in terms of gross domestic product per capita alone. This basic economic measure fails to capture adequately other dimensions that matter to individuals. The Organisation for Economic Co-operation and Development (OECD), for example, provides a comprehensive framework for understanding and measuring people's well-being (OECD 2011, 2020b). The OECD framework for well-being includes several dimensions that relate to the material conditions that affect people's economic options, as well as quality-of-life factors that embody how healthy people are, what they know and can do, and how wholesome and safe their living environments are. The framework also considers how connected and engaged people feel, and how and with whom they spend their time.[9]

1.4.1 Defining Well-Being in Old Age

Three challenges complicate the use of a detailed framework like the OECD's to measure the well-being of older people in developing economies. The first challenge is whether the framework is able to capture the varying social and cultural values and heterogeneous institutional settings that often affect well-being. Second is whether such a framework can be directly applied to measure well-being in the subset of people at the specific life stage called old age. The third is a lack of detailed and standardized data across economies to derive detailed indicators.

Subjective well-being is a state of mind or cognitive assessment of life satisfaction or happiness. Researchers have suggested various subjective measures of well-being—evaluative (assessment of life satisfaction), hedonic (positive or negative

feeling), eudaimonic (meaning or purpose in life), and experiential (feeling during specific activities)—but have raised numerous methodological concerns (Lee and Park 2024). Despite continuing methodological debates, the body of empirical literature on this topic continues to grow. Researchers have studied happiness around the world (Deaton 2008; De Neve et al. 2018; Helliwell et al. 2023), in Europe or the United States (Easterlin 2006; Fonseca et al. 2013, 2014); and in transition economies (Guriev and Melnikov 2018; Clark, Yi, and Huang 2019; Cai, Park, and Yip 2021). Some studies focus on Asian economies, providing an overview of the active pursuit of activities, wellness, and lifestyles that promote health in the region (Park et al. 2021). One widely used direct measure of subjective well-being is a life-satisfaction scale based on survey questions on how satisfied the respondent is with life (Diener et al. 1985). Life satisfaction measures well-being in a positive light, while other examples of survey-based indicators of well-being measure deviation from well-being caused by physical, mental, economic and other distress, and manifested as depression, loneliness, and anxiety. It is important to consider both well-being and "ill-being," as the causal factors may be different. For example, social background affects ill-being more, while social networks affect well-being more (Headey, Holmstrom, and Wearing 1985).

Several dimensions shape the well-being of people in general, but for older people four dimensions are critical (Figure 1.13).[10] The key determinants of well-being and ill-being in older people in Asia can be categorized into four key determinants based on the literature (Ichimura et al. 2017; Teerawichitchainan, Pothisiri, and Long 2015; Nakajima et al. 2024; Kwak and Lee 2024). First, well-being in older people is strongly associated with physical and mental health, especially given vulnerability to chronic illnesses. Good health goes beyond the absence of disease to include physical and mental health, as well as physical mobility

---

[8] Well-being is distinct from wellness, which is largely about physical health. Wellness entails being actively engaged in activities, choices, and lifestyles to achieve a state of holistic health (Global Wellness Institute 2018).

[9] The OECD well-being framework includes over 80 well-being indicators that reflect the 11 dimensions of current well-being and four capitals of future well-being. The 11 dimensions for current well-being are (i) income and wealth, (ii) work and job quality, (iii) housing, (iv) health, (v) knowledge and skills, (vi) environmental quality, (vii) subjective well-being, (viii) safety, (ix) work–life balance, (x) social connections, and (xi) civil engagement. The capitals of future well-being are (i) natural capital, (ii) economic capital, (iii) human capital, and (iv) social capital.

[10] Similarly, Ichimura et al. 2017 found four categories of well-being elements in old age: demographic, economic, social, and health.

and functions (WHO 1948). A second dimension is productivity through work for those who are able and willing to do so; finding fulfillment from work, either paid or unpaid, such as caregiving and volunteering; and contributing to society. A third dimension is economic security, which means having adequate income and wealth including a pension to finance one's consumption in old age. A fourth dimension that enhances older people's well-being is social engagement and meaningful interaction with family.

These four dimensions are interlinked and mutually reinforcing as they affect well-being in old age. As this report explores in the following chapters, health largely determines a person's physical capacity to work. Health includes mental health, which may be affected by social engagement. One's willingness to work may also be affected by the availability of a pension to allow retirement with dignity. Therefore, a shortcoming in one area may hamper the achievement of other elements of well-being, and effective policy reform in one area can positively affect other areas. This argues for well-integrated aging policies and programs.

Quantitative analysis confirms that health, economic security, and social engagement matter to the life satisfaction of older persons in the region. Empirical analysis shows that, among the four dimensions of well-being in old age, self-reported health and physical functionality are by far the most influential determinants of well-being (Kikkawa et al. 2024a). Social engagement in the form of living with a spouse and one's children lifts the well-being of older people as much as having income and assets. Other dimensions, including work and receiving a contributory pension, were not statistically significant, likely reflecting their more complex effects on well-being, which are either positive, negative, or neutral depending on the context (Box 1.2).

Figure 1.13: Four Dimensions of Well-Being in Older People

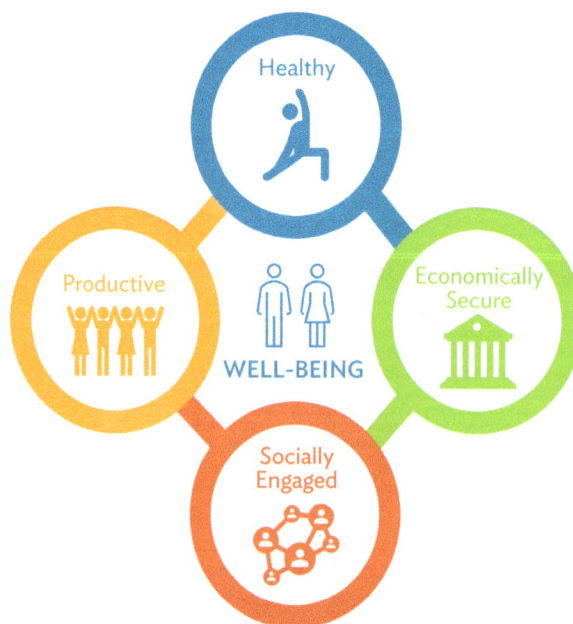

Source: Asian Development Bank.

Box 1.2: Predictors of Well-Being and Life Satisfaction

The predictors of well-being in older Asians are examined using the satisfaction-with-life scale.[a] This indicator is available for five economies included in the Asian Development Policy Report (ADPR) harmonized aging data: India, Malaysia, the People's Republic of China, the Republic of Korea, and Viet Nam. The box figure illustrates the results of a multivariate analysis, validating the significance and magnitude of known predictors of life satisfaction on the four areas of well-being in old age.

Life satisfaction increases with age. An increase in the age of an older person has a statistically significant positive association with life satisfaction scores. The effect is small, but recurs every year. This is consistent with a recognized U-shaped relationship between life satisfaction and age (Blanchflower 2021). No significant difference is found in

life satisfaction in older men versus older women, whichcontrasts with other evidence showing that older women generally report higher life satisfaction than their male peers (Helliwell et al. 2023).

Education is key to an older person's well-being. A higher educational attainment, at least at lower secondary school, is significantly associated with greater life satisfaction in old age. This finding is consistent with studies that show education to be positively correlated with self-reported quality of life (Farzianpour et al. 2015; Schwingel et al. 2009). Education plays a crucial role in well-being through improved income and employment opportunities throughout life and into old age. It also increases one's ability to plan and save for old age.

Life Satisfaction in Older People

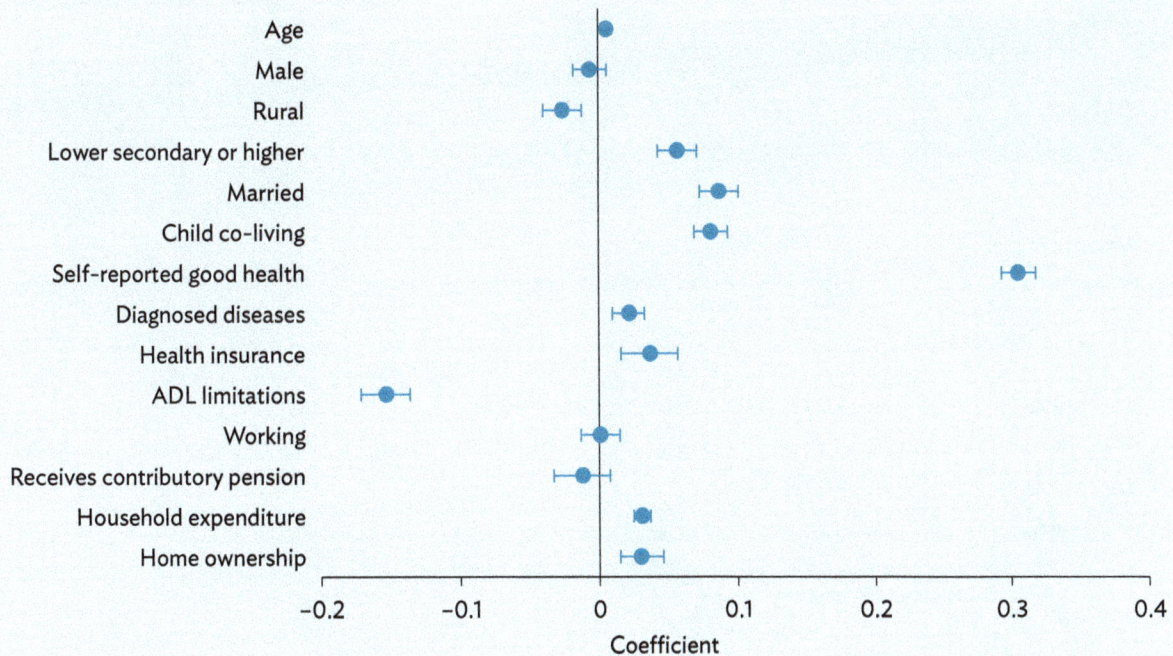

ADL = activity of daily living.

Notes: The dependent variable captures respondents' self-reported life satisfaction on a scale of 1–3, ascending from not satisfied to satisfied and very satisfied (sample mean: 2.35, standard deviation: 0.67). The regression includes an interaction term between working and pension, which is insignificant. Household expenditure is presented as the log of expenditure per household member. The regression is estimated using ordinary least squares. Harmonized sampling weights applied. The sample includes data on older people aged 60+ in India, Malaysia, the People's Republic of China, the Republic of Korea, and Viet Nam. N = 48,565.

Source: Kikkawa et al. (2024a).

continued on next page

Box 1.2 *continued*

Health indicators are the strongest predictors of life satisfaction. Self-assessed good health is significantly associated with a 0.3 point higher life satisfaction score, which is considerable, given that the mean is 2.35, and its standard deviation is 0.67. Also, poor physical health and functional impairment in performing daily living activities are associated with a satisfaction score 0.15 points lower. Counterintuitively, a diagnosis of diabetes, hypertension, or heart disease is associated with greater life satisfaction— one possible explanation being that older people with a diagnosed disease receive more care and attention (Finlay and Kobayashi 2018). In addition, disease diagnosis is consistent with better access to health-care services and a better social and economic circumstance than may be the norm for older Asians.

Paid work and contributory pensions are not associated with the well-being of older persons. Results show no significant association between paid work and well-being, perhaps suggesting that the effect of employment on the well-being of older people depends on the nature of the job or reasons for working. High-quality jobs may increase satisfaction, but this effect may be canceled out by those with low-quality and undesirable jobs. Certainly, low-paying and physically demanding work can undermine the mental and physical health of older people (Henseke 2018).

It may also be true that some people enjoy work, while others prefer retirement. Chapter 3 of this report looks at how work affects well-being in old age. A pension is normally important for providing income in old age, but very low contributory pension coverage in the region, as discussed in Chapter 4 of this report, may explain why pensions have no statistically significant effect on well-being, either positive or negative.

Social engagement matters a lot for an older person's well-being. Being married and living with one's children positively affect life satisfaction. There is large variation across the region, however, in how living arrangements affect well-being in old age. Chapter 5 of this report discusses living arrangements, older people's family and social engagement, and the impact on their well-being.

Some notable differences exist across economies on how various dimensions of well-being affect life satisfaction. Notable variations are associated with gender, educational attainment, urban versus rural residence, and living with one's children, and how they affect life satisfaction.

[a] The scale in the present analysis is ordinal: 1 indicating not satisfied with life, 2 somewhat satisfied, and 3 very satisfied (Diener et al. 1985; Kikkawa et al. 2024a).

References:

Blanchflower, D. G. 2021. Is Happiness U-Shaped Everywhere? Age and Subjective Well-Being in 145 Countries. *Journal of Population Economics*. 34.

Diener, E. D., R. A. Emmons, R. J. Larsen, and S. Griffin. 1985. The Satisfaction with Life Scale. *Journal of Personality Assessment*. 49(1).

Farzianpour F., A. R. Foroushani, A. Badakhshan, M. Gholipour, and M. Hosseini. 2015. Evaluation of Quality of Life and Safety of Seniors in Golestan Province, Iran. *Gerontology and Geriatric Medicine*. 1.

Finlay, J. M. and L. C. Kobayashi. 2018. Social Isolation and Loneliness in Later Life: A Parallel Convergent Mixed-Methods Case Study of Older Adults and Their Residential Contexts in the Minneapolis Metropolitan Area, USA. *Social Science Medicine*. 208.

Helliwell, J., R. Layard, J. D. Sachs, J-E. De Neve, L. B. Aknin, and S. Wang, eds. 2023. *World Happiness Report*. Gallup, the Oxford Wellbeing Research Centre and the United Nations Sustainable Development Solutions Network.

Henseke, G. 2018. Good Jobs, Good Pay, Better Health? The Effects of Job Quality on Health among Older European Workers. *European Journal of Health Economics*. 19(1).

Kikkawa, A., M. Pelli, L. Reiners, and D. Rhein. 2024a. *The Determinants of Well-Being of Older Persons: A Comparative Study across Developing Asia*. Asian Development Bank.

Schwingel, A., M. M. Niti, C. Tang, and T. P. Ng. 2009. Continued Work Employment and Volunteerism and Mental Well-Being of Older Adults: Singapore Longitudinal Ageing Studies. *Age and Ageing*. 38(5).

Source: Kikkawa et al. (2024a).

1.5 Conclusion

The policymakers in Asia and the Pacific must act urgently to improve well-being in old age. Lack of preparedness risks leaving behind older Asians as the region pursues rapid economic progress. However, development that neglects such a large and growing segment of the population cannot be inclusive. Policymakers must work closely with current and future generations of older Asians to improve well-being across four dimensions: health, work and retirement, economic security, and social engagement. Even in younger economies, the time to start preparing is now because the demographic landscape will change dramatically in the future. While absolute poverty among older Asians has declined, the policy objective for Asian governments should be to ensure well-being, defined using a more comprehensive measure of the quality of life.

The changing profile of older people creates both challenges and opportunities. The growing prevalence of living alone, for instance, increases the risk of old-age poverty. On the other hand, improving the educational attainment of older Asians augments their productive capacity and opens up new economic opportunities. Higher productivity not only improves their own well-being, but also expands the productive capacity of the entire economy. This, in turn, helps the economy cope with the economic consequences challenges associated with rising dependency ratios caused by population aging.

This report is organized as follows. The next four chapters present the current state and effect on well-being in old age of physical and mental health (Chapter 2), work and retirement (Chapter 3), financial preparedness and pensions, (Chapter 4), and family, care, and social engagement (Chapter 5). Each chapter discusses progress in the region toward achieving the goal of aging well and identifies priority policy actions. To generate comparable descriptive data and analysis on the state of older people's well-being in the region, the Asian Development Policy Report compiled, harmonized, and merged surveys conducted in nine regional economies on population aging, health, and retirement. Box 1.1 provides more information on the data sources and the data harmonization process.

2

Health of Older People

A key facet of well-being is good health. Good health is not merely the absence of disease. Health is a multidimensional concept that encompasses physical and functional status, including the capacity to perform daily activities, mental health and cognitive functioning, and self-assessed health. The World Health Organization (WHO) defines healthy aging as developing and maintaining the functional ability that enables well-being in old age. The health status of older people varies greatly, compared with younger people. Self-assessments of health provide information about individuals' own perception of their health at a given time, which reflects their underlying medical condition and can be used as a valid indicator of objective health status.[11]

This chapter discusses various dimensions of old-age health to inform policy recommendations. Using available datasets, the analysis begins by looking at cross-country comparisons of the population health status of older people: life expectancy, healthy life expectancy, and the disease burden on older people from infectious disease and noncommunicable disease (NCD), including mental and cognitive disorders.[12] It then presents the physical health, health behavior, functional abilities, mental health, and self-assessed health of older people using the latest available survey data from nine Asian economies, accounting for 82% of older people living in Asia and the Pacific (Chapter 1, Box 1.1). Health-seeking behavior, access to health care, and global and regional policy initiatives on healthy aging, including the role of effective universal health coverage are also examined. Finally, specific policy recommendations are presented.

2.1 Extended Life Expectancy and Health in Older Populations

Life expectancy at birth has risen globally and in Asia. Since 2000, Asia and the Pacific has seen average life expectancy at birth increase by 5.6 years in low- and lower-middle-income economies, 5.2 years in upper-middle-income economies, and 4.4 years in high-income economies. In developing Asia, notable increases in longevity were recorded in Cambodia, up by 12.1 years or 20.6%; the Lao People's Democratic Republic (Lao PDR), by 9.7 years or 16.7%; and Timor-Leste, by 9.7 years or 16.6%. Life expectancy in the region is projected to extend further in the next 3 decades by 4.1 years for men and 3.7 years for women (Chapter 1, Figure 1.5).

The life years gained are not necessarily all healthy years. In the past 2 decades, low- and high-income economies alike have gained in healthy life expectancy at age 60: in Bangladesh by 2.2 years, Maldives 3.1 years, Mongolia 2.3 years, the Republic of Korea (ROK) 3.9 years, Singapore 3.3 years, and Thailand 2.3 years. However, the difference between life expectancy and healthy life expectancy at age 60, or the number of years spent in less-than-full health, has also increased in most economies (Figure 2.1).

---

[11] Lower self-assessed health is associated with functional decline in later age (Kim et al. 2017) and higher mortality (Mossey and Shapiro 1982; Benjamins et al. 2004; Reinwarth et al. 2023). Physical and mental health status influences older people's well-being and satisfaction with life (Kahneman and Krueger 2006; Sun et al. 2016).

[12] An "older person" is aged 60 years or above unless otherwise specified.

Figure 2.1: Average Life Expectancy and Healthy Life Expectancy at Age 60 in 2000 and 2019, by Gender and Economy

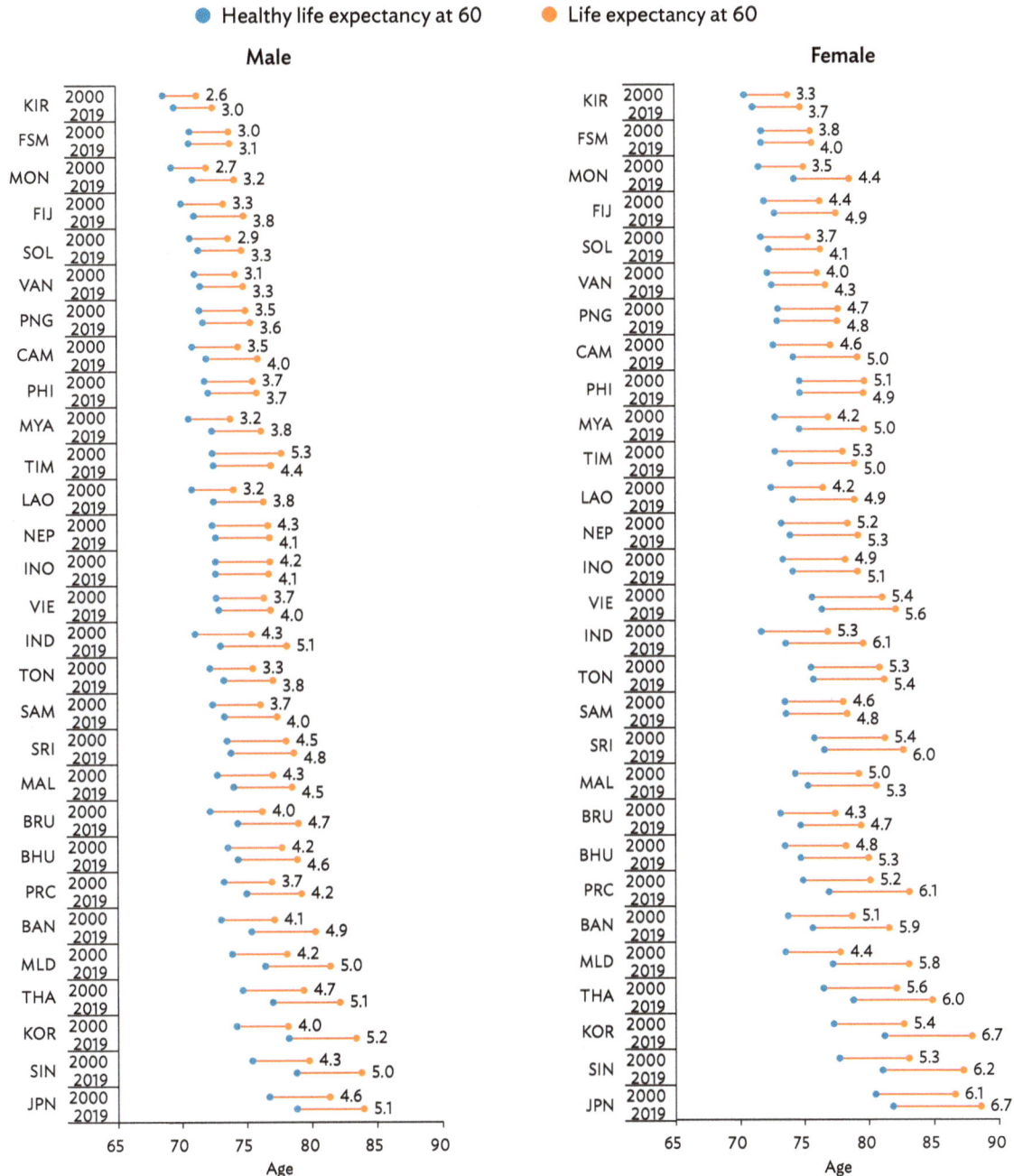

BAN = Bangladesh, BHU = Bhutan, BRU = Brunei Darussalam, CAM = Cambodia, FIJ = Fiji, FSM = Federated States of Micronesia, IND = India, INO = Indonesia, JPN = Japan, KIR = Kiribati, KOR = Republic of Korea, LAO = Lao People's Democratic Republic, MAL = Malaysia, MLD = Maldives, MON = Mongolia, MYA = Myanmar, NEP = Nepal, PHI = Philippines, PNG = Papua New Guinea, PRC = People's Republic of China, SAM = Samoa, SIN = Singapore, SOL = Solomon Islands, SRI = Sri Lanka, THA = Thailand, TIM = Timor-Leste, TON = Tonga, VAN = Vanuatu, VIE = Viet Nam.

Note: Average years in less-than-full health is the difference between life expectancy at age 60, shown as an orange dot, and healthy life expectancy at age 60, shown as a blue dot.

Source: World Health Organization Global Health Observatory.

In Maldives, the average number of years in less-than-full health has increased by 1.5 years for older women and 0.8 years for older men. In Bangladesh, it increased by 0.9 years for older women and 0.8 years for older men. The period in less than full health has increased in more advanced economies as well, for example in the ROK by 1.2 years for older men and 1.3 years for older women. Older women generally suffer longer ill health or disability than men.

The overall disease burden on older people has reduced substantially. Disability-adjusted life years (DALYs)—or the sum of the years lived in ill health or disability, and lost to premature mortality—declined for older people from 2000 to 2019, globally and in all subregions of developing Asia. A significant reduction in DALYs for communicable diseases occurred in developing and lower-income regions. In developing Asia, DALYs per 100,000 people for communicable diseases declined from 12,410 in 2000 to 6,469 in 2019, a reduction of 48%. Within developing Asia, economies in South Asia experienced the largest decline in DALYs for communicable diseases, at 51%, followed by the Pacific at 38% and the Caucasus and Central Asia by 28% (Figure 2.2).

The share of noncommunicable disease burden on older people is rising. While the overall disease burden shrank, the share of NCDs or lifestyle diseases—such as coronary heart disease, stroke, and diabetes—was high and rose in all subregions. In 2 decades, the NCD share in DALYs rose in South Asia from 74% to 81% and in the Pacific from 82% to 87% (Figure 2.3). NCDs are common not only in older people. In many economies, NCD-induced deaths were high in all adult age groups: 20–44, 45–64, and 65+ (Kowal, Ng, and Hoang 2024). This poses a challenge to the goal of healthy aging.

The mental disease burden on older people is rising. About 14% of older people globally live with some form of mental disorder, including depression and substance abuse (WHO 2023). This accounts for 10.6% of all disabilities that affects older people. The share of mental disease DALYs in all disease DALYs for older people changed little in most economies in developing Asia in the past 2 decades but marginally increased in all five subregions—in the Caucasus and Central Asia by 0.4 percentage points, East Asia 0.8 points, South Asia 0.5 points, Southeast Asia 0.3 points, and the Pacific 0.1 points—to account for 1.5%–2.9% of all DALYs. Lack of timely diagnosis may

Figure 2.2: Disease and Injury Burden of Older People, by Subregion in Developing Asia and Type of Disease Burden

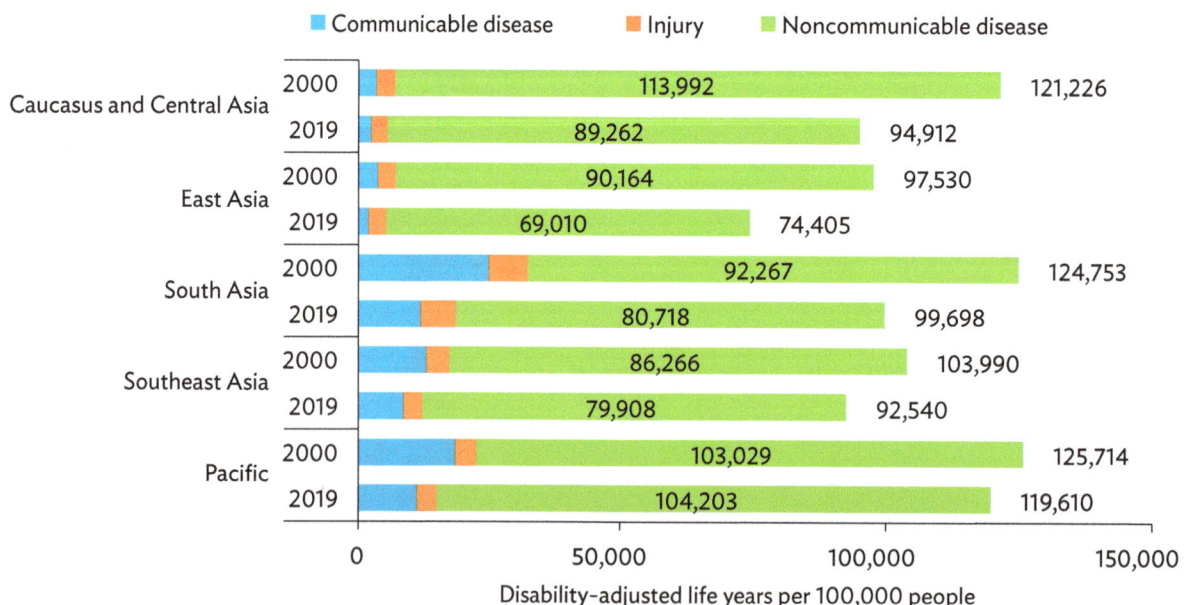

Note: Numbers show disability-adjusted life years per 100,000 people from noncommunicable disease and total.

Source: World Health Organization. 2020. Global Health Estimates 2019.

Figure 2.3: The Share of Disease and Injury Burden of Older People, by Subregion in Developing Asia and Type of Disease Burden

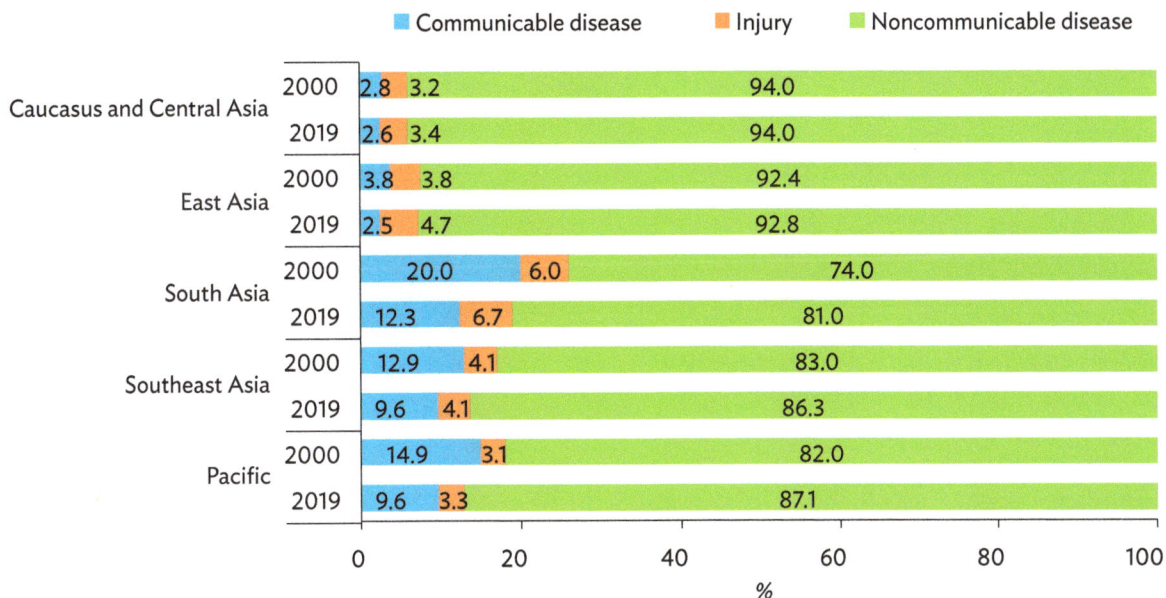

Note: The share of a burden is expressed as the percentage of a disease type to the total divisibility-adjusted life years for people aged 60+.
Source: World Health Organization. 2020. Global Health Estimates 2019.

mean that its prevalence is underestimated. Certainly, the prevalence of poor mental health or elevated depressive symptoms in older people is substantial, especially among the older old, as made evident by survey datasets presented below.

Dementia has become more prevalent among older people. Dementia is indicated by a group of symptoms related to cognitive decline. Dementia of Alzheimer's type is the most common, affecting memory, communication, and thinking. It worsens progressively and interferes with daily living. Southeast Asian economies suffer high incidence of young-onset dementia, defined as younger than 65 years, and these patients, as well as those with moderate-to-severe late-onset dementia caused by restricted blood flow to the brain, show steep decline in cognition (Vipin et al. 2021). Dementia is a major cause of disability and dependence in older people and the seventh most prevalent cause of death globally. In developing Asia, dementia is the seventh most prevalent disease affecting older people. Dementia DALYs per 100,000

population increased in developing Asia by 7.8% in 2 decades, from 8,879 in 2000 to 9,568 in 2019. By subregion, they rose by a large 22.5% in South Asia, and by 12.1% in East Asia and 10.3% in Southeast Asia. They declined marginally in the Caucasus and Central Asia by 0.7% and somewhat more so in the Pacific by 3.7%.

The risk to older people from communicable disease remains high. While the communicable disease share of DALYs declined, communicable disease continues to threaten older people, especially those weakened by illness or otherwise at high risk. Surveys in India and the People's Republic of China (PRC) found older people at heightened risk from gastroenteritis, cholera, malaria, viral hepatitis, tuberculosis, typhoid, dengue, and HIV. In the PRC, for example, older people accounted for 34.6% of tuberculosis cases in 2019, and 34.5% of viral hepatitis C cases, suggesting that older people may be more vulnerable to these infectious diseases because their immune systems have weakened or because they frequently receive blood infusions for treatment

(Chen et al. 2022). In India, 15% of older people were affected in 2018 by diarrhea, 9% by malaria, and 6% by typhoid, with those living in rural areas or with lower educational attainment disproportionately affected (Chauhan et al. 2022).

The coronavirus disease (COVID-19) was a stark reminder of older people's heightened vulnerability to infectious disease. Older people all over the world suffered disproportionately from COVID-19 in terms of the clinical severity of illness and a higher ratio of fatalities to cases. In the PRC, for example, infection rates were twice as high for older people aged 60 years and above than for people aged below 60 years (Chen et al. 2022). Age-specific infection-fatality ratio estimates, before the arrival of vaccines, show exponential increase with age, from 0.0023% at age 7 to 0.0573% at age 30, 1.00% at age 60, and 20.3% at age 90 (Sorensen et al. 2022). National surveys across developing Asia documented an array of health impacts, notably deterioration of physical health in Indonesia and Bangladesh; lower self-assessed health and increased multimorbidity, and greater difficulty performing basic activities of daily living (ADLs, mostly personal hygiene and eating) and instrumental ADLs (IADLs, mostly housekeeping and shopping) in Viet Nam (Giang 2024).

Older people are at increased risk of malnutrition due to physiological decline, multimorbidity, and a lack of nutritious food. About 25% of older adults aged 65 and older are malnourished or at risk of malnutrition (Dent et al. 2023). Malnutrition influences the risk to older people of frailty, cognitive decline, poor quality of life, and mortality. Many studies have found that adherence to a healthy diet in midlife increases the likelihood of healthy aging and maintenance of physical and cognitive function, and reduces depression later in life (Zhou et al. 2023). Risks to malnutrition may be aggravated by rising threats to food security and nutrition from climate change and extreme weather conditions.

Older people are disproportionately threatened by climate change. Storms, floods, heat waves, and other extreme weather events pose a substantial direct health risk to older people. Heat stress, for example, can kill older people who are made more susceptible by heart disease or diabetes (Bell et al. 2016; Harper 2023).

A nationwide study in the PRC found people aged 75 and above to be at the greatest risk of dying from extreme temperatures (Chen et al. 2022). Moreover, air pollution and other environmental hazards can complicate NCDs, particularly heart and respiratory diseases, and undermine cognitive and mental health. Evidence from the PRC found improved air quality to be associated with positive change in lipid profile (Li et al. 2021) and cognitive function (Yao et al. 2022). The mental health of older people can be affected by climate disasters, with older people shown to suffer stress and depression following floods (Erwin et al. 2017).

2.2 Health Status of Older People in Asia: Evidence from Survey Data

Beyond mortality and disease burden, the health status of older people can be assessed by various objective and subjective metrics, collected from social surveys. This chapter sheds light on several aspects of old-age health using micro data from nine Asian economies that account for 82% of Asia's older population, covering NCDs, functional status, mental health, and self-reported health (Chapter 1, Box 1.1). The physical health status of older people is measured using self-reports of diagnosed diseases, while their mental health condition is measured by elevated depressive symptoms reflected in survey responses. Functional status is measured using self-reports of difficulty in performing basic ADLs and more complex IADLs. These impairments undermine older people's ability to live autonomously and independently. Older people's health behavior, use of health-care services, and their access to health insurance are also described, based on available survey data.

Noncommunicable Disease among Older People

Many older people in Asia suffer from one or more NCDs. Self-reports of diagnosed NCDs—hypertension, heart disease, stroke, lung disease, diabetes, and cancer—suggest a clear pattern as the burden becomes heavier starting in middle age. Notably, in the middle-age group aged 45–49, the share of the population diagnosed with at least one NCD ranges from 23% to 37% in different economies, and 5%–10% have multiple NCDs (Figure 2.4). It is important to note that NCDs are often undiagnosed as many people do not get regular checkups, especially in less developed economies, and self-reports may suffer from response biases. In the whole sample across economies, 57% of older people report at least one diagnosed NCD, the highest rate in the PRC at 68%, followed by Viet Nam at 64%, Malaysia and the ROK at 61%, Thailand at 58%, the Philippines at 53%, India at 45%, Indonesia at 42%, and Bangladesh at 38%. Hypertension is the most common NCD afflicting older Asians. Of the nine economies with available data, seven have more than 40% of older people diagnosed with hypertension, with the highest prevalence in Thailand at 55%. The second most common NCD is diabetes, with the highest prevalence in Bangladesh and Malaysia, at 28%, followed by heart disease, which is highest in the PRC, at 25%. As NCD prevalence rises with age, future years may not be healthier for these cohorts unless managed with effective interventions.

Older women suffer more from NCDs. In each economy studied, a higher percentage of older women than men suffer from NCDs. On average in the region, 59% of older women have at least one NCD, highest in Viet Nam at 65%. In addition, about a half of them have multiple NCDs (27%), highest in the PRC at 37%. In all economies except India and the ROK, hypertension and diabetes are more prevalent in older women than men—12 percentage points higher for hypertension in Indonesia and the Philippines, for example, and 11 points higher for diabetes in Bangladesh (Figure 2.5). A higher percentage of older women than men report heart disease in Viet Nam, by 9 percentage points, and in the PRC, by 7 points. Women have a greater risk of developing diabetes and hypertension than men because of their higher body mass index and psychological stress. On average, women expect to live longer, which can mean more years of morbidity. Curative and preventative health services should better reflect gender morbidity patterns and the specific health-care needs of older women. In many cases, NCDs cause physical complications and disability and, in the absence of adequate insurance coverage, can incur high out-of-pocket expenditure for disease management (Hossain, Khanam, and Sarker 2023). Thus, reducing the burdens of NCD can effectively address gender inequality.

Figure 2.4: Share of Older People with One or More NCDs by Age Group and Economy

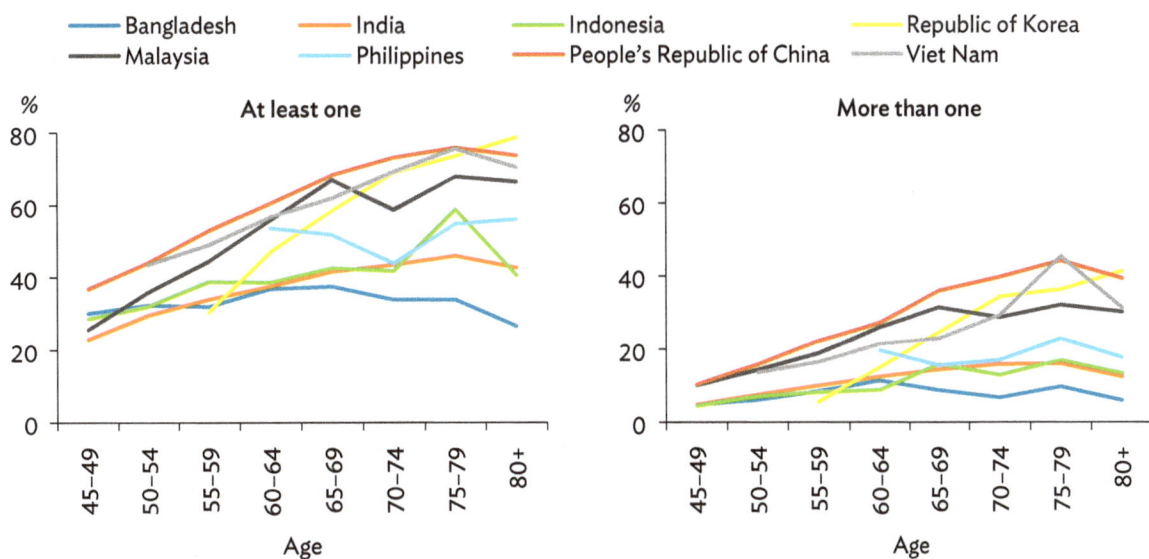

NCD = noncommunicable disease.

Notes: NCDs include hypertension, diabetes, respiratory disease, heart disease, stroke, and cancer. Survey years are 2017-2019, 2021, and 2023.

Source: Chapter 1, Box 1.1.

Figure 2.5: Prevalence of Diagnosed Noncommunicable Disease in Older People, by Gender and Economy

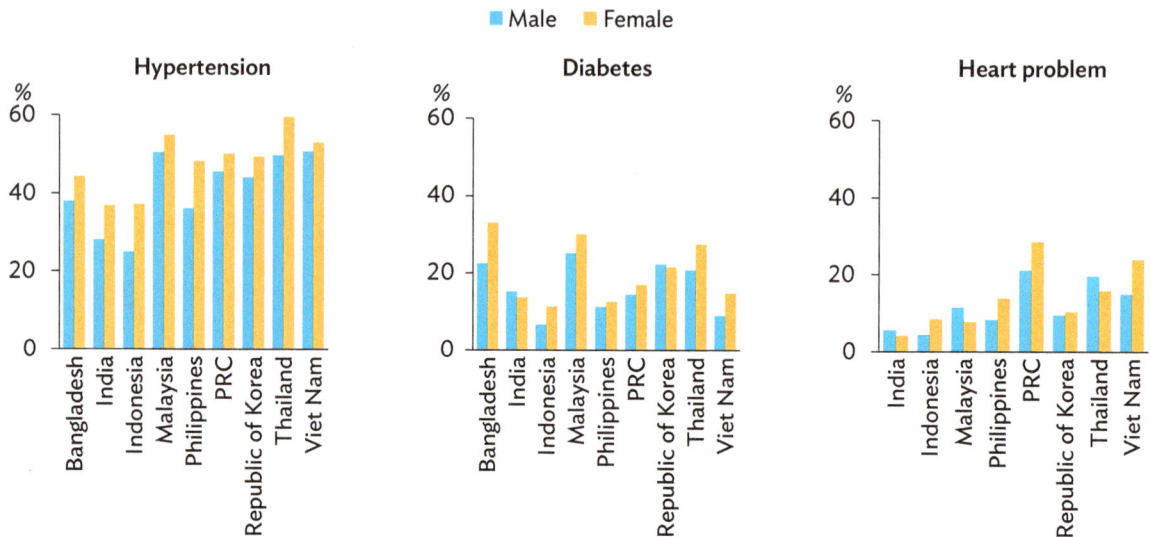

NCD = noncommunicable disease, PRC = People's Republic of China.

Notes: Older people are aged 60 and above. Survey years are 2017–2020, 2021, 2023.

Source: Chapter 1, Box 1.1.

NCD prevalence is higher among older people in urban areas and educated groups. In the PRC, the share of older people with at least one NCD is 70% for urban residents and slightly lower at 66% for rural residents. The gap between urban and rural areas is widest in India at 58% versus 38%, followed by Bangladesh at 48% versus 35%. Diagnosed hypertension and diabetes in particular are more prevalent in older urban residents, with rate differentials widest at 17 percentage points for hypertension in India and 22 points for diabetes in Bangladesh. Gaps are smaller in other economies, but prevalence is high everywhere. Except in Malaysia, the ROK, and Viet Nam, more older people with at least secondary education are diagnosed with at least one NCD than those with lower educational attainment. The gap in NCD prevalence by education is widest in India, at 19 percentage points. Although gaps in NCDs could reflect differences in the shares of persons who are undiagnosed, lifestyle changes associated with increased income and urbanization could raise the risk of NCDs, which need to be addressed by both early diagnosis and management, as well as broader policy interventions to discourage unhealthy consumption.

Unhealthy behavior that adds NCD risk is widespread among older people in the region. While NCDs are caused by a combination of genetic, psychological, social, environmental, and behavioral factors, tobacco and alcohol consumption are two big risk factors, as are unhealthy diets and sedentary lifestyles. The prevalence of risky behaviors are high among older people, and many older people do not exercise or have a healthy diet, undermining their health. Survey data from Indonesia, Malaysia, and the ROK found no more than 40% of older women and men reporting at least one of the following self-care priorities: regular physical exercise, getting enough sleep, or maintaining nutritious diets. In the PRC, 86% of older women and 88% of older men reported positive for at least one of these priorities. The share of older people who are smokers remains very high, with men in the region over six times more likely to smoke than women—53% of older men in Indonesia, 51% in Bangladesh, and 46% in the PRC. Older men report alcohol use more frequently than women, with the rate high at 66% of older men in Viet Nam and 55% in the ROK. Smoking and excess alcohol consumption cause a range of cardiovascular and respiratory diseases, including cancer. Smoking causes hypertension in older adults (Halperin, Gaziano, and Sesso 2008). Male mortality attributable to tobacco consumption has recently been on the rise in Asia (Yang et al. 2019). In the PRC, for example, 20% of all adult deaths in 2010 were attributed to smoking (Chen et al. 2015). Smoking is also a major risk factor for dementia in men (Li et al. 2022).

Reducing risk by preventing NCDs and improving their treatment has significant health and economic benefits. This has potential to lengthen healthy life expectancy (Hu et al. 2019). Smoking cessation at any age reduces mortality risk (Mayor 2016), and by age 50 or 60 restores some lost years to life expectancy (Jha and Peto 2014). In addition to tobacco control and price policies, investment in smoking cessation programs would bring benefits. Community-based health-care programs have achieved promising results in tobacco cessation, blood pressure control, diabetes management, and the uptake of screening for other conditions (Jeet et al. 2017; Kaselitz et al. 2017). Healthy food and diet could minimize the NCD burden. Reducing the intake of saturated fat and salt, for example, can improve blood pressure and reduce the burden from cardiovascular disease, and daily consumption of fruit and vegetables also significantly cuts the risk of cardiovascular disease.

Engaging the community, including community health workers in the primary health care system through health checkups, health screening promotion, home care support, and social care effectively safeguards seniors' health at low cost. Further, primary health care offers economy of scale as the entry point for other health concerns (Hou, Sharma, and Zhao 2023).

Functional Ability

Decline in functional ability worsens with age. Functional impairment as measured by the difficulty in performing basic ADLs such as dressing, bathing, and eating, may arise from complications associated with NCDs and mental illness. Shares of older people reporting some difficulty and needing help with at least one ADL were 20% in the region: 35% in the ROK and Malaysia, 21% in Viet Nam, 16% in the PRC, 13% in India, 9% in Indonesia, 8% in Bangladesh and Thailand, 7% in the Philippines, and 6% in Indonesia. The share of older people reporting difficulty performing three common ADLs ranged from 16% in Viet Nam; 7% in India; and 2%–3% in Bangladesh, Malaysia, and the ROK. As shown in Figures 2.6 and 2.7, ADL impairments are common among older people and rise steeply mostly after age 70

Figure 2.6: Share of Older People Reporting at Least One ADL Limitation by Gender, Age, and Economy

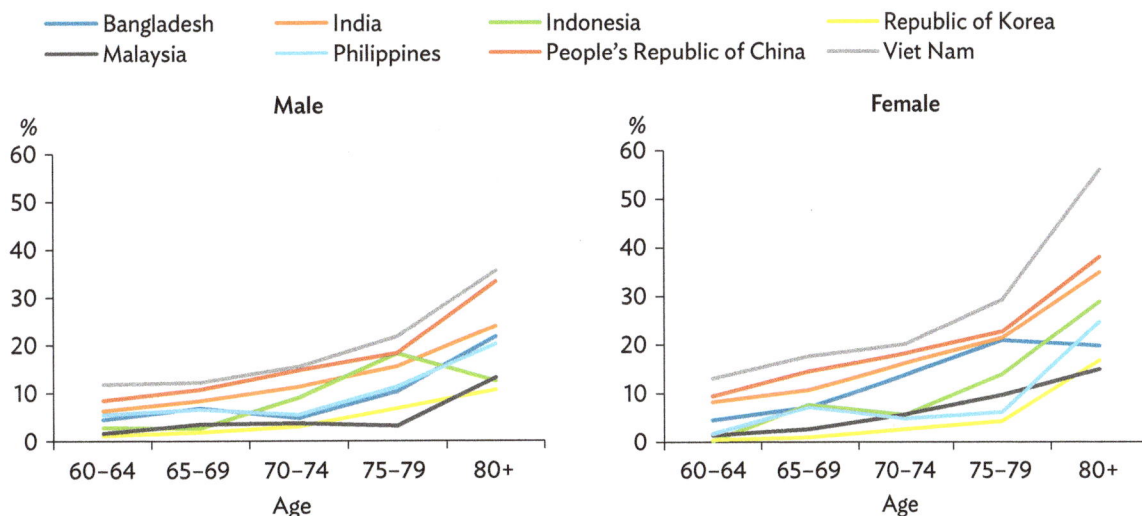

ADL = activity of daily living.

Notes: ADLs include dressing, bathing, and eating. Older people are aged 60 and above. Survey years are 2017–2019, 2021, 2023.

Source: Chapter 1, Box 1.1.

for both genders with few exceptions. ADL impairment can be addressed by improving the management of NCD and providing long-term care solutions.

Challenges to independent living rise steeply with age. Functional impairments are measured by difficulty in performing IADLs, which are more complex activities like preparing food, taking medication, housework, shopping, and using a telephone. Impaired IADLs constrain an individual's ability to live independently and undermine autonomy and quality of life. While IADL reporting often suffers contextual bias, particularly for food preparation, older people reporting some difficulty and needing help on any of these IADLs was highest in Indonesia at 67%, followed by 63% in Bangladesh, 51% in Malaysia, 42% in India, 38% in Viet Nam, 32% in the PRC, 18% in the Philippines, and 9% in the ROK. In Indonesia, for example, 64% of older people report some difficulty in using a telephone, and 14% in taking medication. At the other extreme, difficulty in using a telephone or taking medication was lowest in the Philippines at 4% and the ROK at 3%. The highest share of older persons reporting difficulty in shopping is 37% in Malaysia while the lowest share is 5% in the ROK. Figure 2.8 shows the average share of IADLs in which older people report

difficulties in performing and needing help, by gender, age group, and economy. Functional impairment rises steeply for both genders in very old age, especially in Indonesia, Malaysia, and the Philippines, indicating greater care needs for very old women. Identifying these limitations accurately in older people is important for determining their level of care need and support. These limitations can undermine one's mental health by increasing one's sense of isolation which increase the risk of cognitive decline.

Mental Health

Depressive symptoms are prevalent among older people in the region. Older people are at heightened risk of depression from various factors, including physical illness, loneliness, and social isolation (Chapter 5). In every age group in almost all economies, more women than men are depressed, and the prevalence of depression in older people spikes at about age 70 with few exceptions (Figure 2.9). The share of older people showing elevated depressive symptoms in survey responses was 31% on average in the region, and highest in the PRC, at 43% for women and 30% for men, followed by Malaysia at 36% for

Figure 2.7: Share of Older People Reporting Three Common ADL limitations by Gender, Age and Economy

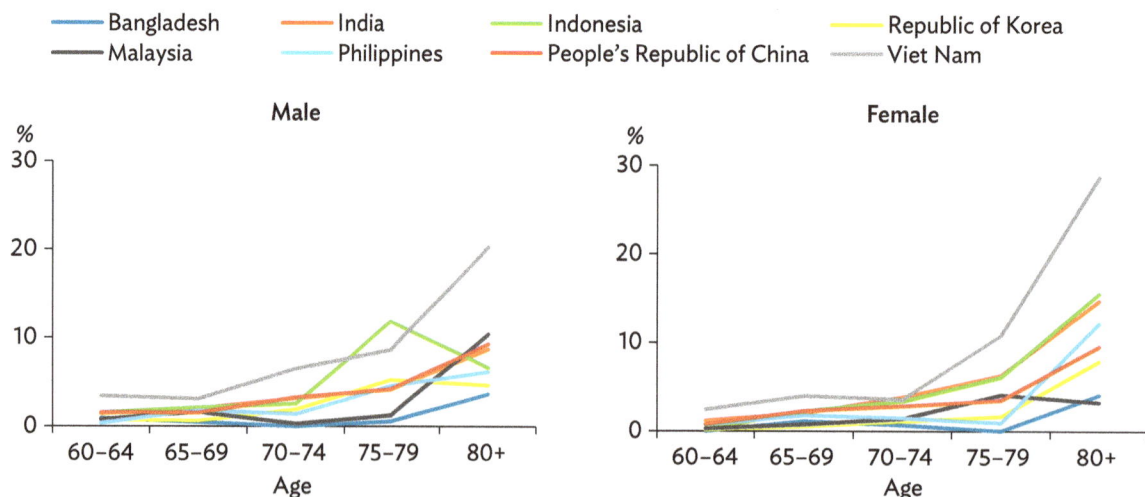

ADL = activity of daily living.
Notes: ADLs include dressing, bathing, and eating. Older people are aged 60 and above. Survey years are 2017–2019, 2021, 2023.
Source: Chapter 1, Box 1.1.

Figure 2.8: Average IADL Limitations by Gender, Age, and Economy

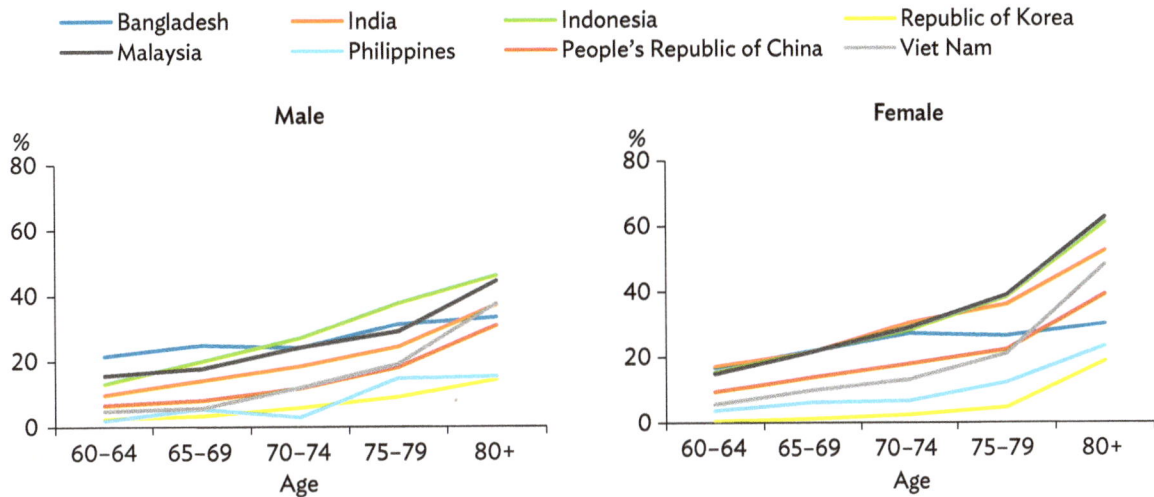

IADL = instrumental activity of daily living.

Notes: Older people are aged 60 and above. IADLs include preparing food, taking medication, housework, shopping, or using a telephone. Average IADL impairment is the average share of IADLs for which older people report difficulty in performing. Survey years are 2017–2019, 2021, 2023.

Source: Chapter 1, Box 1.1.

Figure 2.9: Elevated Depressive Symptoms in Older People by Age Group and Economy

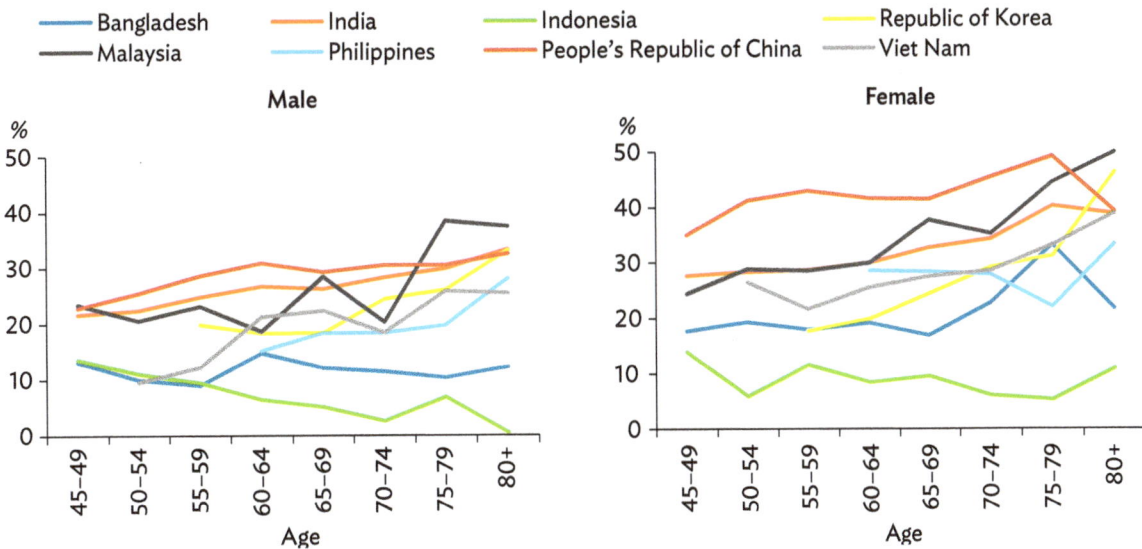

Notes: The presence of elevated depressive symptoms was determined based on the mental health screening module of the respective surveys. Survey years are 2017–2019, 2021, and 2023.

Source: Chapter 1, Box 1.1.

women and 25% for men, India at 33% for women and 28% for men, Viet Nam at 30% for women and 22% for men, and the ROK at 28% for women and 22% for men (Figure 2.9). The shares of older persons with elevated depressive symptoms are lowest in Thailand, at about 6%, and in Indonesia at 8% for women and 5% for men. Urban–rural differences in depressive symptom rates are significant, particularly in Bangladesh,

Malaysia, the Philippines, the PRC, and Viet Nam. The percentage of older people in Bangladesh with elevated depressive symptoms is 6 percentage points higher in urban areas than in rural areas, and in Malaysia 3 points higher, but rates are higher in rural areas by 12 points in the PRC, 8 points in the Philippines, and 7 points in Viet Nam. In all economies, a higher percentage of older people with little education show elevated depressive symptoms than their counterparts with at least secondary education. The gap by educational attainment is widest in the PRC at 17%, followed by 11% in India, the ROK, and Viet Nam.

Poor mental health is associated with functional impairment, NCDs, and other factors. A cross-country analysis of the determinants of elevated depressive symptoms suggests that reporting multiple NCDs and functional impairment are more likely to be depressed. Older people with elevated depressive symptoms report more ADL impairment. Older women in rural areas are more likely to be depressed. Older people who are married or better educated

are less likely to be depressed (Figure 2.11). A study in Malaysia and Viet Nam found that having children and living close to them positively influences mental and physical health, particularly for older women (Rodgers et al. 2024). Functional decline can worsen mental health by undermining self-esteem and a sense of control (Yang 2006) and by worsening isolation (Marmamula et al. 2021). Depression can sap the will and the ability to undertake basic activities. A study in India, for example, found depression prevalence higher among older people in rural areas with comorbidity (Saha et al. 2024). The evidence is strong that depressed individuals are more likely to die earlier than others (Banerjee et al. 2022; Brandão et al. 2019). However, large gaps in the treatment of depression are reported for lack of diagnosis, particularly in low-income settings (Banerjee et al. 2022). While surveys suggest that a large number of older people in the PRC are likely to be depressed, only 2% of them have been diagnosed with a psychological condition by a doctor, and only 1% take medication to treat it (Thornicroft et al. 2017).

Figure 2.10: Elevated Depressive Symptoms in Older People by Gender, Residence, Educational Attainment, and Economy

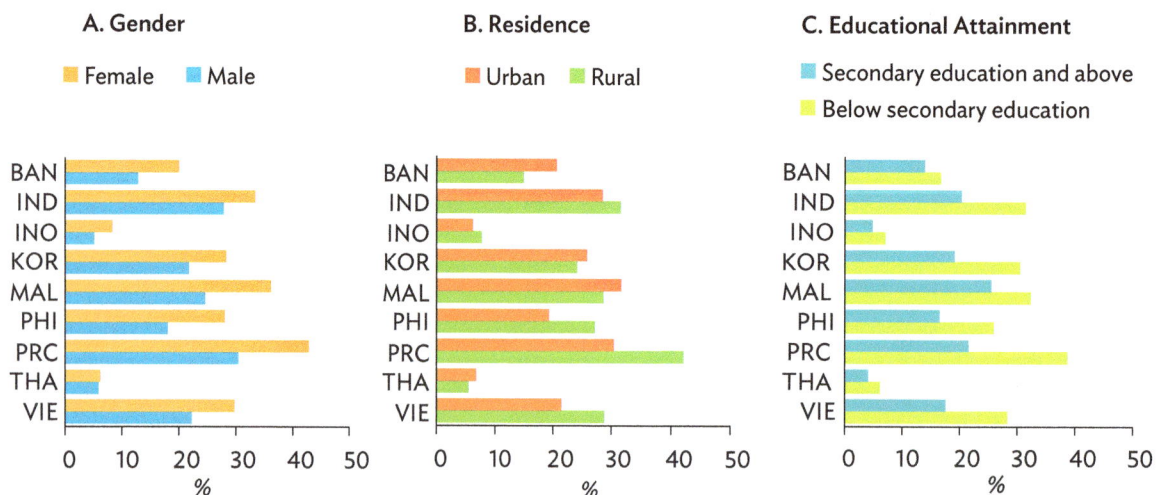

BAN = Bangladesh; IND = India; INO = Indonesia; KOR = Republic of Korea; MAL = Malaysia; PHI = Philippines; PRC = People's Republic of China; THA = Thailand; VIE = Viet Nam.

Notes: Older people are aged 60 and above. The presence of elevated depressive symptoms was determined based on the mental health screening module of the respective survey. Years covered are 2017–2019, 2021 and 2023.

Source: Chapter 1, Box 1.1.

Figure 2.11: Predictors of Depressive Symptoms in Older People in Developing Asia by Gender

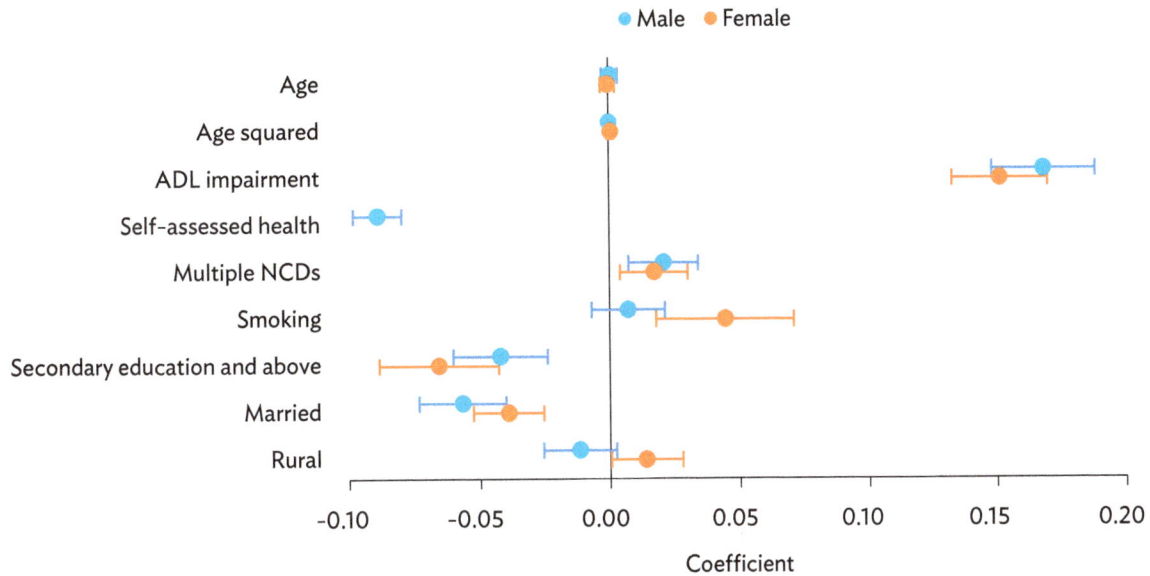

ADL = activity of daily living, NCD = noncommunicative disease.

Notes: The dependent variable is elevated depressive symptoms(=1), and zero otherwise. Eight economies included in the regressions are Bangladesh, India, Indonesia, the Republic of Korea, Malaysia, the Philippines, the People's Republic of China, and Viet Nam. Total observations: 27,330 for male and 31,018 for female. Marginal effects from probit regressions are plotted, for male and female sample. Older people are aged 60 and above. Harmonized sampling weights are applied.

Source: Chapter 1, Box 1.1.

A strong primary health-care system can serve as an entry point to detect and address mental health issues and NCDs. The interplay of mental health conditions, NCDs, and functional impairment suggests the importance of strong primary care. A priority is targeted intervention for older people in rural areas, especially women, to address their mental health and comorbidities. Psychological interventions by nonspecialists such as cognitive behavioral therapists can reduce older people's depressive symptoms in lower- and middle-income settings, as shown in India (Bhat et al. 2022, Dias et al. 2019, Patel et al. 2017). Mental health conditions can also be improved by addressing functional impairments and disabilities. Simply providing eyeglasses or walkers, for example, can permit some older people to venture out of the home, improving their mental health by reducing their sense of isolation and improving their self-esteem (Ye et al. 2022).

Self-Reported Health Status

Poor physical and mental health is associated with lower self-assessed health. A cross-country analysis found that the share of older people who self-assess good health varies considerably. A high 51% of older people in India rated their health as excellent, very good, or good, ranging down to 45% in Indonesia, 41% in the ROK, 42% in Malaysia, 21% in the PRC, 19% in the Philippines, 17% in Thailand, 16% in Bangladesh, and 10% in Viet Nam (Figure 2.12). With regard to gender differences, only in Indonesia and the Philippines did a slightly higher percentage of older women than men assess their health as at least good. Some key determinants of self-assessed health in older people are NCDs and ADL limitations. Educational attainment is associated with higher self-assessed health. Educated people are more likely to be informed about risky behavior and how to care for themselves, and are thus better equipped to safeguard their health (Grossman

1972). Female smokers are likely to report lower self-assessed health, as are older people suffering from depression or ADL limitations or living in rural areas.

Health-Seeking Behavior by Older People

Fewer than half of older people in the region undergo periodic health checkups. Health screening or checkups are primary preventive measures, but only 40% of older people in the region reported having a formal health checkup in the past year. The percentage ranged from 64% in Malaysia to 60% in Thailand, 56% in the PRC, 37% in Indonesia, and 10% in India.[13] The health checkup rate was higher for older people with health insurance, by 2 percentage points in Malaysia, 19 points in Indonesia, and 21 points in the PRC. In Malaysia, about 60% of older people cited lack of necessity as the primary reason for opting out of health screening. If health screening is free and

promoted through awareness campaigns and health literacy education, a greater number of older people can be induced to take part. Regular health screening should be prioritized as it can increase the use of health services and help older people maintain good health. Further, health screening actually reduces older people's expenditure on health care due to improved health (Levine et al. 2019).

Older people's health-care utilization varies with the availability of health insurance across economies. In most economies for which data are available, at least half of older people reported having been hospitalized or using outpatient facilities in the year preceding the survey, with the highest rate in the ROK and Viet Nam at 73% and the lowest in the PRC at 31%. Apart from health status, health-care access and use are influenced by demographics, socioeconomic conditions, urban versus rural residence, and access to health insurance

Figure 2.12: Share of Older People Who Self-Assess Their Health as Excellent, Very Good, or Good, by Gender and Economy

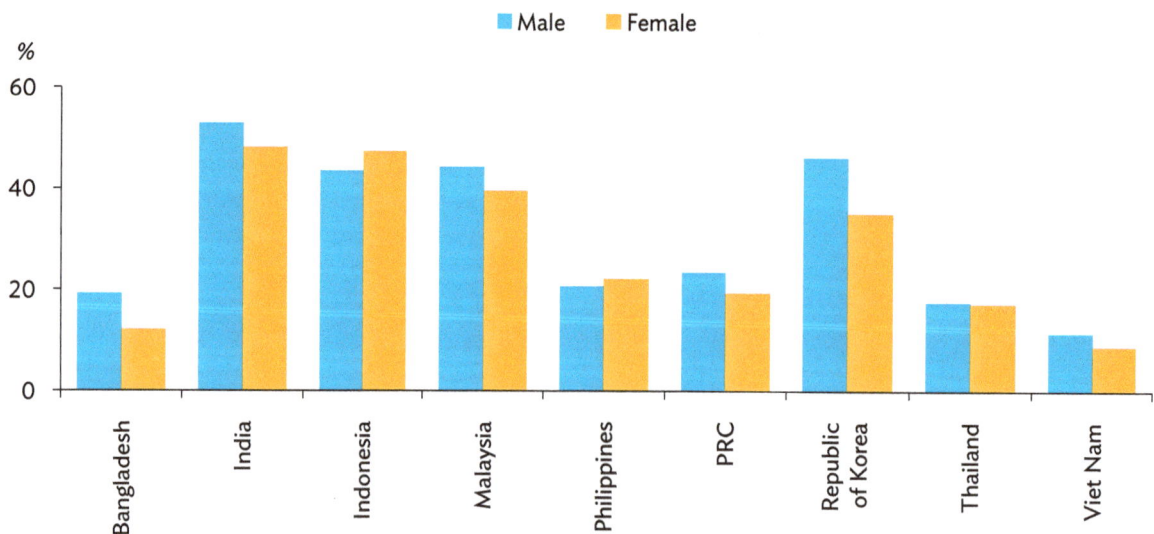

PRC = People's Republic of China.

Notes: Older people are aged 60 and above. Self-assessed health is reported in three categories across economies: (i) excellent, very good, or good; (ii) average or fair; and (iii) poor or very poor. Survey years are 2017–2021, and 2023.

Source: Chapter 1, Box 1.1.

---

[13]   Mobility restrictions during the COVID-19 pandemic kept many older people away from health care and treatment. In Malaysia, only 56% of respondents had a medical checkup in 2020 or 2021, substantially fewer than 74% in 2019 (ADB and SWRC 2023).

(Jiang et al. 2018; Rahaman et al. 2022). Older people who have health insurance are more likely to use health-care services by 41 percentage points in Viet Nam, 20 points in the Philippines, 14 points in the PRC, and 11 points in Indonesia. In some economies, the health-care utilization rates by older people were higher in rural areas than in urban areas: in the ROK, the health-care utilization rate is 77% in rural areas versus 68% in urban areas, and in Thailand the rates are 73% versus 69%. Many health conditions can be detected and managed only by a health-care professional, which is facilitated by maintaining affordable and high-quality community health facilities.

Health checkups and health-care utilization are more frequent for older people with higher educational attainment. The checkup gap between high and low education groups is widest in Indonesia at 30 percentage points, followed by the PRC and Thailand at 14 percentage points (Figure 2.13). Health-care use by the more educated group is higher in all economies except the ROK, where health-care utilization of the low-education group is 16 percentage points higher than the high-education group. Health literacy education can play a key role in promoting preventive behavior and health-seeking behavior, suggesting that governments should invest in promoting health literacy to achieve a more efficient use of health-care resources.

Healthy behavior can be promoted through behavioral intervention. There is great potential for older people to benefit from behavioral nudges that promote physical activity, healthy diets and nutrition, health checkups, adherence to medication regimens, and smoking and alcohol abstention. Studies show a robust association between nutrition in midlife and healthy aging in late life, especially better cognitive and physical function as well as lower depression (Zhou et al. 2023). Examples of effective interventions include positive health messaging to encourage older people to walk (Notthoff and Carstensen 2014); tracking devices that record step counting with financial incentives to boost physical activity of older people (Agarwal et al. 2021); mobile health apps with features that track food consumption, exercise and weight, and provide a virtual behavior-change coach, which have achieved weight loss among older people in the PRC (DeLuca et al. 2020); and pharmacy vouchers to increase health screening for diabetes and hypertension, which effectively increased screening by 31% in Armenia (de Walque et al. 2022). Social and behavioral-change communication to develop and maintain positive health behaviors has the potential to address NCD risks.

Figure 2.13: Checkups and Health-Care Use by Older People, by Educational Attainment

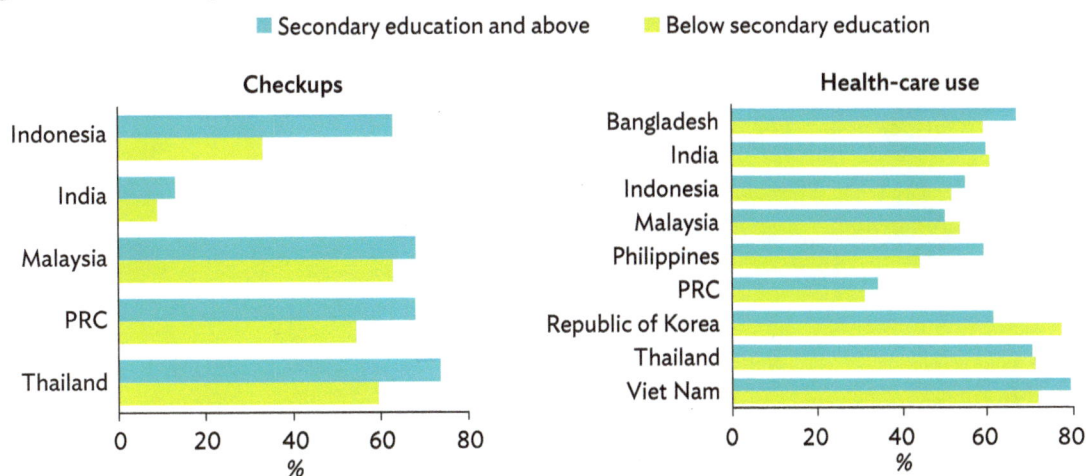

PRC = People's Republic of China.

Notes: Older people are aged 60 and above. Survey years are 2017–2021, and 2023.

Source: Chapter 1, Box 1.1.

2.3 Health System Access, Universal Health Coverage, and Healthy Aging Policies

Older people have large unmet health-care needs. Underutilization of health-care services for any reason—be it cost, quality, or distance—may delay the diagnosis and treatment of preventable disease and thus worsen health outcomes. Surveys conducted in 83 economies across all income levels suggest that many people aged 60–69 do not access health care despite needing it (Kowal et al. 2023). Older people's unmet needs were highest in Indonesia at 43.7%, ranging down to 43.5% in Bangladesh, 37.7% in the Philippines, 29.6% in India, 11.4% in the PRC, and 10.7% in Malaysia (Figure 2.14). Economies with universal health coverage (UHC)—notably the ROK, Thailand, and Viet Nam—had unmet needs for this age group less than 2%, and as low as 0.3% in Viet Nam. The gender gap in unmet need was widest in Bangladesh, at 12.1 percentage points, and the rural–urban gap was widest in Indonesia, also at 12.2 percentage points.

Socioeconomic status influences health-care use. Surveys of self-reported health-care use by older people found unequal access to health care, with a higher percentage of the poorer old in the bottom two quintiles reporting no health-care use (Figure 2.15). In the Philippines, 40% of those who reported no health-care use in the past year were in the poorest quintile. This reflects the need to extend financial protection from high health expenditure while providing UHC, which is discussed later in this chapter.

Health insurance coverage is high for older people in economies with UHC. Access to health insurance, either private or public, is almost 100% in the ROK and Thailand, both of which have achieved UHC. Coverage is lowest in India, at 21%.[14] With the exception of India, older urban residents have higher rates of insurance cover than their rural counterparts, with the gap being widest in Indonesia at 20 percentage points. The Philippines and the PRC stand out for having low coverage of older people in the poorest quintile, who account for 47% and 35% in these two economies, compared with 21%–24% in India, Indonesia, and Viet Nam (Figure 2.15).

Figure 2.14: Prevalence of Unmet Health-Care Needs for People Aged 60–69 by Gender, Residence, and Economy

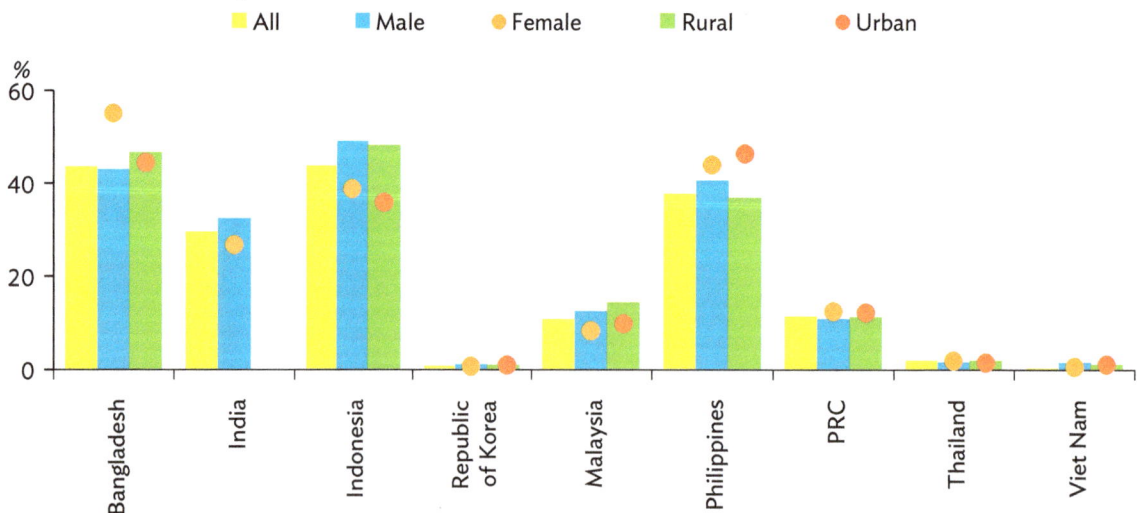

PRC = People's Republic of China.

Note: The survey year is 2017, except for India in 2010 and for Viet Nam in 2019.

Source: Asian Development Bank estimates using data from Kowal et al. (2023).

---

[14]   These data, which are sourced from harmonized data (Chapter 1, Box 1.1), may not reflect the latest health coverage rates for some economies. For example, in the case of India, coverage is expected to have risen in the last few years following the introduction of Ayushman Bharat Pradhan Mantri Jan Arogya Yojana, a new public health assurance scheme.

Figure 2.15: Distribution of Older People with No Health-Care Use, by Wealth Quintile and Economy

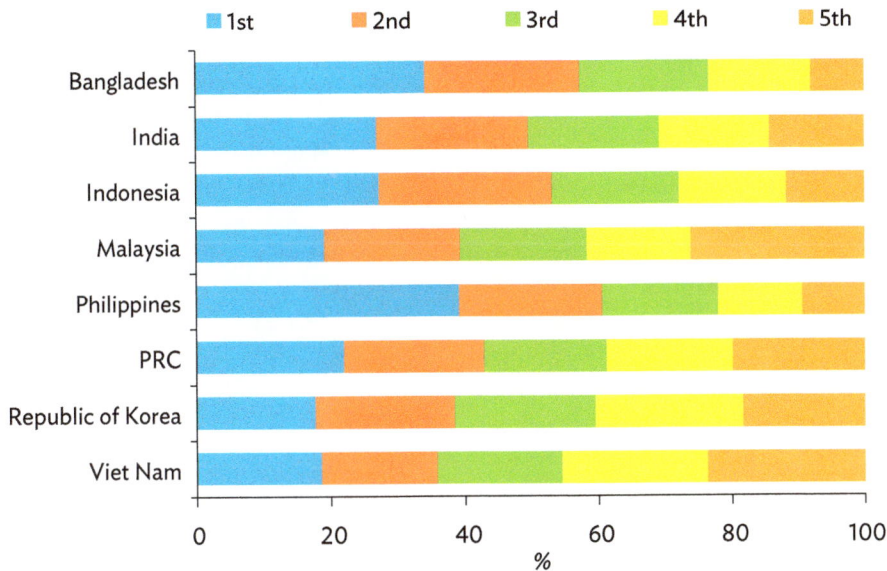

PRC = People's Republic of China.

Notes: Older people are aged 60 and above. Quintiles are numbered from poorest (1st) to wealthiest (5th).

Source: Chapter 1, Box 1.1.

Figure 2.16: Distribution of Older People without Health Insurance, by Wealth Quintile and Economy

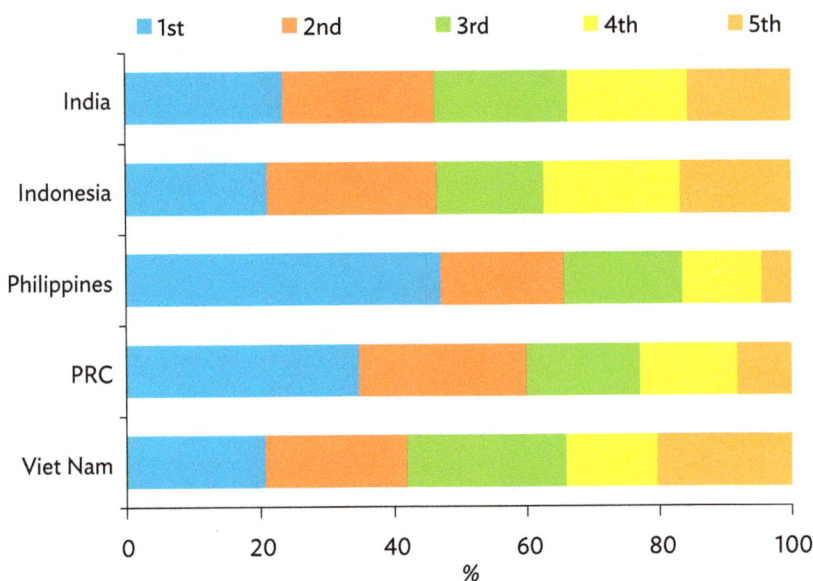

PRC = People's Republic of China.

Notes: Older people are aged 60 and above. Quintiles are numbered from poorest (1st) to wealthiest (5th).

Source: Chapter 1, Box 1.1.

Effectiveness of UHC differs widely across developing Asia. The UHC index is a standardized score of how effectively UHC meets residents' health-care needs throughout their lives. It has 23 indicators in five health-care service domains: promotion, prevention, treatment, rehabilitation, and palliation (GBD 2019 Universal Health Coverage Collaborators 2020). Standardized UHC scores range from 0 to 100, from less to more effective coverage. National scores across the region show differences in the pace of improvement over the past decade (Figure 2.17). Economies with UHC scores above average in developing Asia are Maldives at 67 and Sri Lanka at 66 in South Asia; Malaysia at 67, Thailand at 72, and Viet Nam at 60 in Southeast Asia; the PRC at 70, the ROK at 89, and Taipei,China at 79 in East Asia; and Armenia at 62 in the Caucasus and Central Asia. Large gains in the past decade occurred in five economies in the Caucasus and Central Asia, with the score increasing in the Kyrgyz Republic by 10 points, Kazakhstan by 9, Azerbaijan by 8, Armenia by 7, and Tajikistan by 7. UHC scores also increased in Afghanistan by 8 points and in Sri Lanka by 7; in the PRC in East Asia by 7 points, in the Lao PDR by 9 points, in Myanmar by 8, and in Cambodia by 7. Better access to high-quality health care also reflects progress in UHC.[15]

Despite the improvement in UHC, financial protection remains low in some economies. Financial protection from health expenditure is measured by out-of-pocket health expenditure relative to all household expenditure. If health expenditure is within 10%, the household is considered financially protected. UHC does not uniformly provide high financial protection across economies. In developing Asia, some economies—notably Cambodia, Georgia, Maldives, the PRC, and the ROK—have UHC index scores higher than average or above 50 but also out-of-pocket health expenditure shares higher than 10% or the global average. While the ROK has a UHC score of 89 and Singapore 92, Singapore offers lower-than-average financial protection. In South Asia, Afghanistan, Bangladesh, India, and Nepal have UHC index scores below average and low financial protection, showing poor progress toward UHC. These results highlight the importance of government-led health insurance reform to ensure that health-care service coverage provides financial protection.

To make progress toward implementing a global strategy and action plan for healthy aging, many governments have committed to reform. Governments strive to meet the needs of aging populations by expanding social protection and realizing UHC. A strategy for healthy aging for 2016–2020 was adopted by member states of the World Health Organization (WHO 2017). It outlined five strategic objectives for a world in which all can live long and healthy lives: (i) commitment to national action plans that include all relevant stakeholders, as well as a framework and policies to promote healthy aging; (ii) creating age-friendly communities that promote senior health by removing barriers against good health and well-being; (iii) aligning health-care systems with the shifting burden of disease to meet basic needs and the complex health needs of older people; (iv) creating an integrated and efficient system to provide long-term care for older people; and (v) generating knowledge on healthy aging and how to measure and monitor it to advance the study of healthy aging. Further, WHO member states endorsed a comprehensive mental health action plan for 2013–2030.

An age-friendly environment is important for improving the lives of all older people. To this end, WHO is leading the United Nations' Decade of Healthy Aging, 2021–2030. Age-friendly environments influence social determinants of health and healthy aging by removing the physical and social barriers that hinder older people, thus improving their functional ability. A healthy aging strategy and action plan in the PRC, for example, prioritizes age-friendly environments through home modification and promotes age-friendly communities to facilitate access to health infrastructure, thereby mitigating functional dependency in older people (Chen et al. 2022). A randomized control trial found that home modification reduced disability and improved the quality of life and mental health of older people in the PRC (Szanton et al. 2011).

---

[15] Effective 1 February 2021, ADB placed a temporary hold on sovereign project disbursements and new contracts in Myanmar.

Figure 2.17: Universal Health Coverage Index, by Economy and Subregion

◆ 2010   ■ 2019

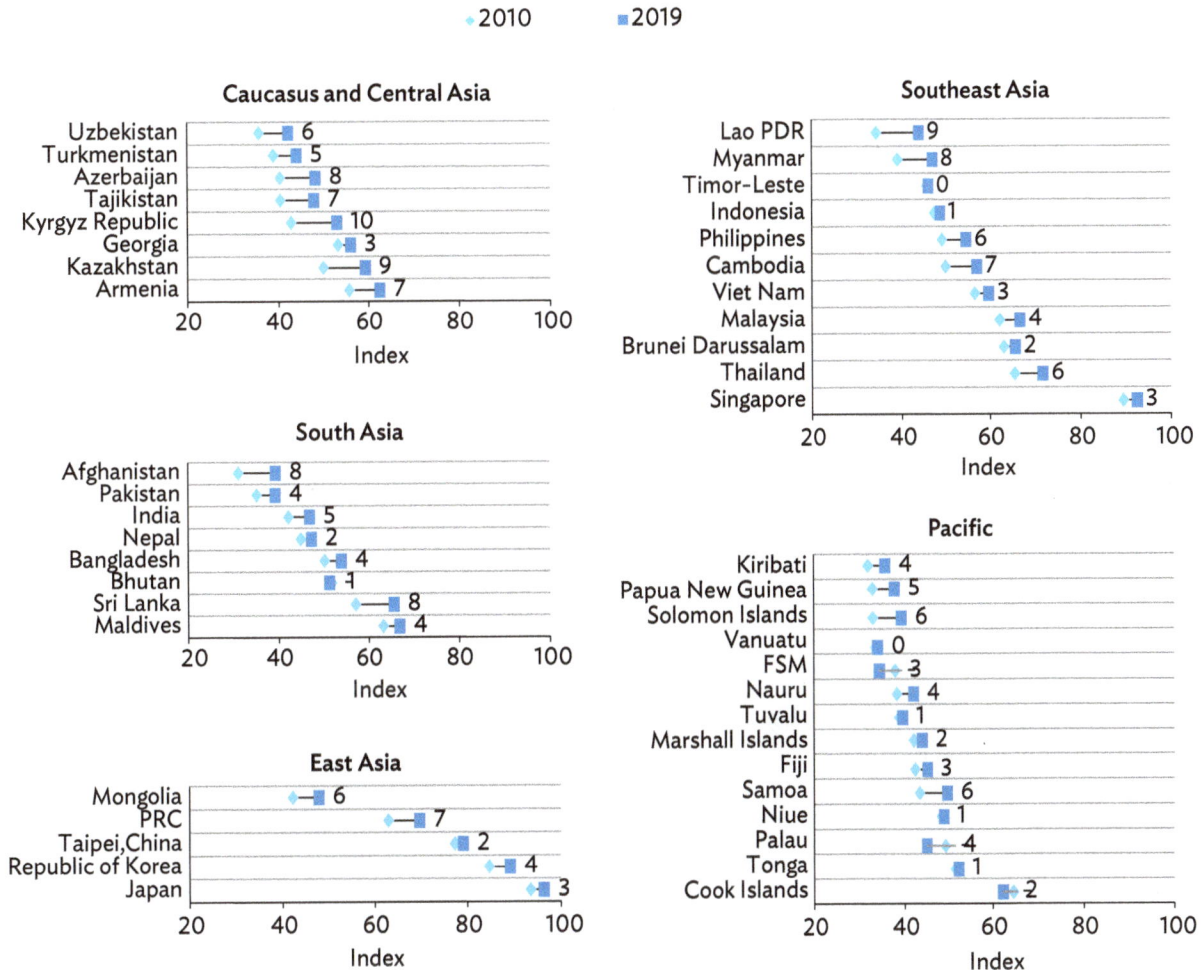

FSM = Federated States of Micronesia, Lao PDR = Lao People's Democratic Republic, PRC = People's Republic of China.

Note: Numbers in figures show point gains or losses from 2010 to 2019.

Source: World Health Organization.

Health and other interventions need to be coordinated to promote older people's health and well-being. NCDs arise from socioeconomic, environmental, and behavioral factors. Studies have linked ambient air pollution to cardiovascular disease, respiratory disease, and lung cancer. Indoor air pollution from fuelwood is associated with diabetes, disabilities, poor sleep quality, and poor cognitive and mental health (Chen et al 2020; Liu, Chen, and Yan 2020). Poor water quality is associated with acute and chronic gastrointestinal infection (Murray et al. 2020). Policies to improve air and water quality and

mitigate other environmental hazards facilitate the prevention and management of chronic disease risk. In the PRC, for example, the implementation of a clean air policy was associated with reduced depression (Chen et al. 2022). Safe water can largely address the problem of waterborne infectious diseases in many parts of the world. Building resilience with measures to adapt to climate change promises to reduce risk to older people's physical and mental health (Chapter 5). Addressing financial insecurity through cash transfers, old age allowances, and social pensions can promote mental health in older people (Alzua et al. 2020; Bando, Galiani, and Gertler 2020).

2.4 Policy Directions to Promote Healthy Aging and Older People's Health

Access to health care and the promotion of lifelong health investment are crucial to healthy aging. Lack of health care is an important impediment to healthy aging. A top priority is to achieve effective UHC, which would extend essential services and interventions to all older people, enabling them to optimize their capacity and functionality. At the same time, the health status of older people reflects health-promoting investment and behavior over their lifetimes. Therefore, policies and incentives are needed to encourage Asians of all ages to pursue healthy lifestyles. Health-care systems must be transformed to foster healthy lives and well-being for Asians of all ages.

2.4.1 Meeting the Diverse Health-Care Needs of Older People

Solid progress in achieving UHC is a priority. Coverage should meet older people's diverse health-care needs, sustaining physical and mental health and functional ability through an integrated approach while adopting innovation and reform to enhance efficiency and prevent financial stress on the health-care system. Reform toward government-led health insurance initiatives is a top priority because insurance enables older people to use health-care services. Expanded access is particularly important for the disadvantaged, those suffering from multiple NCDs, and older women vulnerable to disability. A gender gap in NCD prevalence necessitates primary care for NCDs and interventions tailored to women's specific needs.

Assessable and comprehensive primary health-care systems need to treat and manage NCDs effectively. The primary health-care systems are entry points for equitable NCD care provision and can facilitate community-based and sustainable care over the long term. Access to basic diagnostic tools and essential medicines is essential, as are good medical information and referral systems. A set of primary care NCD

interventions endorsed by WHO includes detection, diagnosis, and care for NCDs such as cardiovascular disease, diabetes, and chronic respiratory diseases, as well as guidance on healthy lifestyles, self-care, and palliative care. This care can be delivered by primary care physicians and other health workers and is feasible in disadvantaged settings. Training for health workers and the availability of affordable basic technologies as well as essential medicines are a prerequisite to effectively delivering NCD care in primary care facilities.

Governments are encouraged to explore cost-effective and pro-poor interventions to address NCDs. Highly cost-effective NCD interventions that can be delivered through primary health-care systems include aspirin prescriptions for acute coronary syndrome and health screenings for the early detection of NCDs (Watkins, Ahmed, and Pickersgill 2024). Such low-cost interventions can be highly effective in preventing premature mortality and, more broadly, improving health in developing Asia, especially among poor people and disadvantaged groups.

Behavioral nudges can help prevent and mange NCDs. Older people can benefit from behavioral nudges that promote physical activity, healthy diets and nutrition, regular health checkups, adherence to medication regiments, and smoking and alcohol abstinence. Examples of effective interventions include positive health messaging; mobile health apps with features that track food consumption, exercise, and weight and provide a virtual behavior-change coaches; and vouchers or subsidies to increase health screening.

Primary care facilities must provide cost-effective mental health services. Mental health services should be made accessible to all communities by integrating them into primary health care. They must follow standard protocol to provide effective mental health care for older people. WHO Mental Health Gap Action Program outlines effective clinical protocols for assessing and managing mental health conditions, including services for neurological disorders and substance abuse in nonspecialized settings, which is cost-effective in low- and middle-income economies. Other low-cost interventions for older people include cognitive behavioral therapy by nonspecialists.

A priority is to leverage mental health technologies in primary health-care settings. The management of mental health conditions can be facilitated with digital mental health apps and mental health platforms such as telehealth and telepsychiatry to enable remote consultations with mental health professionals.

Some mental illness can be abated by addressing functional disability and financial insecurity. Simply providing eyeglasses or walkers that allow older people to venture outside, for example, can improve their mental health by reducing their sense of isolation and improving self-esteem. As financial insecurity causes stress and anxiety, cash transfers, old age allowances, and social pensions can promote mental health.

2.4.2 Promoting Healthy Aging through a Life-Cycle Approach

Investment in health promotion must be strengthened. Adopting a life-cycle approach for the entire population requires investment in health promotion and disease prevention for people of all ages. Free annual health checkups and lifestyle evaluations should be made available to young and old alike, in both rural and urban areas. Another policy tool is highly visible health awareness publicity campaigns targeting NCDs that are supported by adequate coordination between primary health-care providers and other stakeholders.

Digital solutions should be introduced to primary health care to facilitate NCD screening, early detection, monitoring, and management. Integrating digital technology into health care has emerged as a key priority for low- and middle-income economies, as it can enhance connectivity between primary and specialist care providers and thus strengthen person-centered integrated care.

Community-based primary health is an additional tool for effective NCD prevention. Engaging the community, including community health workers, in primary health care through health checkups, health screening promotions, home care support, and social care effectively safeguards older people's health at low cost. These services can be linked to mental

health care to enable early detection of conditions and effective referral of patients to clinical and social services. Innovating and expanding community approaches to build strong primary-care systems for disease prevention and health promotion can yield big dividends for old-age health.

Policies to promote healthy aging must go beyond health-care service delivery. Sin taxes discourage smoking and the unhealthy consumption of alcohol, sugar, and salt, which are common causes of NCDs. Investment in age-friendly physical environments can remove the physical and social barriers that hinder older people, thus improving their functional ability and mental health. Going forward, policymakers must prioritize improving air and water quality and mitigating other environmental hazards. Providing safe water is an effective way to reduce the risk of chronic disease among older Asians. Finally, addressing climate change promises to reduce risks to physical and mental health in old age.

2.5 Conclusion

In recent decades, developing Asia saw significant improvement in health, including for older people. However, increased life expectancy and changes in lifestyle have worsened the prevalence of NCDs and mental disorders. Rising longevity has proved to be a double-edged sword. While healthy longevity improves well-being in old age, longevity in ill health places a heavy strain on health-care systems. The strategic challenge facing regional policymakers is to ensure for current and future cohorts of older people health care that is affordable, sustainable, and high-quality.

Health care and lifelong investment in health are key to older people aging well and in good health. UHC must extend integrated services and interventions to older people so they can optimize their capacity and functional ability. Major threats to older people's health and well-being are posed by the high prevalence of NCDs and mental illness, especially among older women, and from emerging threats from infectious diseases and climate change. Good health is central to aging well, and preparation for this must start early in life. Measures to prevent disease and promote health must reach everyone, of whatever age, gender, or socioeconomic status. Governments must adopt policies and programs that leverage technology-driven solutions and behavioral insights to facilitate NCD and mental illness screening, early detection, monitoring, and management. This is how they can nurture aging yet healthy populations.

3 Work and Retirement of Older Persons

Work can support the well-being of older people. It can be fulfilling and provide a sense of achievement. It can confer social status and sustain social engagement. And it generates income to cover current expenses and save for retirement. In these ways, work contributes directly to well-being while also saving, for the economy as a whole, expenditure on social security. However, sometimes work diminishes well-being. It can be strenuous, taxing, tiring, and detrimental to physical and mental health, especially as an older person's work capacity declines.

Whether work benefits older people or not depends on a number of factors. Decent work in older age can support individual well-being by strengthening financial security, maintaining social connections, and ensuring a sense of self-worth. However, many older workers in Asia and the Pacific work at menial jobs in the informal sector with little choice but to "work till they drop," as they say. Ultimately, how work benefits or harms older workers depends on three key factors: whether or not they work out of necessity, have physical capacity to work, and have opportunities for decent work. It is therefore not so easy to determine the net effect on older people's well-being across an economy.

Informal workers may have little choice but to work. The overwhelming majority of older workers in developing Asia work in the informal sector. Many lack pensions or adequate old-age security benefits and therefore need to keep working for sustenance. Many also lack basic labor protection from injuries on the job or a safety net against disabling illness. Many poor informal workers lack the savings and social support that would allow them to retire, so they keep working despite the strain, sometimes even in ill-health.

At the same time, a growing share of formal sector workers in the region with increased capacity to work are retiring increasingly early. Improved health in older workers means greater capacity to work and reduced strain from working, which makes it more attractive for older people to work longer. However, other changes tend to shorten working lives. Experience in advanced economies shows that high savings derived from rising incomes and better pension coverage militate against a longer working life and make retirement more attractive (Börsch-Supan and Coile 2021). This chapter shows that low statutory retirement age in the region leaves many older people with substantial residual capacity to work. Further, lower mortality rates and better odds for survival into old age can encourage workers to save toward retirement and retire early in good health to enjoy retirement life (Kalemli-Ozcan and Weil 2010). The opposing factors of better health and retirement finance make it difficult to discern trends in labor force participation by older people. Other factors at play are political, institutional, and cultural, as well as the personal circumstances of individuals unrelated to their own health or financial situation, such as the need to be available to provide informal care.

This chapter analyzes the work and retirement patterns of older workers and their motivations. Trends in labor force participation are presented and analyzed considering three dimensions that influence whether older people work: necessity, capacity, and opportunity. Policy insights and recommendations follow the analysis.

3.1 A Snapshot of the Labor Market for Older Workers

The rate at which older people participate in the labor market shows considerable diversity. Differences exist between regional economies, genders, and age cohorts. Factors that help explain differences include an economy's stage of development and structure, in particular employment on and off the farm; the stage of demographic transition; and how much women participate in the labor force. In addition, laws, institutions, and culture play a role in determining whether individuals work in older age.

3.1.1 Labor Force Participation by Older Men and Women

Most men in their late 50s and early 60s continue to work. Labor force participation by men aged 55–64 ranges from 60% to 80% in nearly all of the 34 economies in Figure 3.1. The average share in developing Asia is 73.4%, practically equal to the 74.5% average share of the Organisation for Economic Co-operation and Development (OECD) members. For those aged 65 and above, the rate is 32% in developing Asia, substantially higher than 20.7% in the OECD. Several economies report participation rates over 50% for men 65 and older, notably the Pacific island economies of Tonga and Vanuatu. At the other extreme, low participation is common in the Caucasus and Central Asia, where participation in Armenia, Azerbaijan, Kazakhstan, Turkmenistan, and Uzbekistan is below 10%.

Older women are less likely to work than older men. This is carry-through of lower participation at younger ages. For women aged 55–64, only 12 of 34 economies report a participation rate above 50%. The average in developing Asia is 41.9%, well below 56.1% in the OECD. The participation of this cohort is particularly low in South Asia, below 25.0% in India, Nepal, and Pakistan and not much higher at 28.6% in Bangladesh. A large drop in women's labor force participation after age 65 is notable in the Caucasus and Central Asia, which is also

true for men in the subregion. Labor force participation for all older women in developing Asia is 15.3%, substantially higher than the 11.1% OECD average.

In the past 2 decades, labor force participation has risen for older women but fallen for older men. Across 34 economies, participation by men aged 55–64 fell in 24 economies. For women, the trend is the opposite, with participation increasing in 24 economies. A rise in participation among those aged 65 and over is notable in the rapidly aging economies of Hong Kong, China; Singapore; Sri Lanka; Taipei,China; and Viet Nam. However, considerable diversity exists, as about a third of economies do not follow these trends for either women or men.

The large variation in labor force participation suggests that each economy has its own dynamic. That dynamic reflects the key factors that influence the opportunity and decision to continue working or retire. While better health encourages greater participation, expanded pensions and higher savings from higher wages reduce the need to work and therefore the participation rate. In each economy, a unique interplay of upward and downward pressures determines the net trend over time for each gender and age cohort.

Labor force participation has a U-shaped relationship with economic development. At low stages of development, the participation rate of older people is high (Figure 3.2). As the economy develops, participation falls. It then reaches an inflection point after which it starts to rise again in tandem with higher development. Of 43 Asian economies covered, 9 have gross domestic product (GDP) per capita above $32,684, the inflection point for the group aged 55–64, and 4 have GDP per capita above $64,974, the inflection point for the group aged 65+. The relationship is shown by the fitted lines in Figure 3.2. Asia's developing economies are represented by blue dots, with other economies by orange. In panel A and in panel B, the downward-sloping line indicates participation falling as income rises. Higher income provides more savings and allows for retirement. As economies progress through the middle-income stage, they tend to improve pensions and other old-age social benefits, thereby providing the financial security needed to retire.

Figure 3.1: Labor Force Participation, by Age Group and by Gender, 2021

A. Male

Legend: ■ 2021 ◆ Rate in 2000, indicates rising LFP ◆ Rate in 2000, indicates falling LFP

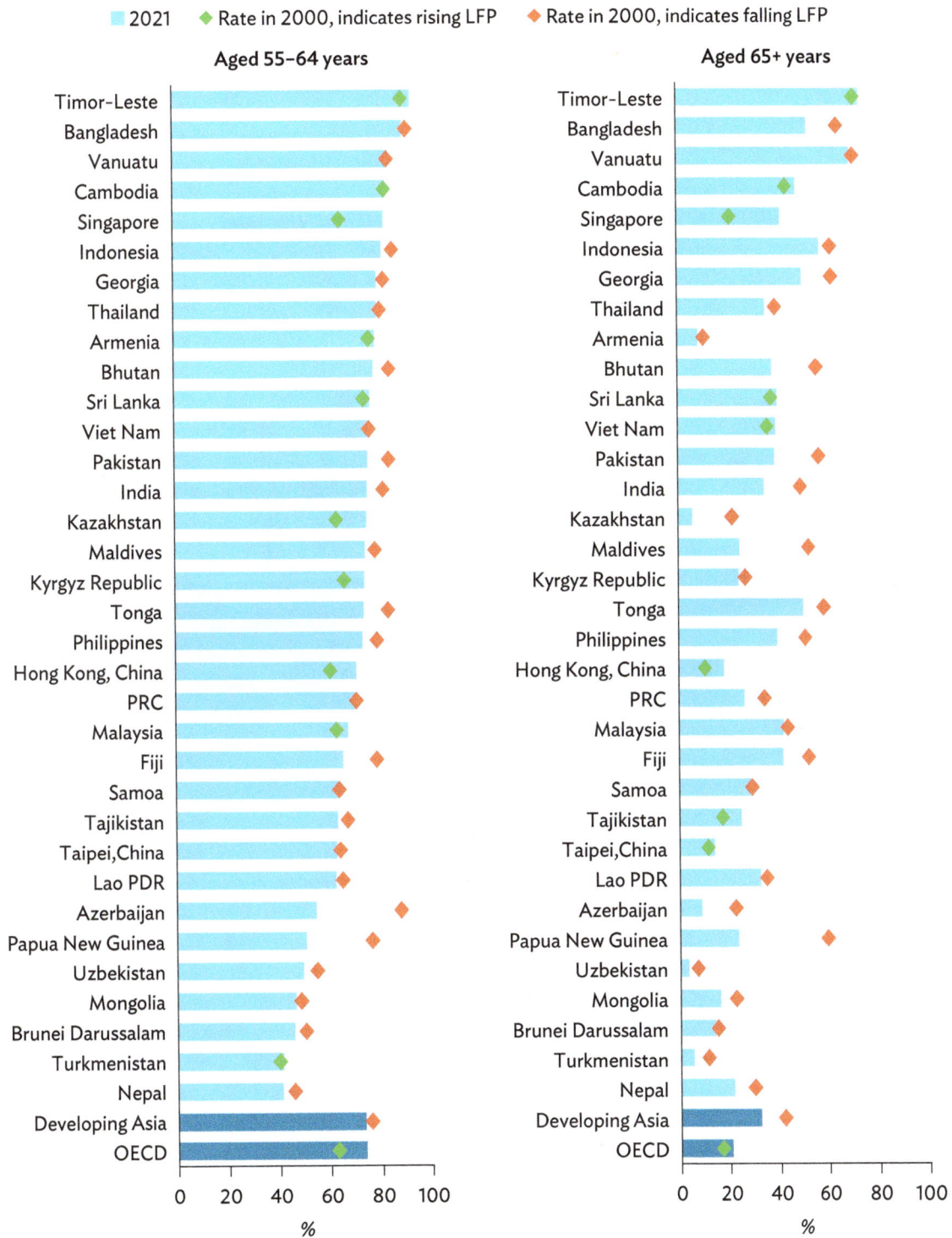

Aged 55–64 years / Aged 65+ years

Countries listed top to bottom: Timor-Leste, Bangladesh, Vanuatu, Cambodia, Singapore, Indonesia, Georgia, Thailand, Armenia, Bhutan, Sri Lanka, Viet Nam, Pakistan, India, Kazakhstan, Maldives, Kyrgyz Republic, Tonga, Philippines, Hong Kong, China, PRC, Malaysia, Fiji, Samoa, Tajikistan, Taipei,China, Lao PDR, Azerbaijan, Papua New Guinea, Uzbekistan, Mongolia, Brunei Darussalam, Turkmenistan, Nepal, Developing Asia, OECD

continued on next page

Figure 3.1 *continued*

B. Female

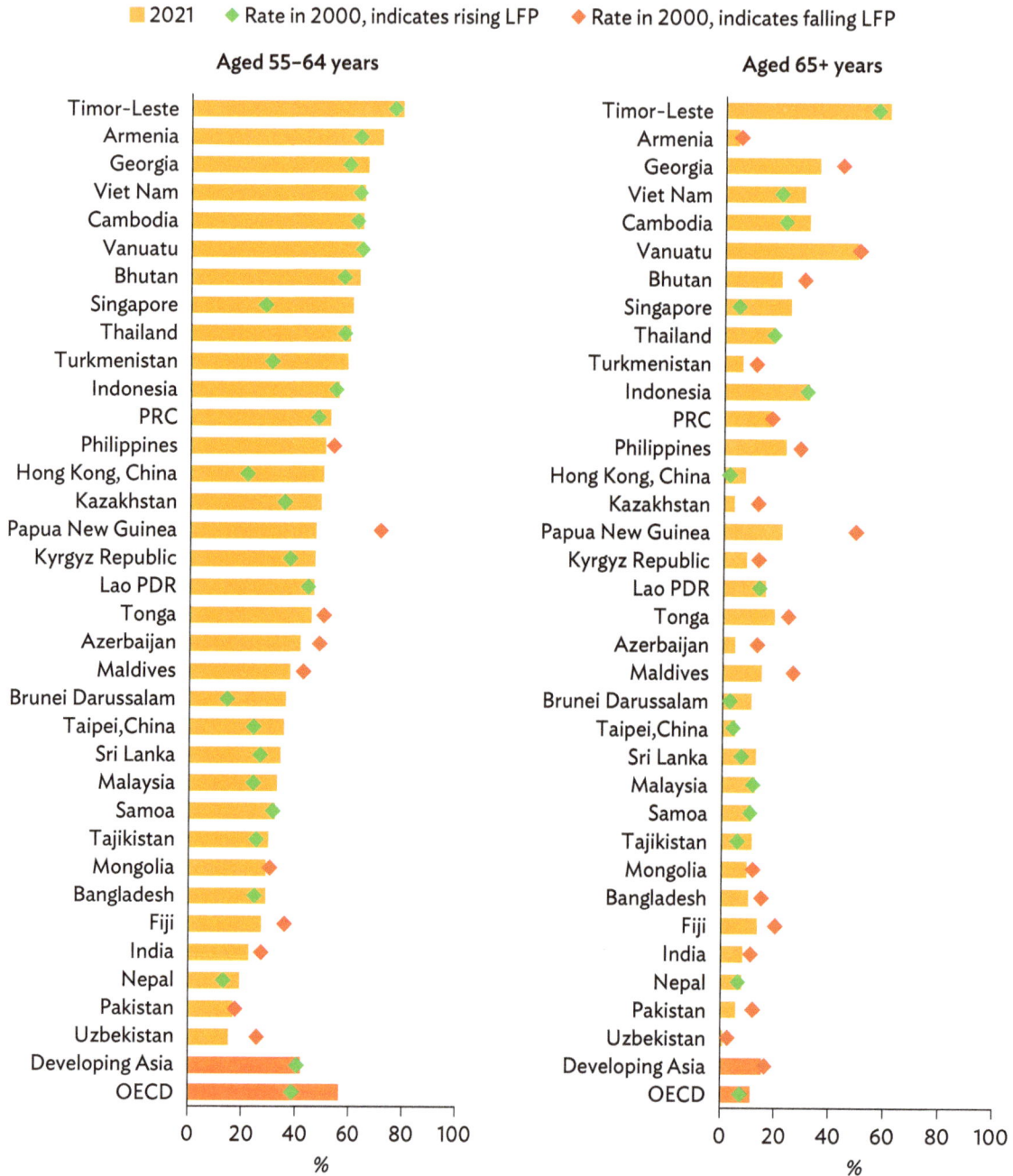

Lao PDR = Lao People's Democratic Republic, LFP = labor force participation, OECD = Organisation for Economic Co-operation and Development, PRC = People's Republic of China.

Notes: The labor force participation rate is based on estimates using models from the International Labour Organization (ILO). OECD includes all its 38 members.

Source: ILO. ILOSTAT.

After the inflection point, income and labor force participation both rise. People in higher-income economies tend to have better health and therefore greater capacity to work into old age. Further, they expect to live longer and so work longer to save more for retirement. An additional factor is that some high-income economies have raised their statutory retirement age, providing scope to work longer. The U-shapes shown here consider men and women together, but the same pattern holds for men and women separately.

The coronavirus disease (COVID-19) undermined the employment of older people. A national survey of older people in Viet Nam found that 14% of older workers suffered salary cuts and/or other income loss; and another 14% lost their jobs to forced resignation, business closure, or early retirement. The economic impact of the pandemic was felt not only in individual employment status but also in income loss for co-living family members. In rapid assessments in Bangladesh, Cambodia, India, Myanmar, Pakistan, the Philippines, and Sri Lanka, 81% of older people said their income was diminished by COVID-19.

Figure 3.2: Labor Force Participation and GDP per Capita, by Age Group, 2021

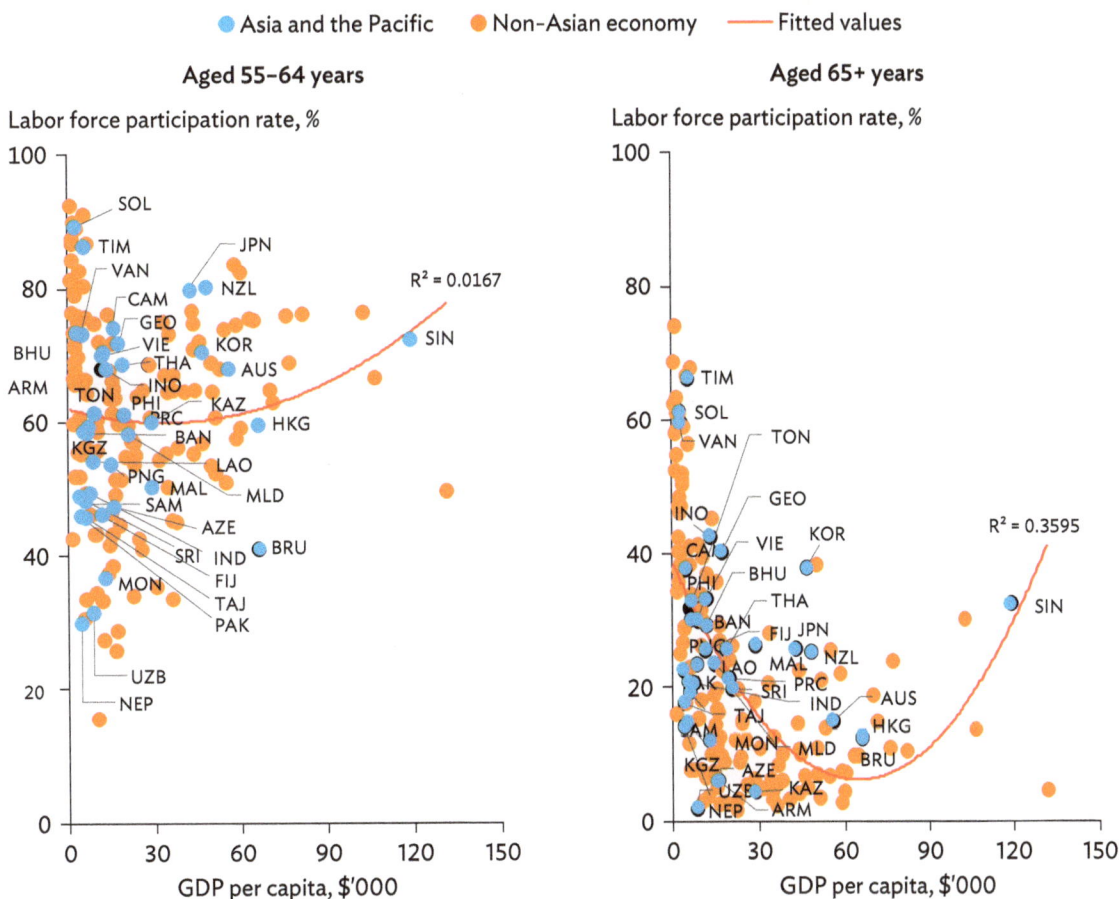

ARM = Armenia; AUS = Australia; AZE = Azerbaijan; BAN = Bangladesh; BHU = Bhutan; BRU = Brunei Darussalam; CAM = Cambodia; FIJ = Fiji; GDP = gross domestic product; GEO = Georgia; HKG = Hong Kong, China; IND = India; INO = Indonesia; JPN = Japan; KAZ = Kazakhstan; KGZ = Kyrgyz Republic; KOR = Republic of Korea; LAO = Lao People's Democratic Republic; MAL = Malaysia; MLD = Maldives; MON = Mongolia; NEP = Nepal; NZL = New Zealand; PAK = Pakistan; PHI = Philippines; PNG = Papua New Guinea; PRC = People's Republic of China; SAM = Samoa; SIN = Singapore; SOL = Solomon Islands; SRI = Sri Lanka; TAJ = Tajikistan; THA = Thailand; TIM = Timor-Leste; TKM = Turkmenistan; TON = Tonga; UZB = Uzbekistan; VAN = Vanuatu; VIE = Viet Nam.

Notes: Labor force participation rate in 2021 is based on estimates using models from the International Labour Organization (ILO). GDP per capita is purchasing power parity in 2021, current United States dollar prices.

Sources: ILO; and World Bank. World Development Indicators.

Among the surveyed older people in these economies, 44% were regularly employed or ran their own business, many in agriculture or petty trade (UNESCAP 2022).

3.1.2   Older Workers in Informal Jobs

An overwhelming majority of older workers work in the informal sector. In economies with available data, an average 94% of people aged 65 and above are informally employed, often in precarious circumstances (Figure 3.3). Work informality among older workers is particularly high in South Asia: 92% in Sri Lanka, 97% in India, and 99% in Bangladesh. The share of informal workers in the older category, especially women, is substantially higher in each economy than the average for all ages. Women who work informally are overrepresented in manufacturing, as family workers and as paid domestic helpers.

3.1.3   Older Worker Employment and Retirement

Many older people in the region, especially men, continue to work until very old age. Among the economies with an employment rate for men in their early 70s exceeding 50%, the Republic of Korea (ROK) recorded 50.8% in 2020 and Indonesia 56.9% in 2022 (Figure 3.3). In line with women's substantially lower labor force participation rate at all ages, the rate at which older women are employed is also lower.

In recent decades, employment rates have changed in various ways for all age groups. Some economies have seen employment rates for both men and women drop substantially, particularly at older ages, possibly as they advance in their stage of economic development (Figure 3.4). This is true of Nepal and the People's Republic of China (PRC) and, to a lesser extent, Fiji and the Philippines. Some economies, like the ROK, have seen substantial increases in employment, particularly among older people and women, possibly as a result of pension reform and policies to promote women's participation in the labor force.

Figure 3.3: Share of Workers Who Work Informally, 2021

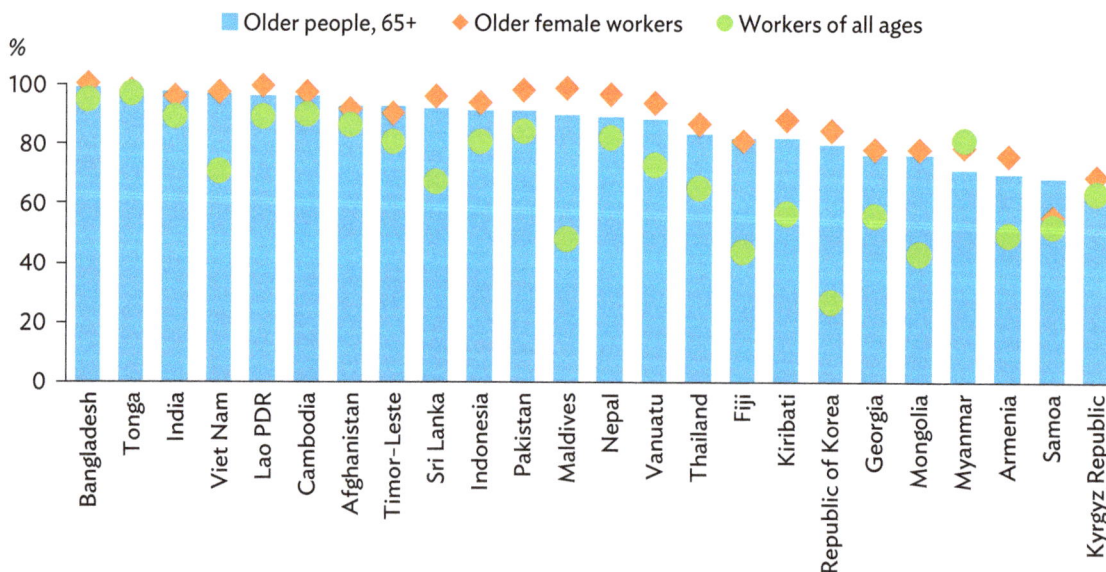

Lao PDR = Lao People's Democratic Republic.

Source: United Nations Economic and Social Commission for Asia and the Pacific. Demographic Changes in Asia and the Pacific (accessed 8 June 2023).

Figure 3.4: Employment Rate, by Gender, Age, and Economy

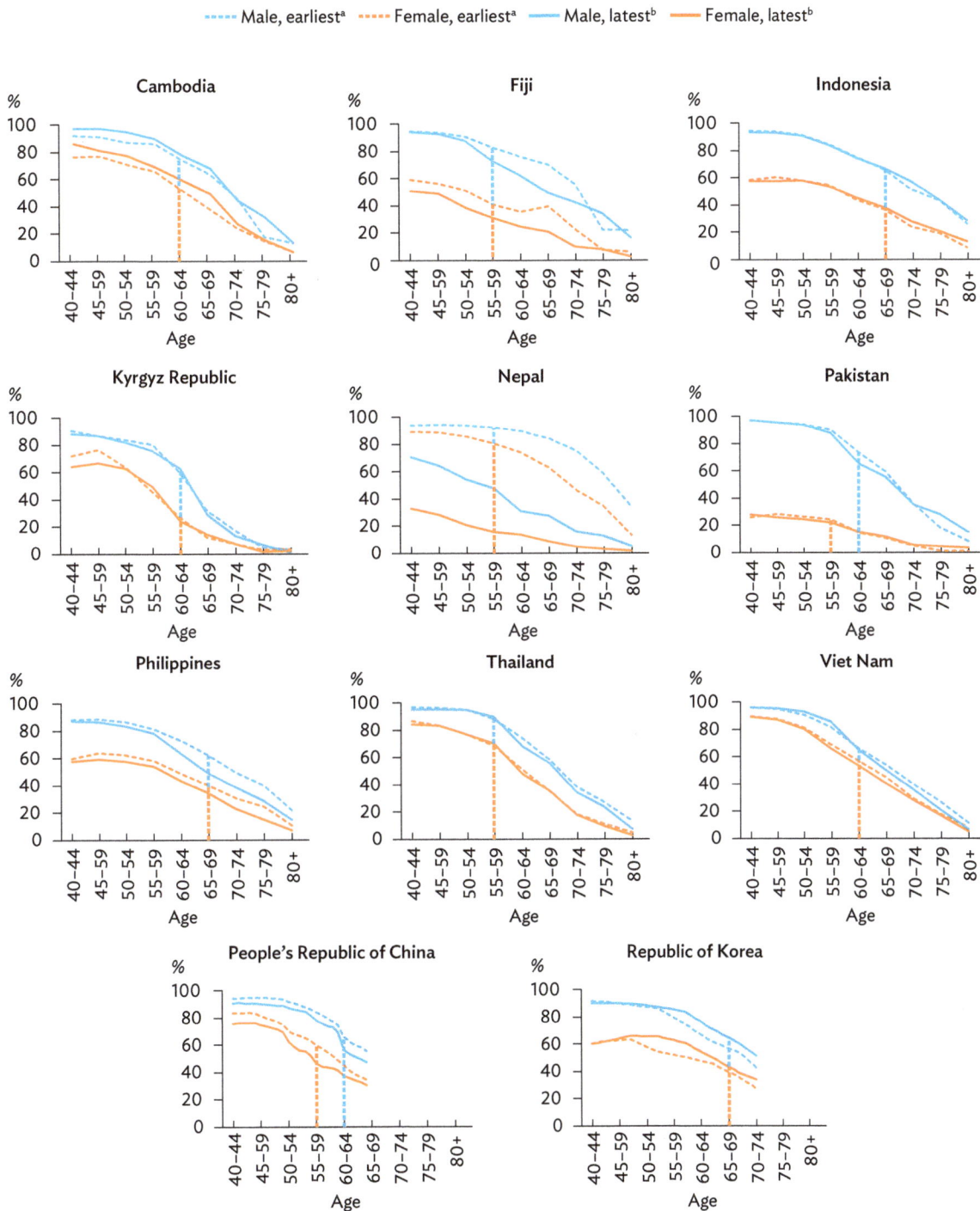

‑ ‑ ‑ ‑ Male, earliest[a] ‑ ‑ ‑ ‑ Female, earliest[a] —— Male, latest[b] —— Female, latest[b]

[a] As of 2000 for the Republic of Korea; 2008 for Nepal; 2009 for Pakistan; 2010 for Fiji, Indonesia, the Kyrgyz Republic, the People's Republic of China; the Philippines, Thailand, and Viet Nam; and 2012 for Cambodia.

[b] As of 2015 for Fiji and the People's Republic of China; 2017 for Nepal and Pakistan; 2018 for the Kyrgyz Republic; 2019 for Cambodia; 2020 for the Republic of Korea; 2021 for the Philippines; and 2022 for Indonesia, Thailand, and Viet Nam.

Notes: Dotted vertical lines represent retirement age for male and female, respectively.

Sources: Asian Development Bank estimates using labor force surveys from national sources.

Most economies have seen relatively little change in employment for either men or women in recent decades. This may reflect opposing forces that mark economic development, as discussed earlier. In addition, experience in advanced economies suggests that pension eligibility in particular imposes an implicit tax on work that lowers labor force participation among older workers (Milligan and Wise 2011). In many economies, income effects may cancel out improved health and job safety.

Where pension coverage is high, employment drops abruptly for the near-old, or those close to the statutory retirement age. Notable economies are the Kyrgyz Republic and the PRC, where many workers exit the labor market at the statutory retirement age. In the PRC, statutory retirement is set at a younger age for women, triggering their earlier exit. Women in Pakistan similarly have an earlier statutory retirement age than men, but with less impact on retirement given women's low labor force participation. Overall, employment rates for women still lag in many economies. While Cambodia and the Philippines, and especially Japan and the ROK, see convergence in employment rates for men and women, in most economies the gap is large and shows no sign of converging, as women's employment rates have changed little in recent years.

Older workers with only primary education are likely to remain in the labor market beyond the statutory retirement age (Figure 3.5). Workers with tertiary education, by contrast, exhibit a marked drop in employment at about the statutory retirement age, having recorded a high employment rate during their prime working age. This distinct pattern of labor force participation by educational attainment implies that highly educated workers, who have employment-linked pensions or other retirement assets, are able to retire, while less-educated workers continue to work out of necessity because they have no such support for retirement.

Average actual retirement age varies substantially across economies. Average retirement age for older adults is relatively high in Bangladesh and the ROK at

63 years but lower in the PRC at 54 and in Viet Nam at 52. Substantial use of early retirement options in the PRC, where the statutory retirement age for men is 60 and pension coverage is relatively high, recalls trends observed in OECD economies in the 1980s and 1990s. In the PRC—as in many developing economies—productivity has risen rapidly, partly because younger workers entering the labor force tend to be significantly more productive than older ones. Fang, Qiu, and Zhang (2022) showed that these productivity differences are the reason behind early retirement, as there is little demand for less-productive older workers who receive higher wages than younger, more productive colleagues. Early retirement may subside as productivity differences between older and younger workers narrow, spurred by all workers' greater educational attainment and acquisition of skills.

Women retire earlier than men in all economies, and retirement comes late for workers with the lowest educational attainment. The retirement age gap by gender is particularly wide in the PRC at 7 years and much narrower in Indonesia at 2 years and in Malaysia at 1 year (Figure 3.6). All three economies maintain different statutory retirement ages by gender. The gender difference in retirement is also low, at less than 1 year, in Bangladesh and India where the employment rate for women of prime working age is generally low and there is a single retirement age for both genders. On average across the economies presented here, workers with incomplete elementary schooling tend to retire 2 years later than those with upper secondary and tertiary education. However, individual economies display substantial differences: the education-retirement gap is wide in Indonesia and the ROK but much narrower in the other economies—and even reversed in the PRC. On average, workers living in rural areas, where work informality is more pervasive, retire 1.4 years later than those in urban areas. For the ROK and Indonesia, the gap is greater, with rural workers retiring 4 years later than urban workers. The education and residence gaps are in line with the perceived necessity to continue working for longer due to lack of financial preparedness for retirement.

Figure 3.5: Labor Force Participation, by Age, Educational Attainment, and Economy

——— Primary   ——— Secondary   ——— Tertiary

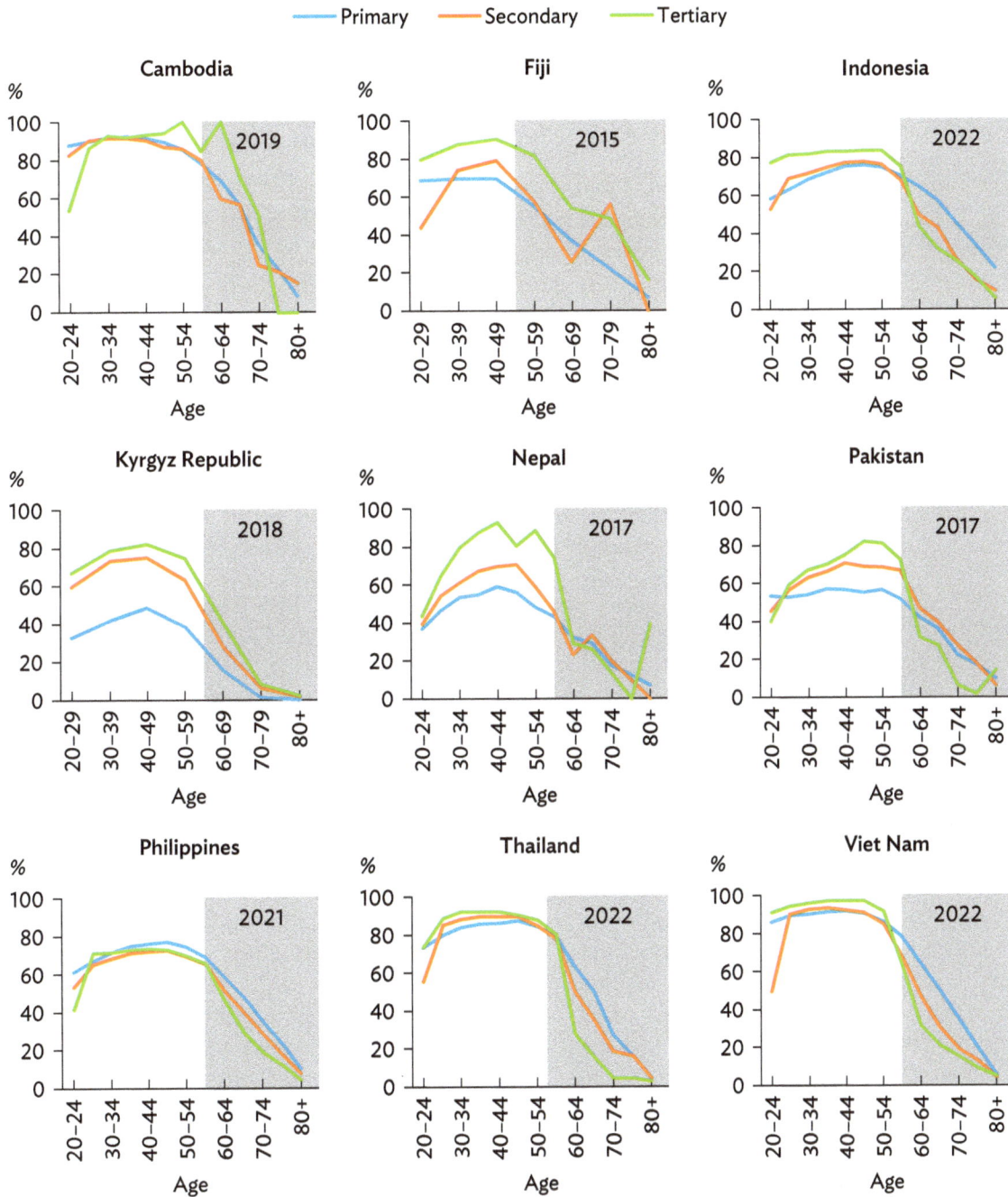

Notes: Shaded area is beyond statutory retirement age. The year in the upper right corner is the survey year.

Source: Asian Development Bank estimates using labor force surveys from various economies.

Figure 3.6: Average Actual Retirement Age, by Economy

A. By gender

B. By residence

C. By educational attainment

■ Tertiary and above
■ Upper secondary and vocational
■ Elementary and lower secondary
■ Less than elementary

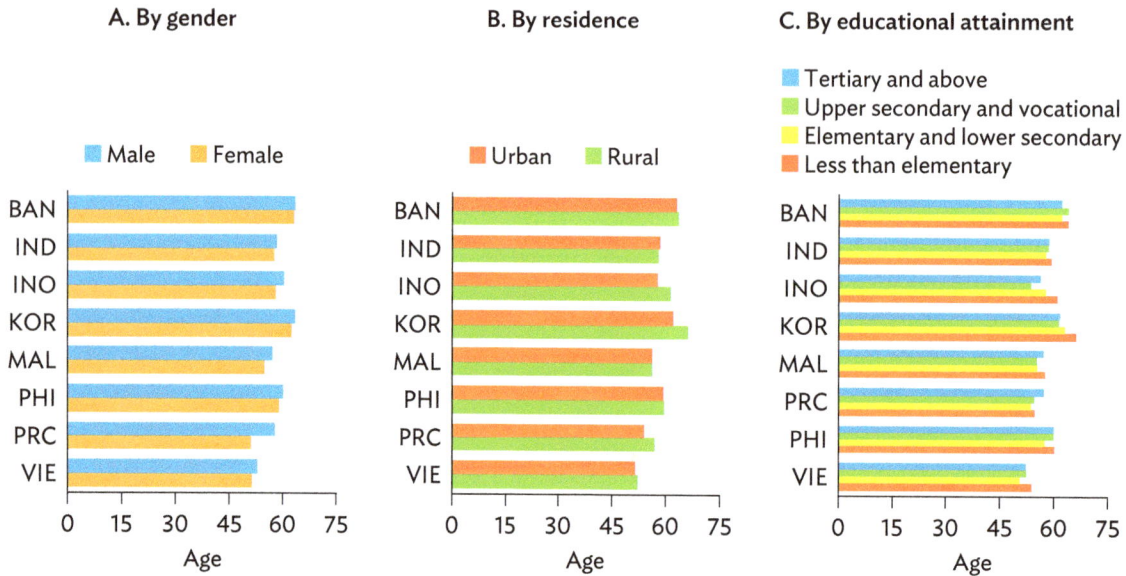

BAN = Bangladesh, IND = India, INO = Indonesia, KOR = Republic of Korea, MAL = Malaysia, PHI = Philippines, PRC = People's Republic of China, VIE = Viet Nam.

Notes: These are reported actual retirement age of those who are retired, not currently working, and 40 years old and above. Survey years are 2017–2019, 2021, and 2023.

Source: Chapter 1, Box 1.1.

3.2 Well-Being and Work in Old Age

Decent work can benefit well-being in old age in many ways. Work in old age may be positive for individual well-being for financial reasons and for maintaining social connections and creating a sense of self-worth (Mori et al. 2024). In fact, older workers tend to be more satisfied with their jobs than younger workers. Figure 3.7 shows job satisfaction to be surprisingly high, which probably reflects in part the difficulty of measuring it, but in almost all economies, job satisfaction tends to improve with age. Certainly, there may be self-selection issues, as those who remain employed in old age, especially after 80, may gain greater satisfaction from work than those who retire. In developing economies, however, where many older workers work until very old age, high job satisfaction may reflect appreciation toward simply having a job.

Many older workers in the region do not have desirable jobs but still "work till they drop." Because

they lack the safety net to retire with dignity, they are forced to continue working, risking their health and jeopardizing their well-being. Governments thus face a dual problem and need to strike a balance between allowing older workers to retire with dignity and promoting decent work for those older workers who are willing and able to work.

Work benefits older workers or not depending on necessity, capacity, and opportunity. The decision to continue working is ultimately a choice between leisure and work made by weighing pros and cons. As workers age, factors like health, the presence or absence of social support and savings, and demand for work play greater roles in the decision (Figure 3.8). These factors largely determine how working in old age affects well-being.

3.2.1 Work Necessity in Old Age

Most older workers work out of necessity if they do not have the financial or social means to retire. In some cases, work can jeopardize their physical

Figure 3.7: Job Satisfaction in Selected Economies, by Age Group

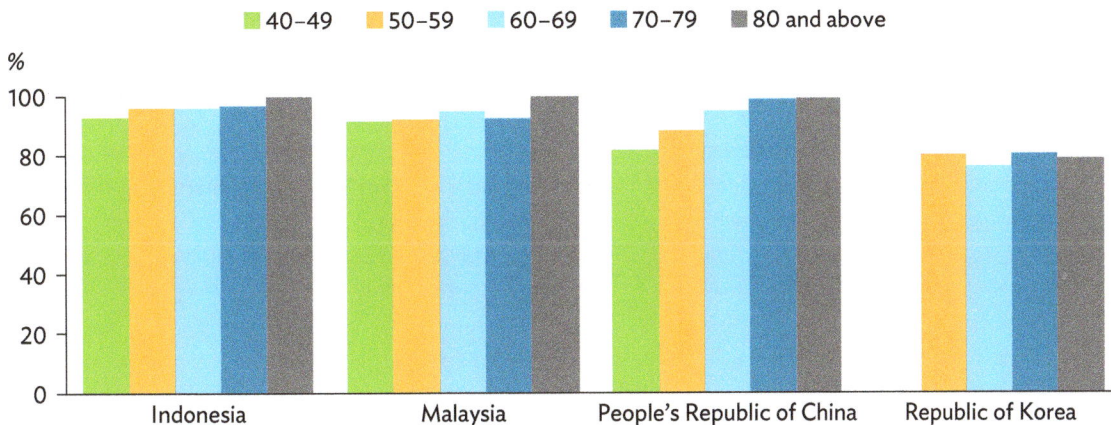

Notes: The figure shows the share of workers who self-report being satisfied with their jobs. Job satisfaction in Indonesia and the Republic of Korea means agreeing or strongly agreeing with the statement, "I am satisfied with my job." In Malaysia agreeing with that statement, as opposed to being neutral or disagreeing; and in the People's Republic of China responding as somewhat satisfied, satisfied, or very satisfied with the job. Survey years are 2018, 2021, and 2023.

Source: Chapter 1, Box 1.1.

Figure 3.8: Three Factors Governing How Work Affects Well-Being in Old Age

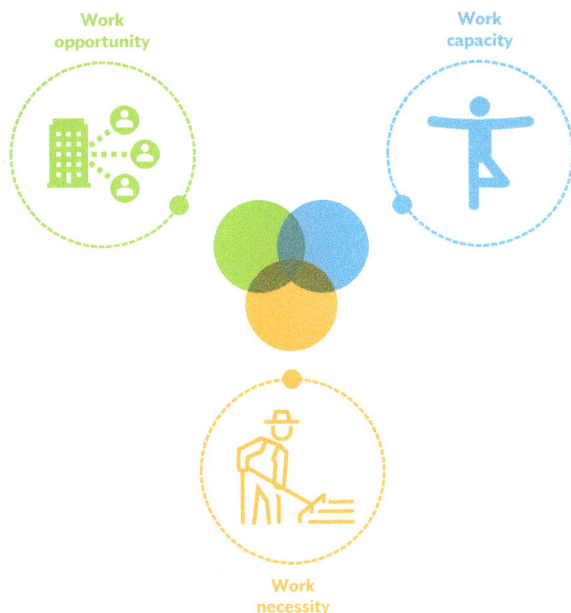

Source: Asian Development Bank.

and mental well-being. Informal workers generally lack contributory pensions or other safety nets that would allow them to retire with dignity. Many of them work simply because they need the money to provide for themselves and their families. While not all older workers in the informal sector work out of necessity, and not all those who work out of necessity jeopardize their well-being, the large shares of older workers in informal employment can indicate their vulnerability.

Widespread informality for older workers can reflect a transition from formal to informal work as they age. In Viet Nam, a cohort analysis based on data from multiple years of the national labor force survey suggests that the share of mature workers in informal employment has grown over time as they age. This pattern is most pronounced for women in their 40s, for whom informality doubled from 14% in 2007 to 28% in 2017, while informality for men rose from 20% to 24% (Kikkawa and Gaspar 2022). A similar trend is reported in Indonesia, where informally employed workers tend to continue to work informally as they age while formal workers gradually move into the informal sector or exit the labor force (Kudrna, Le, and Piggott 2020). Meanwhile, the situation in Sri Lanka is somewhat more upbeat, as the share of the mature labor force in their early 40s working without a pension or provident fund decreased from 31% in 2006 to 28% in 2017 for men, and from 23% to 20% for women.

Agriculture employs most older workers in several economies, which explains widespread informality. The share of older workers in agriculture increases with age. The share of aged 60 and older is particularly high in Bangladesh, Cambodia, Indonesia, Pakistan, and Viet Nam, where it exceeds 50% (Figure 3.9). Across all economies, the share is highest in the 75–79 age group, as their exodus from the labor force is more pronounced in other sectors. Farm employment tends to be informal, which means scant pension coverage and no statutory retirement age. Many farmworkers are farm owners themselves, who usually continue to work on their farms until late in life. Farms may be passed on to the next generation, with the older generation continuing to help out with chores and at peak seasons.

The average age of farmworkers is rising as the region's populations age and economic development draws younger workers away. In Thailand, the average age of farmworkers increased by about 5 years in the past decade to 48, as did the average age in Viet Nam to 46. In Fiji, it rose by 2 years to 43, as in the Kyrgyz Republic to 39. The experience of economies with advanced aging suggests that agriculture may remain the major sector employing older people, especially as fewer young workers choose to work in it. In Japan, farmers are now in their late 60s on average (MAFF 2021). The adoption of technology to automate farmwork can reduce its physical intensity and thus help older people work longer in the sector (ADB 2019). In addition to technology adoption, measures to mitigate the adverse impact of climate change on aging agricultural workers merit greater attention. Other initiatives should ensure access for older farmers to agricultural credit with which to procure technology. They can do so by identifying alternative collateral and using big data to enhance lending models to reduce and diversify risk. Models may enhance collaboration with microcredit and agricultural cooperatives because these local actors possess information with which to assess older farmers' creditworthiness in given circumstances. Training and technical advice may be provided to older farmers.

Urban and rural workers have distinctly different retirement patterns, largely reflecting formal versus informal employment. Employment rates for workers in urban areas decline abruptly upon reaching statutory retirement age (Figure 3.10). As discussed, this drop in employment is spurred by old-age pension entitlement. However, workers in rural areas show little discontinuity in employment rates as they age. Again, this suggests a lack of pension entitlement, which highlights the importance of supporting vulnerable older workers in rural areas.

High informality leaves many older workers with neither a clear plan to retire nor financial preparedness for it. Chapter 4 of this report shows that the share of financially prepared workers in the near-retirement group varies widely between economies and depends heavily on having the financial means derived from wealth and other public and private sources, on household composition for cross-subsidization, and on educational attainment, which closely relates to financial literacy. Given a strong education gradient in informality, it is likely that many informal workers are financially ill-prepared to retire and must continue to work no matter what. In fact, survey data from Indonesian and Malaysian working adults reflect this reality (Figure 3.11). Over 40% of respondents in Malaysia and over 15% in Indonesia have not given much thought to retirement. Interestingly, this share is comparable between workers aged 60–69 and those 70+. A quarter of respondents aged 60 or more plan to work until their health fails in Malaysia, a share that exceeds 40% in Indonesia. Workers in all age groups would benefit from guidance on thinking about and planning their remaining working life and how to transition to retirement.

Figure 3.9: Share of Employment, by Sector and Age

- ■ Agriculture, forestry, and fishing
- ■ Manufacturing
- ■ Other industries
- ■ Other services
- ■ Public services
- ■ Real estate and other business activities
- ■ Transportation, information technology, and finance
- ■ Wholesale and retail trade

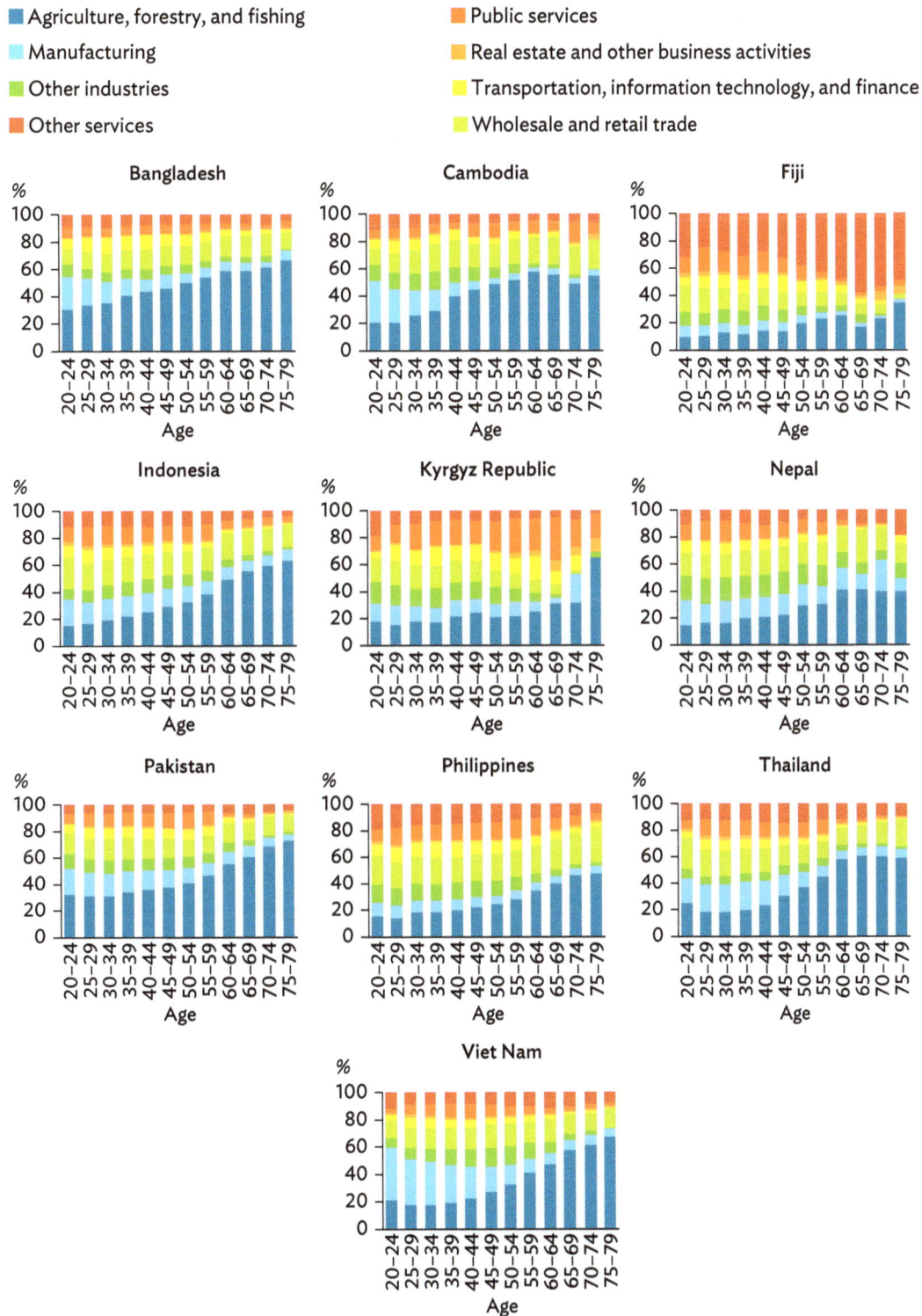

Note: As of 2010 for Bangladesh; as of 2015 for Fiji; as of 2017 for Nepal and Pakistan; as of 2018 for the Kyrgyz Republic; as of 2019 for Cambodia; as of 2021 for the Philippines; and as of 2022 for Indonesia, Thailand, and Viet Nam.

Source: Asian Development Bank estimations using labor force surveys from national sources.

Figure 3.10: Employment Rate, by Residence and Age

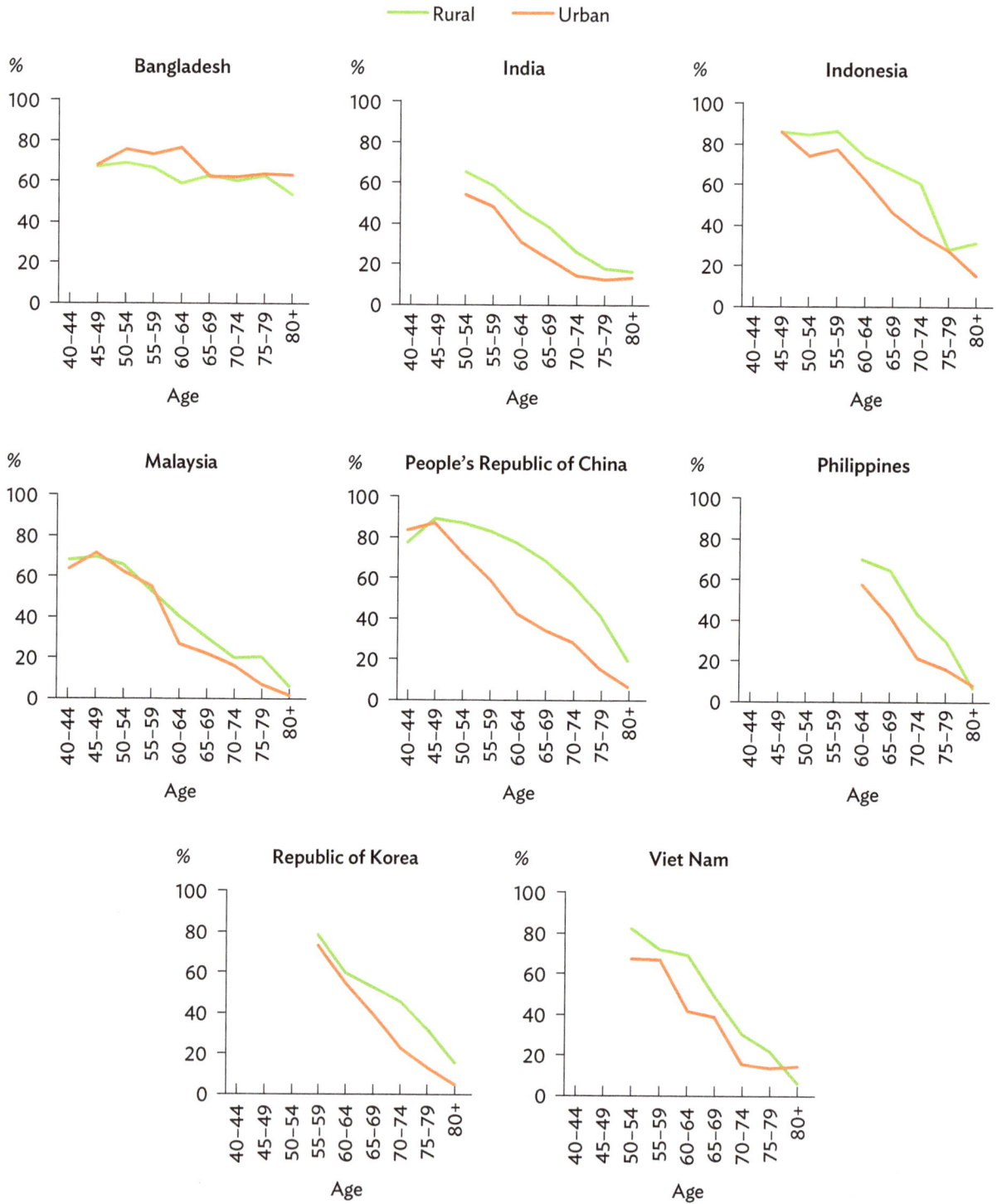

Note: Survey years are 2017–2019, 2021, and 2023.

Source: Chapter 1, Box 1.1.

Figure 3.11: Retirement Prospects and Plans

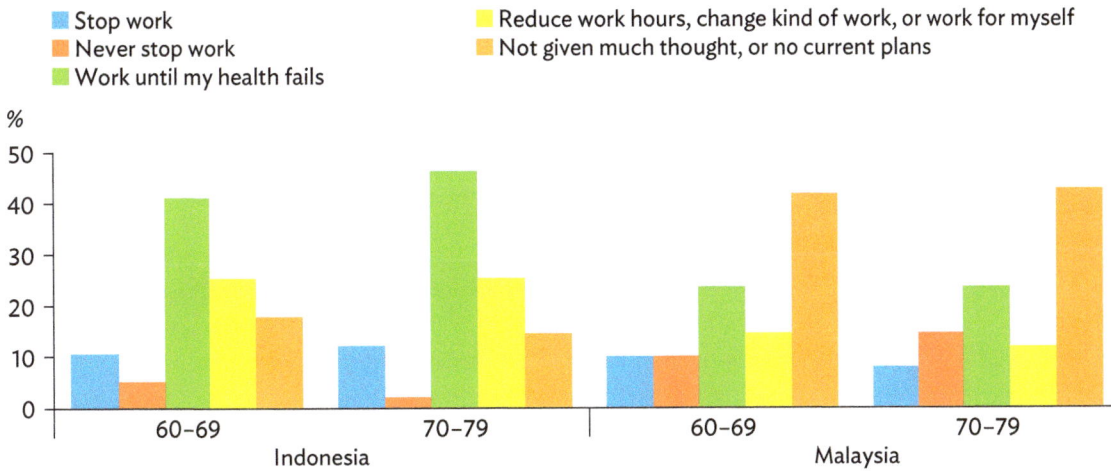

Legend:
- Stop work
- Never stop work
- Work until my health fails
- Reduce work hours, change kind of work, or work for myself
- Not given much thought, or no current plans

Note: Survey years are 2021 and 2023.
Source: Chapter 1, Box 1.1.

3.2.2   Work Capacity in Old Age

Improved health and longevity in Asia and the Pacific mean that more people are healthy enough in old age to keep working. Poor health is associated with early withdrawal from the labor force (Mitra et al. 2020; van Rijn et al. 2014; Kim and Mitra 2022). The region has witnessed great improvement in health and longevity over recent decades, allowing many older workers to work for longer. One question is whether workers have the mental and physical capacity to work past the current retirement age.[16]

Health capacity to work is, broadly, how much a person can work given his or her health status. An older cohort's additional health capacity to work can be estimated using a method laid out by Milligan and

Wise (2015). The method quantifies it by comparing the employment rate of different cohorts that have the same mortality rate. If a cohort of older people today work less than past workers with the same mortality rate, they are considered to have untapped health capacity to work.[17]

In most economies, older cohorts have additional health capacity to work. Figure 3.12 shows that the health capacity of men and women aged 55–69 has increased in the past 15 years in eight Asian economies.[18] The PRC had the largest increase in health capacity to work among the economies analyzed here, with men gaining 2.2 years of additional work capacity and women 2.9 years, despite data limitations that allowed estimates for only the 55–64 age group. Malaysia recorded 2.2 more years for men but only 0.4

[16]   Capacity for work is a complex concept that includes physical and mental health, physical and cognitive functionality, and human capital aspects such as education and skills. Capacity for work can mean different things, as does disability, depending on the individual and the context. The focus here is on health capacity to work.

[17]   The model relies on several assumptions described in detail in Milligan and Wise (2015). A key assumption is that mortality is a good proxy for health status. The validity of this assumption can be checked by comparing mortality rates by age group with other measures of health such as self-assessed health status (Kikkawa et al. 2024b). The Milligan and Wise method also assumes that all increases in life expectancy translate into additional years of capacity to work. As the method is calculated relative to a base year, results may vary depending on the year selected. For this reason, it is best to interpret the results as providing only an approximation of how long people can work.

[18]   As estimates for individual economies used different baseline and endline years, results are standardized to measure the additional work capacity created over the period of 15 years. Standardization assumes that additional work capacity increases in a linear manner over time.

years for women. Older men in India gained 1.9 years and women 0.9 years. As in the PRC, older women outpaced men in Thailand, gaining 1.8 years to men's 1.3 years. Meanwhile, older men in Indonesia and older women in Japan lost work capacity.

Caution is required when interpreting the results for female health capacity to work (Oshio, Usui, and Shimizutani 2020). In Japan, Indonesia, Malaysia, and the ROK, women added little additional health capacity to work or even lost capacity, but this result demands scrutiny. Employment rates for women in the region have increased largely from higher labor force participation, mainly a dividend from cultural shifts and a transition from unpaid to paid work. However, the model mechanically subtracts increased employment at all mortality levels from additional health capacity to work, which may be misleading.

Older people's additional health capacity to work can inform estimates of their untapped capacity. To overcome some of the limitations of the previous model, one can estimate the share of older people who do not work but could work, estimating their capacity with a regression-based simulation method developed in Cutler, Meara, and Richards-Shubik (2013). The method uses data on people nearing retirement age to obtain parameters of association between their employment status and their health and other characteristics.[19] These parameters are then used to estimate their work capacity.

A large majority of men in their 60s have untapped health capacity to work. Men's health capacity to work in their early 60s is estimated at about 80% or more in all of the economies analyzed, indicated in Figure 3.13 by the height of combined blue and orange

Figure 3.12: Additional Years of Work Capacity in Older Persons Aged 55–69

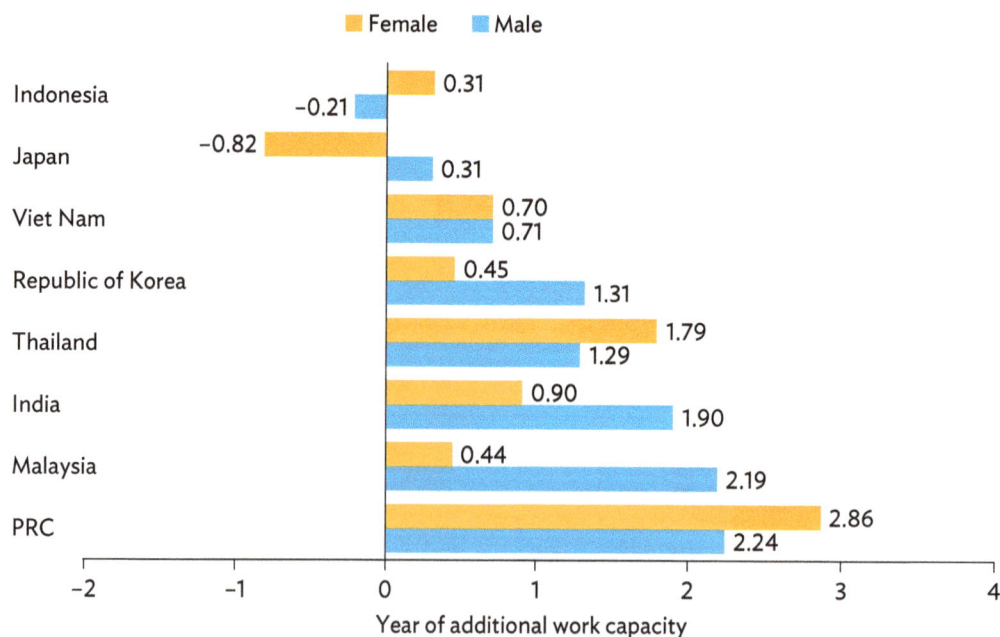

PRC = People's Republic of China.

Note: Data for the PRC are for ages 55–65.

Sources: Asian Development Bank estimates using Chen and Park (2024); Giang, Kikkawa, and Park (2024); Lee et al. (2024); Mansor, Awang, and Park (2024); Oshio Shimizutani, and Kikkawa (2024); Suriastini, Wijayanti, and Oktarina (2024); Zhao et al. (2024); Longitudinal Ageing Study in India (2019); and International Labour Organization. Labor Force Survey 2000 and 2019 data.

---

[19]   Near-retirement age is 50–59 for men except in Indonesia, which uses 50–54. For women, it is 50–59 except in Indonesia and Viet Nam, which use 50–54.

bars for those working and not. Among those who are healthy to work, the share not working, or untapped work capacity, ranges from 10% in Viet Nam (7.8% of total population not working when 77.8% having capacity to work) to 22.6% in India. Men in their mid to late 60s have health capacity only slightly lower and much greater untapped capacity, ranging from 24.8% in Indonesia to 37.1% in Thailand.

Women in their 60s have substantial untapped health capacity to work. Estimated work capacity is lower for women than for men, in part because the association between health and employment is looser for women as, in many economies, many healthy women are not gainfully employed (Figure 3.13). However, estimates suggest that women have more untapped health capacity to work than do men. These results need to be interpreted with caution because the statutory retirement age for women in some economies is lower than for men, notably in Indonesia, the PRC, and Viet Nam, and some women retire before it. Tapping older women's work capacity will require addressing their disproportionate burden of informal care, which constrains their time available to take up paid jobs.

Figure 3.13: Untapped Work Capacity, by Age Group, and Gender

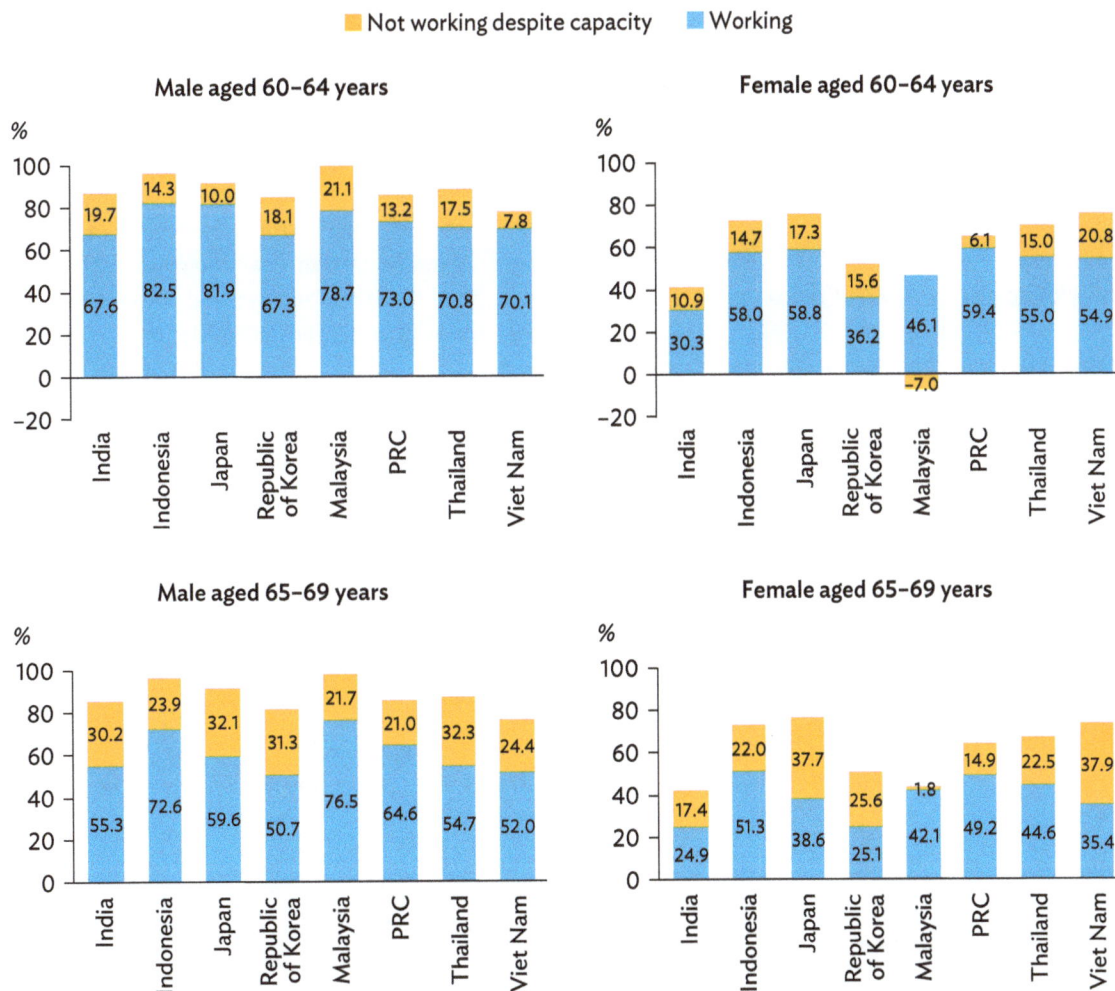

PRC = People's Republic of China.

Note: Untapped capacity to work is defined as people with health capacity to work but do not work.

Sources: Asian Development Bank estimates using Chen and Park (2024); Giang, Kikkawa, and Park (2024); Lee et al. (2024); Mansor, Awang, and Park (2024); Oshio, Shimizutani, and Kikkawa (2024); Suriastini, Wijayanti, and Oktarina (2024); and Zhao et al. (2024); and methodology from Cutler, Meara, and Richards-Shubik (2013).

Untapped work capacity is greater for urban residents than for rural residents. It is also greater among well-educated people than among less-educated people and among formal workers than among informal workers (Kikkawa et al. 2024b). This finding is consistent with the general observation that formal sector jobs are more likely to be held by educated people with savings, pensions, and retirement benefits. They are therefore more likely to retire despite possessing the capacity to work. In contrast, most jobs in the rural areas are in agriculture or otherwise informal, with the consequent lack of pension coverage inhibiting the ability to retire.

Untapped work capacity can become a silver dividend in economies that encourage older people to stay in the labor force. Better physical health is a key factor generating an additional year of capacity to work in some Asian economies. This silver dividend can be tapped by promoting the employment of older workers. If fully realized, the dividend could raise GDP by an average of 0.9% across the eight economies shown in the table in Box 3.1.

3.2.3   Work Opportunity in Old Age

Older people who want to work and have the capacity to do so need the opportunity. Labor force data suggest that workers continue in their usual informal pursuits for many years into old age without a specific retirement age (Figure 3.5). Older people can benefit from working, but only when work is adequate and adaptable to their needs and capacity. This means having the opportunity to work in jobs that are less physically demanding and do not jeopardize their health. It also requires that jobs offer schedule flexibility, possibly allowing them to transition toward retirement. Generally, ensuring that older workers have opportunities to thrive in the labor market requires that ageism be addressed.

3.2.3.1   Shifting Older Workers into Jobs with Lower Physical Demands

Older workers typically work in agriculture, which generally offers poor-quality jobs that can cause job strain (Shoghik et al. 2022). The risk of accidents is high from difficult working conditions, physical fatigue, and little or no abidance by occupational health and safety regulations. Further, the physical health and cognitive functions of older people are known to be disproportionately affected by rising temperatures under environmental degradation and climate change (Fritz 2022; Lai et al. 2022), inducing higher mortality rates (Yu, Lei, and Wang 2019). Older agricultural workers who spend many hours outside may be particularly vulnerable to these environmental factors and would thus benefit from measures to mitigate and adapt to climate change.

Technological advances in agriculture may enable older workers to prolong their careers. Mechanization may reduce fatalities, injuries, and work-related ill-health. Many older farmers in the region have already adopted machinery such as four-wheel tractors for tillage and combine harvesters (Srisompun, Charoenrat, and Thipayanet 2014). The government can help older workers absorb new information and overcome difficulties in adjusting to new ways of working through lifelong learning programs in coordination with agricultural cooperatives and training centers. Some farm technologies may need to be adapted to the capacities and needs of older farmers (Anriquez and Stloukal 2008).

Older people lack the agricultural credit and investment they need to procure farm technology. Many loan programs target young farmers but not older ones. To tackle credit constraints on older farmers in the region, financial institutions are encouraged to explore ways to offer more credit by reducing and diversifying risk through, for example, acceptance of alternative collateral, the use of big data to enhance lending models, and the provision of training and technical advice to older farmers. Support for microcredit and agricultural cooperatives may be considered, as these local actors can garner the information needed to assess older farmers' creditworthiness.

Older workers may increasingly be ready to shift toward less demanding jobs. Chapter 1 of this report shows that years of schooling and literacy have increased substantially in recent decades (Figure 1.8). Importantly, future generations of older workers will be better educated than current cohorts (Figure 3.14). In every economy in the region, the share of older people with at least upper secondary education will

Box 3.1: Silver Dividend from Untapped Capacity for Work

A silver dividend is growth potential generated by untapped work capacity in older people. The dividend was estimated for seven Asian economies using a method described in Cutler, Meara, and Richards-Shubik (2013). This method was supplemented with calculations to estimate the contribution to gross domestic product (GDP).

Untapped work capacity is valued at the minimum wage to calculate the contribution to GDP. This low wage is used to account for downward pressure on wages that may be exerted by increased labor supply from older people—probably a conservative estimate (Matsukura et al 2018). However, another assumption, that older people work full time, may provide an upward bias.[a] Possible fiscal savings as more people remain in work are not considered.

Results suggest the silver dividend may be high in more aged societies, such as Japan and the Republic of Korea. GDP could increase by 1.4% and 1.5%. In emerging economies with aging populations, the effect may also be sizable. For example, it may raise GDP in India by 1.5%, Viet Nam by 1.1%, and Thailand by 0.9%. More moderate contributions, at 0.4% or lower, are likely in Indonesia, Malaysia, and the PRC.

References

Chen, Z. and A. Park. 2024. Understanding the Health Capacity to Work among Older Persons in Rural and Urban Areas in the People's Republic of China. *Asian Development Review*. 41(1).

Cutler, D. M., E. Meara, and S. Richards-Shubik. 2013. *Health and Work Capacity of Older Adults: Estimates and Implications for Social Security Policy.* Social Science Research Network.

Giang, L. T., A. Kikkawa, and D. Park. 2024. Health Capacity to Work Among Older Adults in Viet Nam. *Asian Development Review*. 41(1).

Gubert J., K. Milligan, and D. A. Wise. 2009. Social Security Programs and Retirement around the World: The Relationship to Youth Employment, Introduction and Summary. *NBER Working Papers* 14647. National Bureau of Economic Research.

Kondo, A. 2016. Effects of Increased Elderly Employment on Other Workers' Employment and Elderly's Earnings in Japan. *IZA Journal Labor Policy*. 5(2).

Lee, S.-H., C-K. Park, H. K. Kim, and D. Park. 2024. Health Capacity to Work at Older Ages in the Republic of Korea. *Asian Development Review*. 41(1).

Matsukura, R., S. Shimizutani, N. Mitsuyama, S.-H. Lee, and N. Ogawa. 2018. Untapped Work Capacity among Old Persons and their Potential Contributions to the "Silver Dividend" in Japan. *Journal of the Economics of Ageing*. 12.

Mansor, N., H. Awang, and D. Park. 2024. Health Capacity to Work among Older Malaysians. *Asian Development Review*. 41(1).

Oshio, T., S. Shimizutani, and A. Kikkawa. 2024. Health Capacity to Work among Older Japanese Persons. *Asian Development Review*. 41(1).

Suriastini, N. W., I. Y. Wijayanti, and D. Oktarina. 2024. Older People's Capacity to Work in Indonesia. *Asian Development Review*. 41(1).

Zhao, J., C. K. Law, J. Piggott, and V. S. Yiengprugsawan. 2024. Health Capacity to Work among Older People in Thailand. *Asian Development Review*. 41(1).

Value of Untapped Work Capacity, Aged 60–69

Economy	$ million	Year	Increase in GDP if Untapped Work Capacity Is Utilized, %
India	43,388	2019	1.5
Indonesia	3,044	2014	0.3
Japan	69,646	2019	1.4
Republic of Korea	25,464	2020	1.5
Malaysia	674	2020	0.2
PRC	59,292	2018	0.4
Thailand	3,712	2015	0.9
Viet Nam	2,973	2019	1.1
Average			0.9

GDP = gross domestic product, PRC = People's Republic of China.

Sources: Asian Development Bank estimates using Chen and Park (2024); Giang, Kikkawa, and Park (2024); International Labour Organization. ILOSTAT. Wages and Working Time Statistics Database. Lee et al. (2024); Mansor, Awang, and Park (2024); Oshio, Shimizutani, and Kikkawa (2024); Suriastini, Wijayanti, and Oktarina (2024); and Zhao et al. (2024).

[a] Increased labor supply from older workers arguably has potential to displace younger workers. Not taking this effect into account may create more upward bias, but evidence for it in developing Asia is scant. Empirical evidence from advanced economies is mixed, generally suggesting no direct impact (Kondo 2016; Gubert, Milligan, and Wise 2009).

Source: Kikkawa A., T. Oshio, Y. Sawada. S. Shimizutani, N. Ogawa, A. Park, and T. Sonobe. 2024. Health Capacity to Work among Older Persons in Asia: Key Findings from a Regional Comparative Study. *Asian Development Review*. 41(1).

Figure 3.14: Share of the Population Aged 40–64 with Post-Secondary and Upper Education

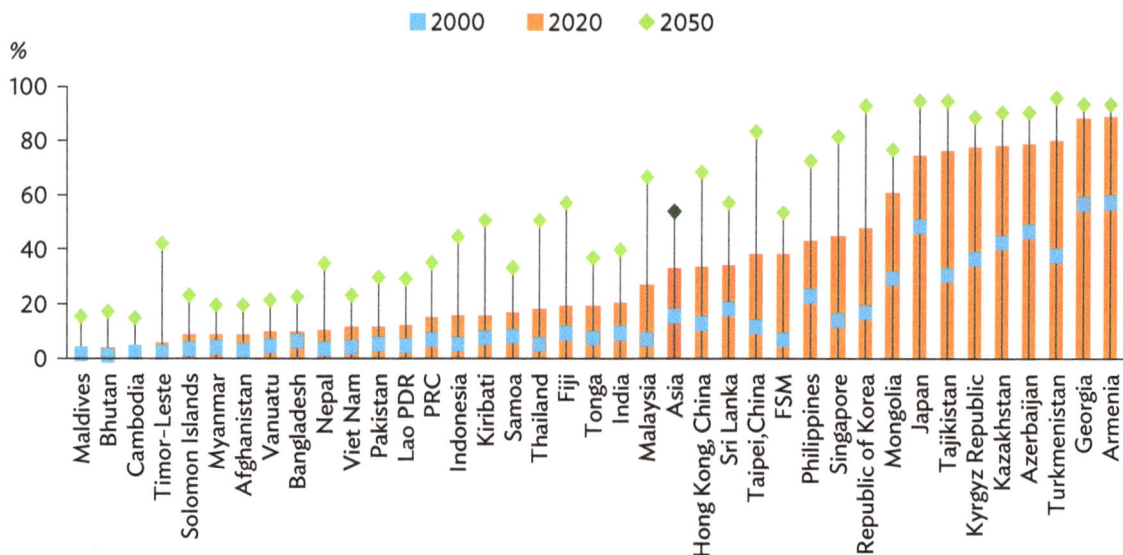

FSM = Federated States of Micronesia, Lao PDR = Lao People's Democratic Republic, PRC = People's Republic of China.
Source: Wittgenstein Centre for Demography and Global Human Capital. Wittgenstein Centre Human Capital Data Explorer.

increase by 2050, despite substantial variation in the share of people attaining that level of education. This will give older people better access to decent jobs and enhanced capacity for training and reskilling. However, policymakers must implement lifelong learning and address the silver digital divide to help workers translate formal education into productive job skills that ensure continued employability.

Skills development and lifelong learning can make older workers more attractive to employers. By providing training programs tailored to older adults, several economies in Asia enable them to acquire the skills and knowledge necessary to navigate the rapidly evolving job market. However, employers are often reluctant to engage older workers and provide training because returns on training are expected to be low (OECD 2019b). It is thus important to encourage lifelong learning and the acquisition of skills, rather than providing training only late in life. In Singapore, support for older workers relies on early intervention through the Professional Conversion Program, which helps mid-career workers reskill and transition into new industries or occupations. The program offers training and salary support to help individuals acquire the skills necessary for successful job conversion. In

Kazakhstan, older workers nearing or above retirement age are included in the formal education system through silver universities. This allows them to pursue continuing education, acquire new knowledge, and enhance their personal and professional development.

Studies on how training makes older workers more employable and productive have found effects varying from small to moderately positive (Picchio and van Ours 2013; Charness and Czaja 2006). Evaluation must take into account possible bias as people self-select into training. Little evidence exists on how effective Asian initiatives are that aim to make mature workers more employable. In the ROK, training in information and communication technology has been found effective at mitigating productivity decline among well-educated older workers (Lee, Kwak, and Song 2022). Training on the job can help retain employees and has been shown to improve the employability of older workers in the ROK (Lee, Han, and Song 2019). Evidence from advanced economies shows that success lies in formulating effective programs that suit the needs, learning patterns, and interests of mature workers and encourages them to enroll in them throughout their careers, not just when nearing retirement age, and in encouraging employers to invest in the skills of mature workers.

3.2.3.2 Creating Opportunities for Older Workers in Flexible Jobs

Flexible employment allows older workers to balance their work and personal lives and accommodate their unique circumstances. Ensuring the availability of full-time and part-time positions allows older workers to choose the work hours that best suit their circumstances and desired commitment. Holistic approaches allow older workers to remain active in the labor force while alleviating the burden of demanding roles, thus enabling them to continue to contribute their valuable expertise and skills. Allen et al. (2023) found that more flexible work arrangements weakened negative stereotypes about older workers and mitigated their influence on work matters. Further, flexible work arrangements may play a role, however minor, in alleviating risks to seniors' work engagement from mental and social challenges. In Switzerland, workplace flexibility was found to keep older workers in their careers in knowledge-intensive industries up to and beyond retirement age (Jansen et al. 2019).

In some economies and sectors, older workers have few opportunities to work flexible hours. Figure 3.15 shows that, as workers age, working hours shorten at varying speeds in different economies. Across all sectors, the

Figure 3.15: Wage Rate and Work Hours for Older Workers by Economy and Gender

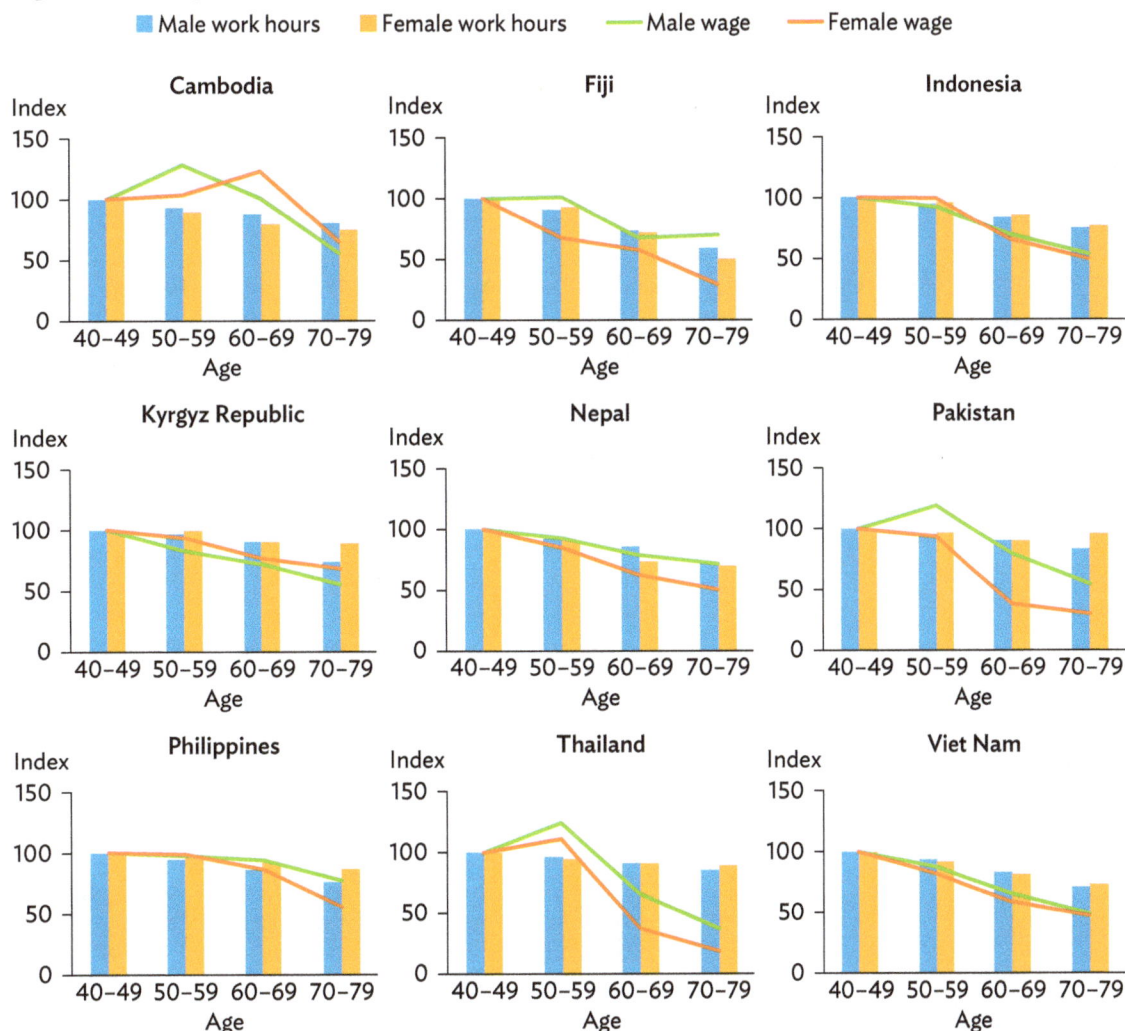

Note: The wage and work hours index base is age 40–49 = 100.

Source: Asian Development Bank estimates using labor force surveys from national sources.

differences in working hours between prime-age workers and workers aged 55–64 in professional, administrative, and wholesale services are small. Older workers in agriculture, manufacturing, and mining, however, work substantially less than workers in prime age. This may be because the work is taxing, and does not necessarily reflect greater flexibility. In fact, little overlap seems to exist between working in an age-friendly job and the opportunity to work shorter hours. Some sectors in the region offer considerable scope for improved flexibility in working hours.

Governments in Asia and the Pacific are exploring policies to promote more flexible work arrangements. In Singapore, the New Part-Time Re-employment Grant supports employers who offer part-time reemployment, flexible work arrangements, and structured career planning to older workers (Table 3.1). Employers can receive funding to implement part-time reemployment policies for their older employees. A more targeted initiative is the Senior Worker Early

Adopter Grant, which encourages employers to adopt flexible work arrangements and age-friendly practices. In Japan, grants are offered to employers to subsidize the cost of human resources system reform to accommodate flexible and age-friendly jobs with a specific target to support the employment of workers aged 65 and above.

3.2.3.3 Matching Older Workers to New Jobs

Older workers may struggle to find jobs. How older workers go about searching for jobs—and how hard they search—determines a lot about their opportunities in the labor market. Older workers search for jobs in somewhat different ways than younger workers. Their search tends to be less intense, partly because the chance of success and financial gains from a job search are often lower, as discussed in more detail below, and they use different channels (Guillemyn and Horemans 2023). Additionally, as job searches move increasingly online, older jobseekers may struggle to keep up.

Table 3.1: Programs and Policies Promoting Special Working Arrangements for Older Workers in Selected Asian Economies

Program or Policy	Implementing Economy	Year of Implementation	Description
New Part-Time Re-employment Grant	Singapore	2020	The program supports employers who offer part-time reemployment, flexible work arrangements, and structured career planning to senior workers. Employers can receive funding to implement part-time reemployment policies for their older employees. To be eligible for the grant, companies need to have at least one senior worker aged 60+ at the time of application.
Senior Worker Early Adopter Grant	Singapore	2020	The program encourages employers to adopt flexible work arrangements and age-friendly practices. By voluntarily committing to hiring and retaining older workers, companies can receive financial support through the grant. Since February 2021, eligible companies have been able to receive up to S$125,000 if their own retirement and reemployment ages exceed minimum statutory requirements.
65 Years and Older Employment Promotion Subsidy	Japan	2019	The subsidy is a grant to employers to facilitate lifelong employment, in which older workers can work regardless of age as long as they have the will and ability to work. In line with promoting flexible work for older workers, one program provides grants that allow continued employment for older workers but without a fixed term.

Source: Asian Development Bank compilation based on national sources.

Dedicated matching programs or agencies can be created to help older workers find jobs. New initiatives increasingly create programs or agencies that identify employment opportunities for older workers and match them with the seniors on their roster (Box 3.2). Japan's Silver Human Resource Center, for example, matches the skills and experience of older people with paid service needs in households, businesses, and community organizations. The work on offer is commonly tutoring, housekeeping, gardening, babysitting, and building management. These increasingly popular programs are run by government, civil, and community organizations. These matching programs especially benefit older female job seekers who prefer flexible jobs close to home.

3.2.3.4 Combating Ageism

Age discrimination or ageism, can diminish the retention of older workers in the workforce. Ageism can become manifest at various stages of employment and career development, affecting recruitment, retention, promotion, skill development, and dismissal.[20] Ageism is widespread in the labor markets of developing Asia, where job advertisements often specify an age requirement and many employers force people into early retirement.

A major cause of ageism in Asia and the Pacific is the belief that older workers take jobs from the young. Employment rates for older and younger workers tend to rise and fall in tandem, globally and in

---

Box 3.2: Examples of Public Placement Services for Older People

Silver Human Resources Centers (SHRCs) were first established in Tokyo in 1975. They provide job-matching and training services to older individuals. To meet the needs of older people including retirees, they offer temporary, short-term, or other light work. By leveraging their expertise and connections, the centers effectively bridge the gap between seniors seeking employment and employers looking for experienced and capable individuals. As of 2021, more than 1,300 SHRC locations had registered almost 700,000 older people. Research has found that a light work schedule of one or two times a week acquired through the SHRC significantly improved the well-being of older Japanese (Morishita-Suzuki, Nakamura-Uehara, and Ishibashi 2023).

In 2004, the Republic of Korea introduced the Senior Employment and Social Participation Support Program. Through it, the government provides supplemental income security and social participation in old age by creating and providing social jobs that match the aptitudes and abilities of senior citizens. The program had 840,000 participants in 2021. A systematic literature review of the program outcome shows that the majority of program participants are women (Koh and Lee 2023).

Centre for Seniors in Singapore operates a program called Employment Support for Seniors. It offers career advisory services that help seniors identify career options and become job-ready, and offers job-matching services for citizens and permanent residents of Singapore aged 50+ who are currently unemployed. In 2022, the center achieved 2,229 placements (Centre for Seniors 2022).

References

Centre for Seniors. 2022. *Annual Report 2022*.

Koh, Y. B. and Y. Lee. 2023. Evaluating the Senior Employment and Social Activity Support Program in Korea: A Systematic Review of Satisfaction. *Innovation in Aging 7*. (Supplement 1).

Morishita-Suzuki, K., M. Nakamura-Uehara, and T. Ishibashi. 2023. The Improvement Effect of Working through the Silver Human Resources Center on Pre-Frailty among Older People: A Two-year Follow-Up Study. *BMC Geriatrics*. 23(265).

---

[20] Ageism encompasses stereotypes, prejudice, and discrimination based purely on age toward others or oneself, most typically older people (WHO 2021a). It can be perpetrated at the personal, group, and institutional level (Marques et al. 2020). Sometimes it manifests as intergenerational conflict over public or family resource allocation.

the region—a positive correlation that may reflect skill complementarity between older and younger workers (Gruber and Wise 2010; Kalwij, Kapteyn, and de Vos 2010; Munnell and Wu 2012; OECD 2013; World Bank 2015). While there can be unintended negative consequences for younger workers from reform that forces firms to retain older workers,[21] reform is likely to be beneficial on balance, providing incentives for employers to ensure that older workers are well matched to their jobs and able to stay productive. Recent evidence confirms that multigenerational workforces are more productive (OECD 2020a).

Some economies legally prohibit age discrimination in the workplace. Age discrimination is banned by law in almost all OECD economies, and advances are being made in Asia and the Pacific. Laws that prevent age discrimination by imposing fines and shaming violators have been implemented in the Philippines; the ROK; and Taipei,China. Biases against hiring older workers are likely to persist in economies where such legislation is lacking. In Indonesia, for example, almost all job vacancy advertisements specify an upper age limit (Awaliyah et al. 2017). It is essential that governments in the region implement and enforce antidiscrimination legislation.

Enforcing antidiscrimination legislation can be complex, but technological advances and awareness campaigns may help. Laws against age discrimination in the workplace are hampered by the difficulty of proving discrimination and the cost and procedural barriers to bringing a case to court (OECD 2019b). However, increased digitalization in the job market may enable more efficient mechanisms to detect discrimination in job ads (Burn et al. 2023) and allow the implementation of age-blind selection processes (OECD 2019b). Awareness campaigns and initiatives that promote best practices and consultation and cooperate with social partners are needed to change employers' attitudes toward older workers.

3.2.3.5 Retaining Older Workers in the Labor Force

A perceived or actual gap between the cost of employing older workers and their productivity can hamper their hiring and retention. Such gaps can be a consequence of compensation and promotion based on seniority. As older employees enjoy wage that rises out of step with their productivity, seniority systems can create barriers to employing older workers and reduce their retention rate (Frimmel et al. 2018; OECD 2018a). As a result, in the ROK, where seniority is culturally ingrained in the workplace, few workers retain their jobs after the age of 55 or 60 (OECD 2018a, 2018b). Policymakers and firms can consider transitioning away from seniority systems toward performance-based compensation and promotion. One option to reform seniority is to introduce a ceiling age for managerial posts, as in Japan with the "post off" system (Box 3.3). However, rigid implementation of such system can be a disincentive to older workers. Comprehensive reform to assess workforce performance across age groups may be more desirable, complemented by offering a smooth transition from work to retirement.

Some economies in the region offer wage subsidies and tax breaks to promote the employment of older workers. Wage subsidies or tax breaks aim to close the gap between the pay and productivity of older workers. In the ROK, the Age-Friendly Enterprises program provides financial support to companies that hire a specified number of individuals aged 60 or over in eligible occupational categories in which they can work competitively. What little data exists on wage subsidies for older workers generally suggest only modest effects (Huttunen, Pirttilä, and Uusitalo 2013; Albanese and Cockx 2019), mostly benefiting older women (Boockmann et al. 2012; Freire 2018). As wage subsidies are costly and substantially disrupt the labor market, they are rarely a cost-effective way to boost the employment of older workers across the board. To be effective, wage subsidies need to target disadvantaged

---

[21]   Empirical evidence of the impact of delayed retirement on youth employment is mixed. In Italy, strong employment protection for older workers and reform that raised the retirement age during a period of shrinking employment were found to crowd out younger and prime-age workers (Boeri, Garibaldi, and Moen 2022; Bertoni and Brunello 2021). In Japan, the Elderly Employment Stabilization Law, which mandates that employers must retain incumbents until they become eligible for pensions, did not crowd out younger workers but prompted employers to cut the wages of older workers and reduce the number of female part-time workers (Kondo 2016).

Box 3.3: Transition from Seniority Systems to Performance-Based Compensation in Japan

In response to Japan's aging workforce, numerous public and firm-level initiatives have been implemented to promote the continued employment of older workers. The "post off" system was first introduced to firms in the late 1980s as an attempt to facilitate the retention of older workforce in Japan where seniority-based promotion is widely practiced (Rudline 2022). Under this system, managers in their 50s, typically between 55 and 58, are required to step down from managerial roles and take on rank-and-file posts a few years prior to their retirement, regardless of their potential and contributions to the organization (Yatabe 2017).

The primary rationale for this system lies in its ability to facilitate organizational restructuring, enable internal promotion for younger managers, and foster generational change (Rudline 2022). Another reason for this human resources practice is to hold down labor costs incurred when employees' salaries rise more quickly than their marginal productivity, as is the case in Japan's seniority-based wage system.

Despite good intentions, the system has undesirable repercussions. With career advancement barred and income decreased, among other indignities, many workers caught by the system in their late 50s lose motivation. Many older white-collar workers cease to hold positions reflecting their professional skills, experience, and expertise (Debroux 2022). Further, they lose interest in programs

to upgrade their skills (Yatabe 2017). Perhaps in response to these problems, some companies have discontinued the system and implemented instead a more meritocratic standardized evaluation at every level of the organization. This move has boosted employee morale and encouraged older workers to extend their employment, fostering a more inclusive and dynamic workforce.

While initiatives such as the post off system aimed to address labor market challenges arising from an aging population, they revealed shortcomings in maintaining employee motivation and using experienced workers to their full potential. Recent trends indicate growing recognition of the value of retaining and reintegrating older employees for their institutional knowledge and potential to contribute to a more diverse and dynamic workforce. As Japan continues to navigate these complexities, fostering an inclusive environment that maximizes the contributions of all generations will be essential for its future success.

References

Debroux, P. 2022. Employment of Senior Workers in Japan. *Contemporary Japan*. 34(1).

Rudline, P. 2022. It's No Longer "Post Off" for Japanese Employees in Their Late 50s. *LinkedIn*. 21 November.

Yatabe, K. 2017. Nihon Kigyo ni Okeru Teinen Seido no Jittai to Mondai Ten. *Seikei Kenkyu*. 53(4).

older workers, such as low-wage earners and jobseekers who have been unemployed for a long time (OECD 2019b). Tax breaks may be less disruptive than wage subsidies, offering incentives to hire older workers and formalize their employment. The Government of Thailand grants firms a tax deduction worth twice the cost incurred in employing people aged 60 and above (World Bank 2021). Malaysian income tax rules allow employers to claim further deductions on remuneration paid to older Malaysian employees. This program is slated for evaluation in 2025, which should provide new evidence on how effectively tax breaks promote older worker employment.

3.3 Policies for Productive Aging

Policies that promote productive aging and employment should take into account the heterogeneity of older workers and emerging trends. The strain of work may undermine the well-being of some older people who continue to work because they lack the financial resources to retire. Support is needed to make work less strenuous through the adoption of age-friendly technology and work flexibility. Basic labor protection against illness, accidents, and disability—and access to pensions and savings opportunities—would allow these older workers to retire with dignity and improved well-being. At the same time, improved health and the benefits of working make many people able and willing to work longer. Governments and employers can lower barriers to working in old age and impart skills to make older workers more employable. Parallel needs to help some workers continue to work and help others to retire can be viewed as brackets to effective government and employer policy.

3.3.1   Supporting Informal Workers' Career and Retirement Transition

Governments are encouraged to improve working conditions for older workers, notably in agriculture. This can be done by making work more age-friendly and encouraging older workers to shift to less demanding tasks, depending on their capacity and preference. Investment should promote the adoption of technology and mechanization through training conducted in collaboration with agricultural cooperatives and training centers. Other initiatives should secure for older farmers agricultural credit with which to procure technology. This can be done by identifying alternative collateral and using big data to enhance lending models to reduce and diversify risk. Models may enhance collaboration with microcredit and agricultural cooperatives because these local actors possess information with which to assess older farmers' creditworthiness. Training and technical advice may be provided to older farmers.

Governments must do more to extend basic labor protection to all workers, including informal workers and the self-employed. Measures in the workplace to prevent accidents and illness can, along with insurance against accidents and illness, paid leave, and pensions, smooth career progress and retirement transitions and protect workers from health shocks and income loss.

3.3.2   Raising the Statutory Retirement Age and Making It More Flexible

Policymakers are encouraged to review their statutory retirement age periodically. This call for action is particularly relevant in economies that have kept the same retirement age for a long time despite significant change in older workers' health and preferences. In most economies, the retirement age is substantially lower than the average healthy life expectancy. This is particularly true for women in

many economies of developing Asia, as the statutory retirement age for women tends to be lower than for men despite women enjoying longer healthy life expectancy, as discussed in the following chapter (Chapter 4, Table 4.2 and Box 4.2). A rising trend is to build into pension design automatic adjustment of the pensionable age in response to changing life expectancy (Chapter 4, Box 4.3).

Revising the mandatory retirement age requires careful consideration of various factors. While raising the age for mandatory retirement and pension eligibility is an attractive response to lengthening life expectancy, governments must thoroughly evaluate the capacity of older individuals to work. Any increase in retirement age should be paired with safeguards to bridge any gap that may open up for individuals between salary and pension. Flexible retirement that allows workers to retire gradually or within an age range, or to defer retirement, may better suit individual needs and preferences. Revisiting gender differences in retirement age is essential, but pension entitlement should take into account that many women engage in unpaid work and caregiving throughout their working lives. Building a political consensus through close consultation with the public on retirement age is a necessary step. So is disseminating information to workers of all ages to help them set realistic expectations about future retirement needs, taking into account future changes in retirement age and pension policies, and to raise awareness of the advantages of planning career and retirement paths in anticipation of an extended working life.

3.3.3   Innovative Action to Generate and Expand Employment for Older People

Better retention of older workers requires that gaps between pay and productivity be closed. Such gaps arise when older workers' wage increases outpace their productivity growth. Governments can improve the retention of older workers by aligning wages with productivity. One option is targeted incentives such as subsidies and especially tax breaks to encourage firms to employ and retain older workers. Such incentives need to be carefully designed, however, and targeted to specific groups to be cost-effective and minimize labor market distortion. Another option is to move away from wage increases based on seniority toward compensation based on performance. This can lighten the burden of hiring older workers and promote their retention. More generally, governments should encourage firms to revisit such human resources practices as promotions based on seniority and carefully assess possible consequences before legislating age-differentiated employment protection. Once employment protection and human resources practices become age-neutral, policymakers should consider disallowing firm-mandated retirement ages.

Older workers would benefit from job-search and matching support. Older workers are likely to struggle to find jobs, especially outside of their usual sector and occupation. Governments should ensure that older and other disadvantaged workers are served by mainstream placement organizations and public employment services. These services must be inclusive and tailored to the needs of older workers. Services and platforms that are specific to older workers could then complement and supplement these mainstream services, offering in addition volunteer options and very flexible work arrangements.

Age discrimination needs to be addressed. Legislation that prohibits age discrimination in recruitment and the workplace must be adopted to set sound standards for age-neutral recruitment and employment. Enforcement must be carefully monitored. To address more subtle yet pervasive discriminatory practices, it is crucial to foster a change in culture and employers' attitudes. Age discrimination can be tackled through awareness campaigns, management training, and employee engagement.

3.3.4 Older Workers' Employability Enhanced through a Lifelong Approach to Skills Development

Investing in high-quality education and lifelong skills development is critical. Older workers lose productivity partly for lack of upskilling and reskilling to adapt to rapidly changing labor markets and technological advances. Rising cohorts of older workers will have higher educational attainment, but translating this into greater employability requires a lifelong approach to learning. Governments should

support firms' provision of upskilling on the job that facilitates the workers' own periodic review and upgrade of their skills.

Skills should be formally recognized after being acquired by older workers on the job and outside of the formal education system. Some economies have certification systems that formally recognize skills and knowledge from prior work experience, formal and informal training, and other life experience. This allows workers to cite their competencies when job hunting or pursuing formal education and training. SkillsFuture in Singapore is one such lifelong learning program (Government of Singapore 2024).

Training needs to be adapted to the needs of older workers. It is crucial that older people receive training that fits their schedule and recognizes that they may not have been retrained for several years. Apprentice-style training that combines short classroom sessions with learning on the job has been found effective for older workers (OECD 2019a). Intergenerational learning groups are useful, particularly for tackling information and communication technology. Age-divided learning, on the other hand, can perpetuate stigma and difference (CEDEFOP 2012).

3.4 Conclusion

The employment and retirement patterns of older workers show wide heterogeneity across and within economies. Policies should take into account this heterogeneity and emerging trends. The employment and retirement paths of older workers differ in the formal and informal sectors of many economies and will continue to differ for years to come. Women and rural workers are disproportionately present in the informal group, which often excludes them from labor and social protection.

More targeted policies are needed to bridge inequity by improving the quality of jobs held by older informal workers. In the short term, governments with large informal economies are encouraged to ensure labor rights and basic pension access to older informal workers and offer them a smooth transition to less physically demanding work and more flexibility. This can be accomplished in agriculture through automation, skills development, and, as a prerequisite, better access to credit. Meanwhile, a smaller but growing number of older workers in formal employment are able and willing to work but are forced to retire before they are ready by an outdated statutory retirement age. Older workers in the formal sector stand to benefit from a more flexible retirement age and reform to human resources practices based on seniority that would align older workers' salaries with their productivity. Formal and informal workers alike stand to benefit from lifelong learning that imparts digital and other marketable skills. This learning should not begin in old age, but much earlier in working life. As the job market for older workers is elusive, governments can offer specialized placement services for them and incentives to employers to hire and retain them.

Employment and labor-protection policies geared toward productive aging promise to enhance the well-being of older people and contain the macroeconomic costs of population aging. Governments of economies that are at an advanced stage of aging, and consequently have an aging and contracting workforce, are aligning their policies on investing in human capital and technology adoption to collect a silver demographic dividend provided by longer service of skilled workers. The time is ripe for many rapidly aging economies in developing Asia to review existing policies and make the most of such valuable investments.

4

Economic Security in Old Age and Pensions

Sufficient financial resources for a decent living are a prerequisite to well-being in old age. Poverty and economic deprivation significantly diminish life satisfaction and mental wellness (Ridley et al. 2020). Financial risk and uncertainty generally increase later in life with deteriorating health and loss of wage income. Family transfers are a key source of income for older Asians, supplemented by income from working. Going forward, contributory and social pensions are set to play a bigger role in the region to safeguard old-age economic security.

This chapter reviews the major sources of income for older people in the region. They are most notably family transfers, income from working, and contributory and social pension benefits. It then examines financial preparedness, which determines old-age economic security. Finally, it considers the current state of Asian pension systems, in particular their coverage and benefit adequacy.

4.1 Income and Asset Profiles of Older People and Their Families

4.1.1 Income Streams for Older Households and Individuals

Financial preparedness in old age can be measured by comparing retirement financial resources with anticipated consumption. More precisely, preparedness can be evaluated by determining whether the value of all retirement financial resources

is adequate to meet anticipated consumption needs in a person's remaining years (Ehrlich and Liu 2024). Retirement financial resources are various incomes and assets owned individually and collectively by household members. Incomes commonly reported by older people are mainly transfers from family, wages and business receipts, and pensions.

Family transfers are a major source of income for households with older people. Figure 4.1 presents average distributions of major household income sources for three types of households in selected Asian economies: without older people, mixed old and young members, and older people only (Albert et al. 2024). It shows that the percentage of personal transfers and pension contributions in total income increases with the share of older members in the household. Reliance on transfers in older households is particularly heavy in the Lao People's Democratic Republic (Lao PDR) at 71.8% and Cambodia at 61.5%.

Wages and business income are important to mixed households and older households. They provide a fifth of income for older households in Cambodia, the Lao PDR, and Thailand, and nearly two-fifths in the Philippines. In Georgia, pensions provide nearly two-thirds of older household income, suggesting exceptionally broad coverage and extensive pension support.

A separate survey of older individuals confirmed that transfers from families are the most common type of income (Figure 4.2). Transfers of cash and in kind are followed by wages and then by contributory and social pensions. Shares of older people that report receiving transfers from children and other family members are 83% in the People's Republic of China (PRC) and Viet Nam, 64% in the Republic of Korea (ROK), and 50% in Indonesia. This share tends to increase with age in

Figure 4.1: Distribution of Income Sources by Type of Household in Selected Economies

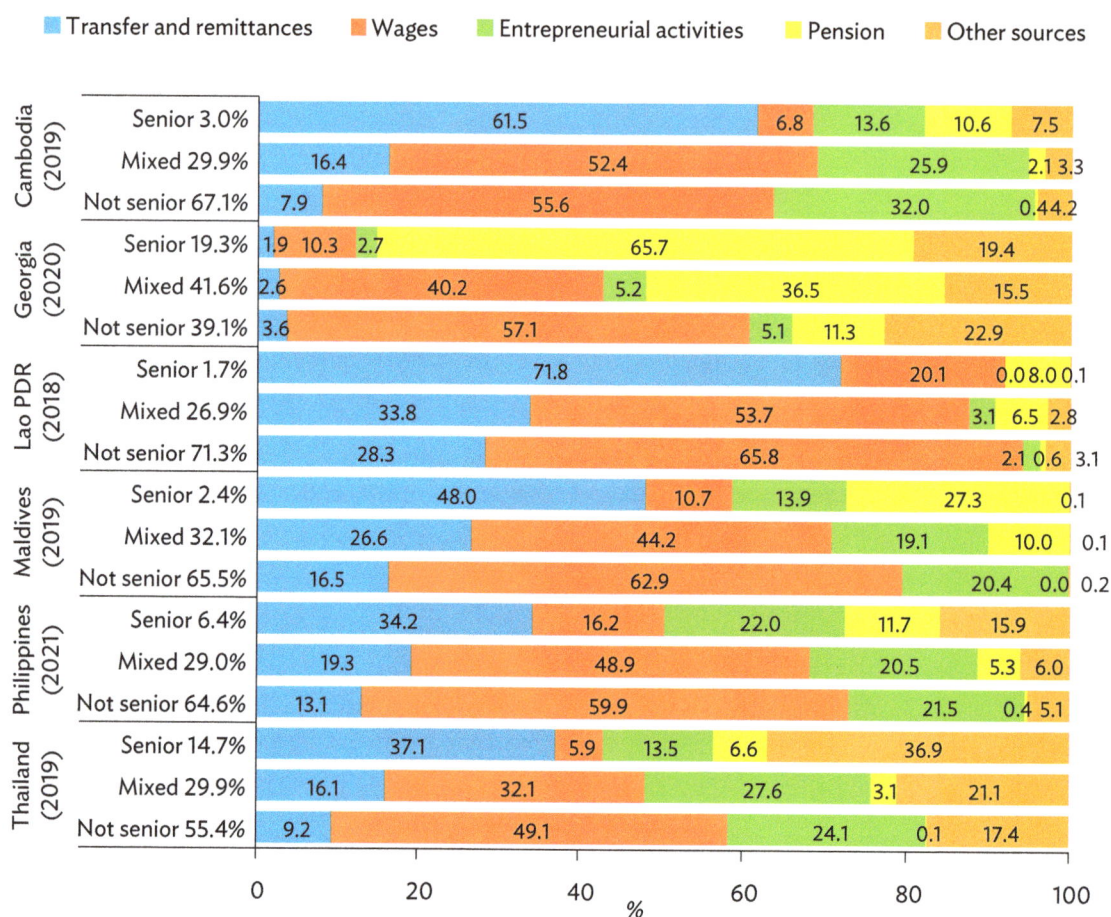

Legend: ■ Transfer and remittances ■ Wages ■ Entrepreneurial activities ■ Pension ■ Other sources

Economy	Household type	Transfer and remittances	Wages	Entrepreneurial activities	Pension	Other sources
Cambodia (2019)	Senior 3.0%	61.5	6.8	13.6	10.6	7.5
	Mixed 29.9%	16.4	52.4	25.9	2.1	3.3
	Not senior 67.1%	7.9	55.6	32.0	0.4	4.2
Georgia (2020)	Senior 19.3%	1.9	10.3	2.7	65.7	19.4
	Mixed 41.6%	2.6	40.2	5.2	36.5	15.5
	Not senior 39.1%	3.6	57.1	5.1	11.3	22.9
Lao PDR (2018)	Senior 1.7%	71.8	20.1	0.0	8.0	0.1
	Mixed 26.9%	33.8	53.7	3.1	6.5	2.8
	Not senior 71.3%	28.3	65.8	2.1	0.6	3.1
Maldives (2019)	Senior 2.4%	48.0	10.7	13.9	27.3	0.1
	Mixed 32.1%	26.6	44.2	19.1	10.0	0.1
	Not senior 65.5%	16.5	62.9	20.4	0.0	0.2
Philippines (2021)	Senior 6.4%	34.2	16.2	22.0	11.7	15.9
	Mixed 29.0%	19.3	48.9	20.5	5.3	6.0
	Not senior 64.6%	13.1	59.9	21.5	0.4	5.1
Thailand (2019)	Senior 14.7%	37.1	5.9	13.5	6.6	36.9
	Mixed 29.9%	16.1	32.1	27.6	3.1	21.1
	Not senior 55.4%	9.2	49.1	24.1	0.1	17.4

%

Lao PDR = Lao People's Democratic Republic.

Notes: Years are the latest available. Percentages of household type shares may not total 100% because of rounding. Other income sources include drawdown from savings, asset sales, and interest income.

Sources: Cambodia Socio Economic Survey 2019; Georgia Household Incomes and Expenditures Survey 2020; Lao PDR Expenditure Consumption Survey 2018; Maldives Household Income and Expenditure Survey 2019; Philippine Family Income and Expenditure Survey 2021; and Thailand Household Socio-Economic Survey 2019.

many economies, presumably compensating for the loss of other income after retirement. Cash transfers to older people from their children are reciprocal, as older people also give money to their children (Figure 4.3). Transfers to children tend to decline as parents age, while transfers from children increase.

In some economies, large shares of older people work for money. The percentage of wage earners in Bangladesh is 62%, India 34%, and Indonesia 55% (Figure 4.2). The share of working older people declines with age but remains high until their 70s and 80s in many economies. (Chapter 3 of this report discusses patterns of labor force participation). Across economies, older people who work are less likely to be covered by contributory pensions. While many economies in the region do not penalize pensioners for working, pension design must take into consideration how pensions affect work incentives (Box 4.1). In economies with high contributory pension coverage, older people's participation in the labor force is generally lower.

Figure 4.2: Share of Older People Reporting Income from Family Transfers, Wages, and Social and Contributory Pensions

■ Wages   ■ Social pensions   ■ Contributory pensions   ■ Family transfers

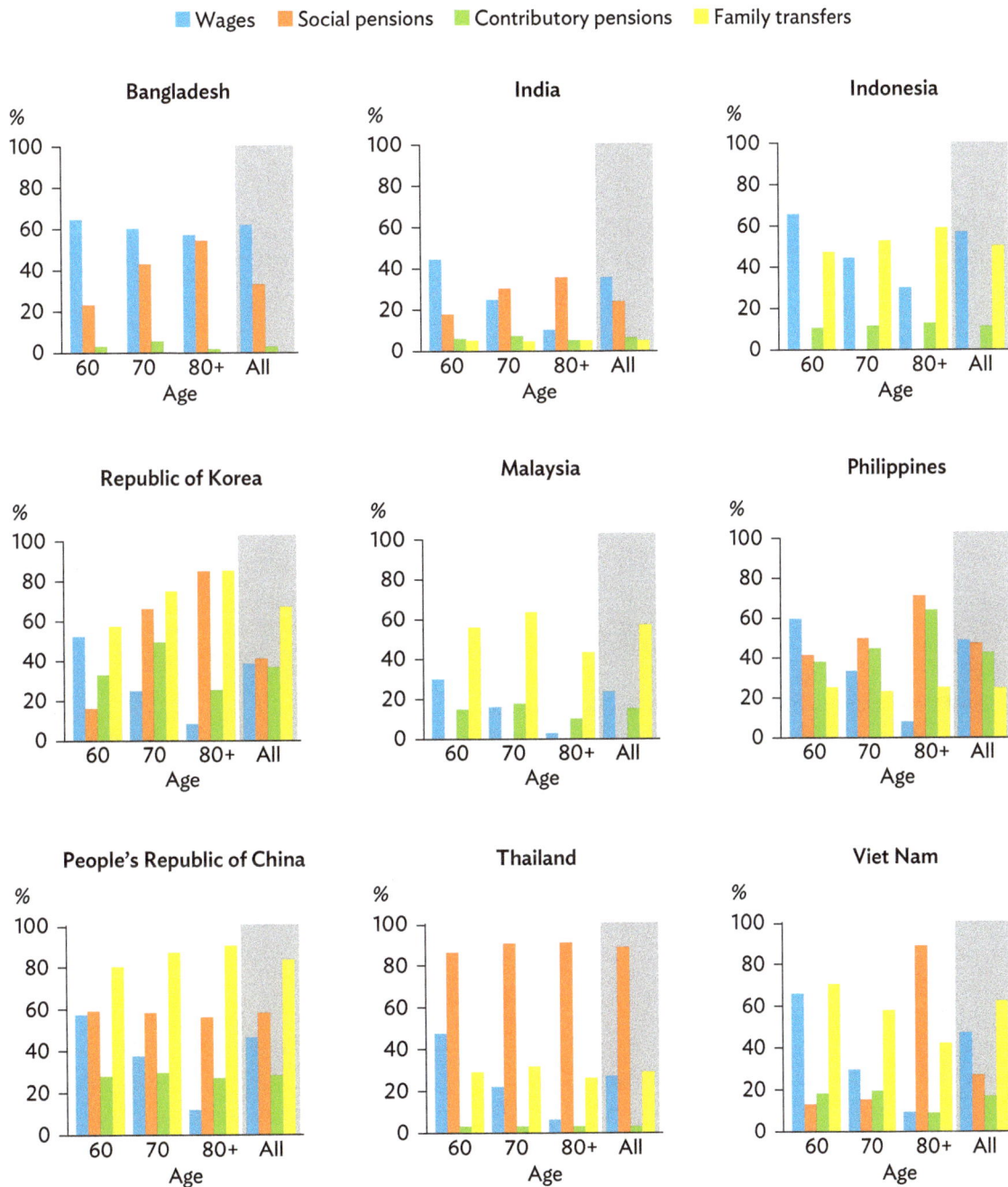

Notes: Older people are aged 60 and above. Contributory pensions include private/occupational and public pensions and those funded by national provident funds. Family transfer information is not available for Bangladesh. Survey years are 2017–2021, and 2023.

Source: Chapter 1, Box 1.1.

Figure 4.3: Share of Transfers Between Older People and Their Children, by Age Group and Economy

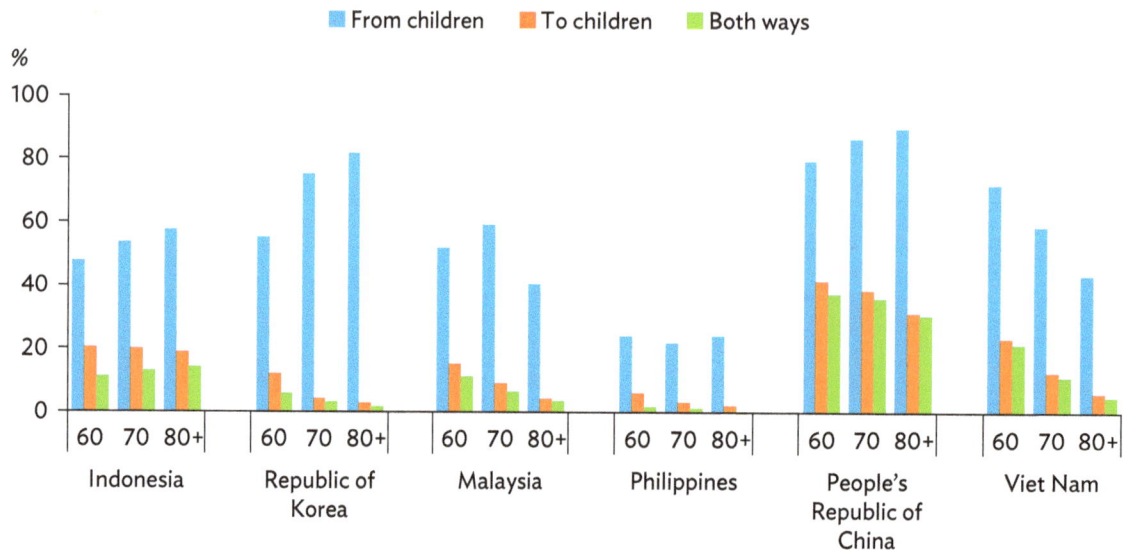

Notes: Older people are aged 60 and above. Transfer percentages are based on monthly amounts to and from children living outside of the household. Survey years are 2018, 2019, 2021, and 2023.

Source: Chapter 1, Box 1.1.

Pension income is less common than private transfers and wages in almost all economies with available data (Figure 4.2). Across the region, pension coverage is higher for urban residents than rural, and for the formal sector than the informal. Of the two pension streams, social pensions, or noncontributory cash assistance for older people, are more widely available than contributory pensions. Social pensions go to 86% of older people in Thailand and 58% in the PRC but only 44% in the Philippines, 40% in the ROK, and 28% in Viet Nam.[22] Contributory pensions in the region are mainly restricted to former employees of large firms and state offices and enterprises. Coverage of older people ranges down from 40% in the Philippines to 35% in the ROK, 28% in the PRC, 17% in Viet Nam, 14% in Malaysia, 10% in Indonesia, 6% in India, 4% in Thailand, and 3% in Bangladesh. The share of older people in the region receiving neither contributory nor social pensions is 40% on average but higher at 90% in Indonesia, 85% in Malaysia, 71% in India, and 66% in Bangladesh.

Coverage of contributory pensions typically increases with individual wealth. Very few individuals in the bottom wealth quintile, based on expenditure, receive contributory pensions in developing Asia. Exceptions are 37% in the Philippines, which has an extensive social security system that includes pensions, and 31% in the ROK, which has a national contributory pension. Lower rates are 6% in Malaysia, 7% in the PRC and 5% in Viet Nam. Individuals in the highest wealth quintile are up to 10 times more likely to receive contributory pensions than those in the lowest quintile (Figure 4.4). In Bangladesh, the PRC, and Viet Nam, more than half of those receiving contributory pensions are in the wealthiest quintile. Yet coverage remains low even in that quintile, ranging from 9% in Bangladesh, 12% in India, to 68% in the PRC.

Noncontributory social pensions have some redistribution effects, but their coverage of wealthier groups is also high. Social pension coverage is significantly higher than that of contributory pensions,

---

[22]   The distinction between contributory and social pensions is not always clear-cut. In the PRC, for instance, social pensions have a small contributory element.

Figure 4.4: Share of Older People Receiving Contributory and Social Pensions, by Wealth Quintile

■ Contributory pension   ■ Social pension

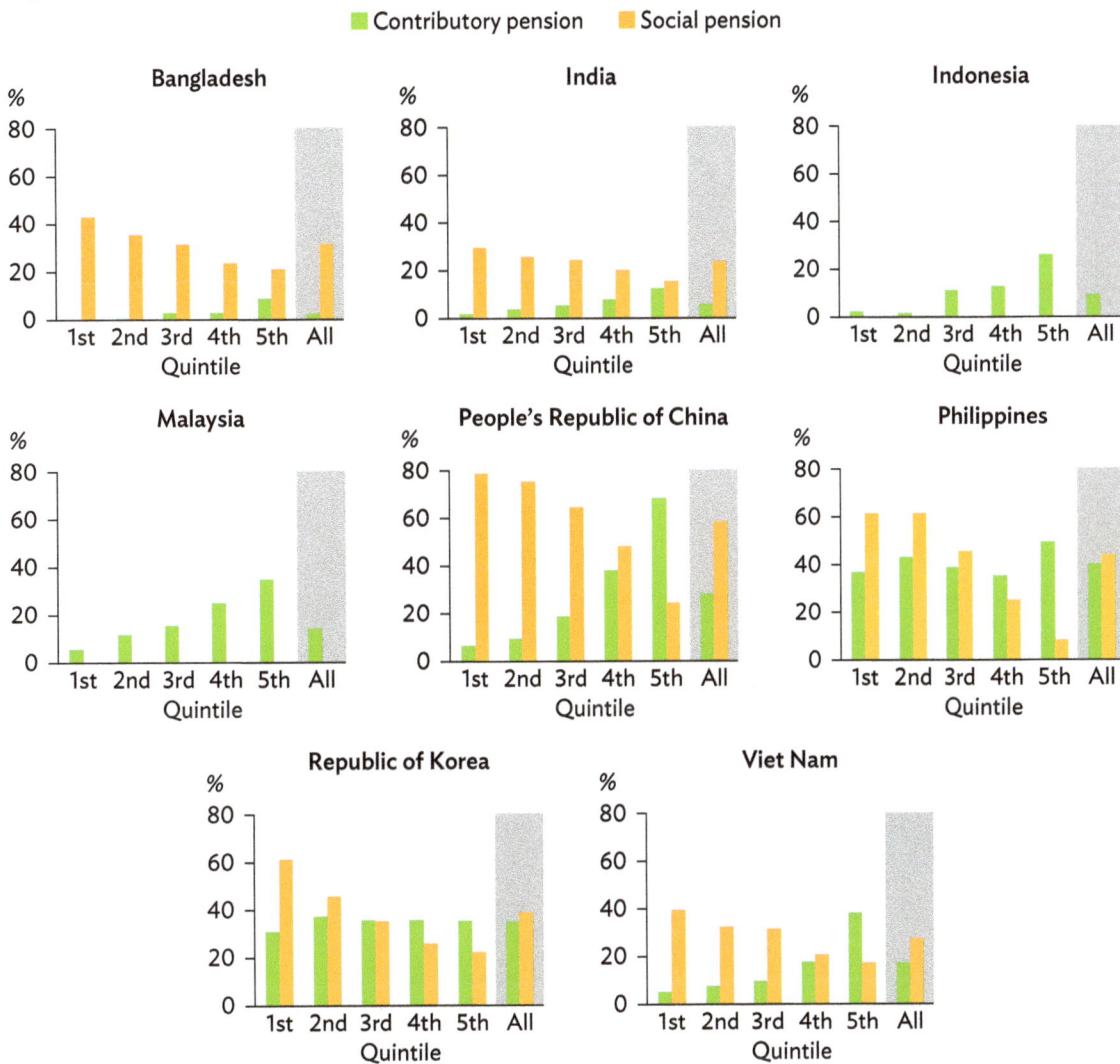

Notes: Older people are aged 60 and above. Quintiles are numbered from poorest (1st) to wealthiest (5th), and based on expenditure except in the Philippines, where asset data are used. Contributory pensions include both private and public occupational pensions and national provident funds. Social pension data are not available for Indonesia and Malaysia. Survey years are 2017–2019, 2021, and 2023.

Source: Chapter 1, Box 1.1.

reaching 58% in the PRC, 45% in the Philippines, 39% in the ROK, 32% in Bangladesh, and 24% in India. Social pension coverage in the poorest quintile exceeds 30% across the region, with the PRC having the highest at 79%, followed by the Philippines and the ROK at 61%, but lower in other economies: Bangladesh at 43% and India at 30%. Yet many governments extend social pensions to the wealthiest groups: 24% in the PRC, 22% in Bangladesh, 17% in Viet Nam, and 15% in India. Social pensions can tamp down the need for family transfers, but only marginally as coverage is low in some economies and benefits are generally small across economies.

Older women are more likely to receive social pensions but less likely to receive contributory pensions. The gender gap in contributory pensions is wide in many economies (Figure 4.5). In India, the coverage rate for men is 76 percentage points higher than that of women, and in Bangladesh 62 points higher. This can be explained by women's lower rate of participation in the labor force, their consequently lower contributions, and pensions' low survivor benefits (Figure 4.5 and Box 4.2). Social pensions, meanwhile, show greater gender equity, which is partly explained by women's longer life expectancy. Contributory pension coverage is significantly higher for urban residents, while the opposite is generally true of social pensions.

Figure 4.5: Distribution of Older People Receiving Contributory and Social Pensions

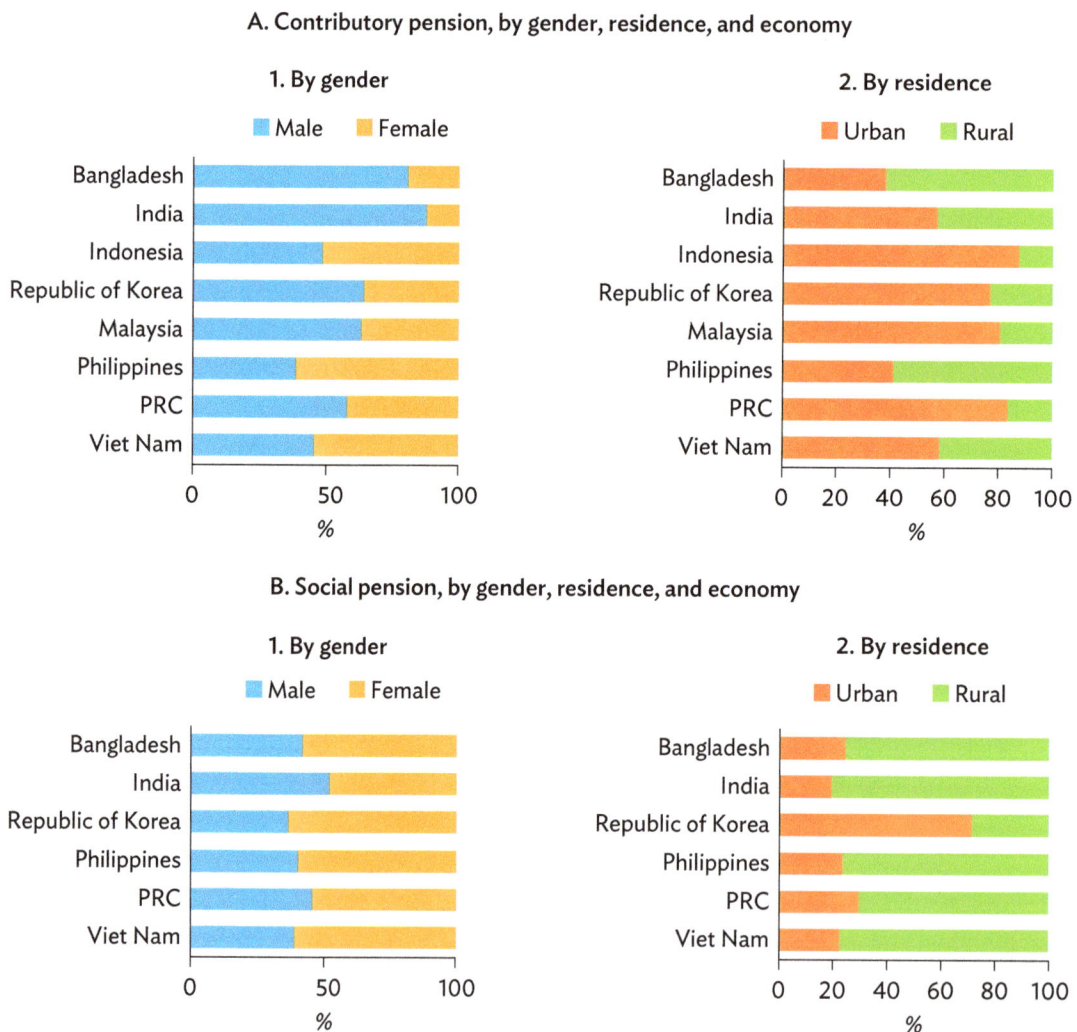

A. Contributory pension, by gender, residence, and economy

1. By gender

2. By residence

B. Social pension, by gender, residence, and economy

1. By gender

2. By residence

PRC = People's Republic of China.

Note: Older people are aged 60 and above. Survey years are 2017–2019, 2021, and 2023.

Source: Chapter 1, Box 1.1.

Box 4.1: Pensions and Work Incentives

Pension systems present financial incentives that affect work and retirement decisions (Gruber and Wise 1998, 1999). Policymakers in Asia and the Pacific must therefore design pensions carefully. In the People's Republic of China (PRC), for example, the probability that urban workers withdraw from the workforce increases with receipt of a contributory pension, with about 40% of both men and women retiring, but the impact of hybrid social pensions is lower (Zhang, Giles, and Zhao 2014). The probability of retirement increases upon receiving a contributory pension among urban workers in the PRC as well as urban and rural men in Indonesia (O'Keefe, Giles, and Yang 2021). In Thailand, a social pension slightly more generous than the regional norm has an observable impact (Badiani-Magnusson 2016; Huang and Giles 2017).

It is unsurprising that older workers who can retire early with reasonable incomes choose to do so. Policymakers need to balance pension systems such that older people are protected but also encouraged to work and continue to contribute to the pension system. The most obvious policy lever is the age of access to a pension, which should be fair while ensuring long-term sustainability and considering impact on the labor market (Chomik and Whitehouse 2010). In many regional economies, access ages for both social and contributory pensions are low, even taking into account differences in life expectancy (Table 4.2). Access ages could be raised and linked to life expectancy measures.

Another policy lever is the extent to which contributory pensions require workers to retire to receive them. Such work or earnings tests are common, but some wealthy economies have sought to remove them: notably Norway, the United Kingdom, the United States, and, most recently, Denmark. In Asia and the Pacific, provident funds impose no such work tests, though they are retained in some defined benefit programs, as in the Philippines for those aged 60–65. Many economies in the Caucasus and Central

Asia removed such tests as part of pension reform during their post-Soviet transition. Models based on advanced economies suggest that removing work tests can delay retirement and lengthen work lives but reduce the claiming age and lower work intensity (Song and Manchester 2007; Blundell, French, and Tetlow 2016). Policymakers may therefore wish to complement the abolition of work tests with mechanisms that offer increased pensions if claimed later. To calm political opposition stirred by raising the retirement age, policymakers can provide financial incentives while still allowing retirement at the current retirement age.

References

Badiani-Magnusson, R. 2016. Estimating the Impact of Thailand's Elderly Social Pension on Well-Being. Mimeo. World Bank.

Blundell, R., E. French, and G. Tetlow. 2016. Retirement Incentives and Labor Supply. In Piggott, J. and A. Woodland, eds. *Handbook of the Economics of Population Aging, Vol. 1.* North-Holland.

Chomik, R. and E. Whitehouse. 2010. *Trends in Pension Eligibility Ages and Life Expectancy, 1950–2050.* Organisation for Economic Co-operation and Development.

Gruber, J. and D. Wise. 1998. Social Security and Retirement: An International Comparison. *American Economic Review.* 88(2).

——. 1999. *Social Security and Retirement around the World.* National Bureau of Economic Research.

Huang, Y. and J. Giles. 2017. Universal Social Pension and Spousal Labor Supply in Rural Thailand. Mimeo. World Bank.

O'Keefe, P., J. Giles, and H. Yang. 2021. Ageing, Work and Retirement in China, East and Southeast Asia. *China: An International Journal.* 19(3).

Song, J. G. and J. Manchester. 2007. New Evidence on Earnings and Benefit Claims following Changes in the Retirement Earnings Test in 2000. *Journal of Public Economics.* 91(3-4).

Zhang C., J. Giles, and Y. Zhao. 2014. A Policy Evaluation of China's New Rural Pension Programme: Income, Poverty, Expenditure, Subjective Well-Being and Labour Supply. *China Economic Quarterly.* 14(1).

Source: Asian Development Bank.

Box 4.2: Gender Dimensions of Pension Systems in Developing Asia

Public pensions offer significantly different financial protection by gender. This is true around the world, including in Asia and the Pacific, and arises from several factors. First is a gender gap in labor force participation, with women working less but often overrepresented in the informal sector. This means that fewer women than men are primary members of contributory pension programs. A second factor is the gender wage gap and consequently lower women's contributions to pensions even if they put in a full work history. In East Asia and the Pacific, the gender wage gap in 2015 was about a fifth, and in South Asia a third (UN Women 2015). Yet another factor is lower pension contributions as paid work must compete with caring for children, older parents, and often grandchildren. This gap may be wider in economies with an official retirement age for women lower than that for men, as in Bangladesh, Georgia, Kazakhstan, the Lao People's Democratic Republic (Lao PDR), Pakistan, the People's Republic of China (PRC), Uzbekistan, and Viet Nam. This is especially common in economies with a socialist legacy. In defined contribution systems, women's longer average lifespan means lower average benefits across years in retirement or, alternatively, greater likelihood of exhausting lump-sum payouts.

Some negative gender outcomes from inadequate coverage are partly offset in most Asian systems. Offsetting features are survivor benefits for the spouses of male pension contributors in defined benefit systems, or spouses' inheritance of undrawn accumulation in provident funds or defined contribution programs, though most provident fund accumulations are exhausted before they can be passed on to a spouse. Most defined benefit programs in the region have survivor benefits, though design varies across economies in the degree of financial protection offered. In Indonesia, the PRC, and Thailand, the survivor benefit is paid as a lump sum and hence does not assure financial protection throughout old age. Other economies pay lifetime benefits of differing amounts: in the Malaysian civil service program and the Philippines equal to the full benefit owed to the deceased, and in Kazakhstan, Mongolia, the Republic of Korea, and Uzbekistan an amount set by other benchmarks—in Viet Nam, a percentage of the minimum wage, and in Kazakhstan calculated using the benefit owed to the deceased adjusted by other factors. Broadly, the protection provided by survivor programs is only as strong as coverage and adequacy limitations allow the contributory system to be.

Many features of benefit design can benefit or disadvantage women. A contributory system is likely to favor women if benefit design is redistributive. A long vesting period, on the other hand, is less likely to be met by women who interrupt their careers for caring or childrearing responsibilities—a work pattern commonly seen in Hong Kong, China; Timor-Leste; and Viet Nam. Because of their longer life expectancy, women receive lower monthly benefits in economies that take into account gender mortality rates when computing annuities, notably Hong Kong, China; India; Indonesia; Malaysia; and Singapore.[a] Lower ages for pension access can mean that women retire early, having saved less for a longer retirement.[b] Gender differences in pension outcomes cannot be comprehensively addressed through contributory programs, which are inequitable by design.

Reference

UN Women. 2015. *Protecting Women's Income Security in Old Age: Toward Gender-Responsive Pension Systems.* United Nations.

[a] Only a few member economies of the Organisation for Economic Co-operation and Development (OECD) allow consideration of mortality rates, allowing instead for annuity contracts to cross-subsidize between sexes.

[b] Lower access ages for women are still offered in the Lao PDR, Mongolia, the PRC, and Viet Nam but have been phased out in nearly all OECD economies.

Source: Asian Development Bank.

Figure 4.6: Share of Older People Who Own Their Home, Land, and Financial Assets, by Age and Economy

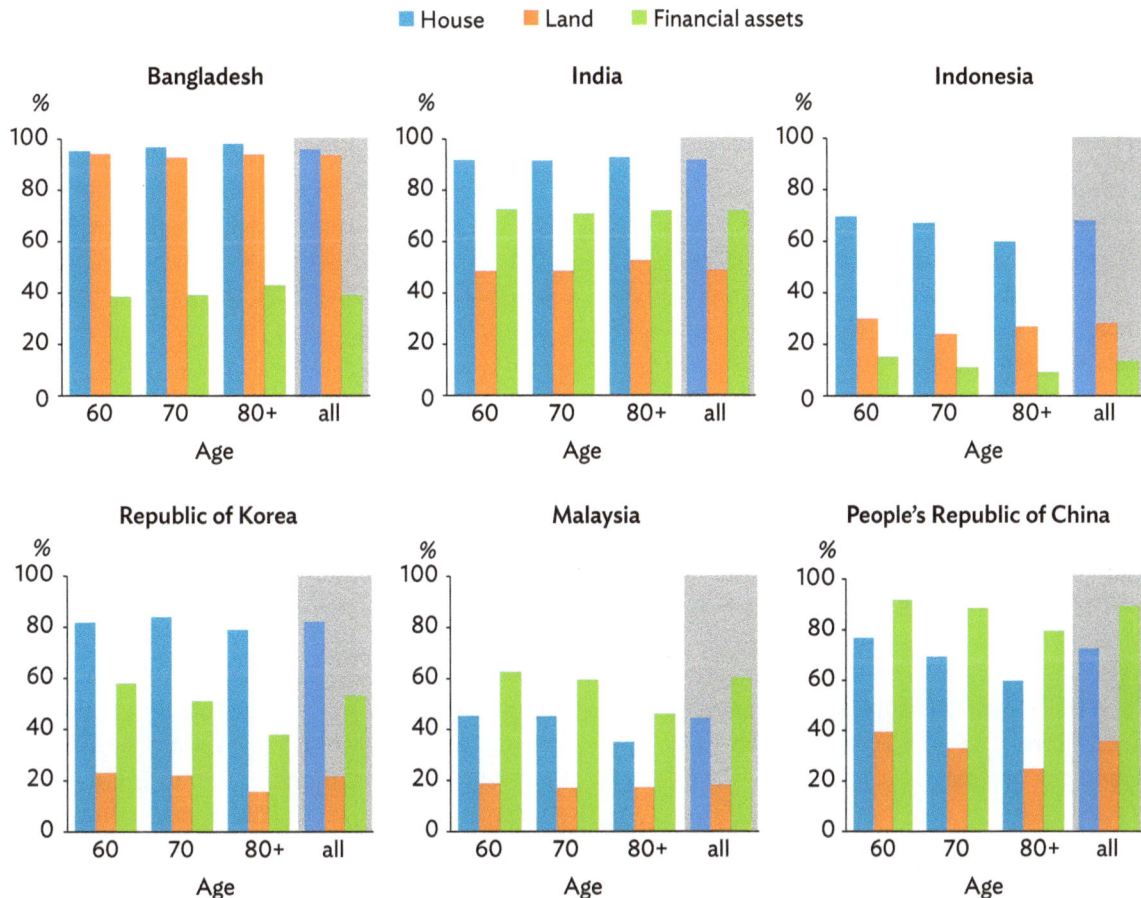

Notes: Older people are aged 60 and above. Individuals were asked about ownership of their home, land, and financial assets in Indonesia, Malaysia, and the Republic of Korea (ROK). In Bangladesh and India, households were surveyed, and in the People's Republic of China married couples. The ROK data lump together land and real estate ownership. Financial assets include savings, bank accounts, stocks, and other financial instruments. Survey years: 2017, 2018, 2021, and 2023.

Source: Chapter 1, Box 1.1.

4.1.2   Assets Held by Older People

Assets can provide economic security in old age. They also facilitate intergenerational transfers, affecting the support older adults can offer to their families. Older people may hold many types of assets but most commonly their homes. Home ownership exceeds 80% in Bangladesh, India, the ROK, and Viet Nam, but is lower in Malaysia at 44% (Figure 4.6). Property ownership other than one's residence is also important. Cash savings are held by many older people: 87% in the PRC, 60% in Malaysia, and 53% in the ROK, but only 28% in Bangladesh, 25% in Viet Nam, and

9% in Indonesia. Asset holding declines with age but not by much. Mechanisms by older Asians to derive consumption income from their homes include renting them out and taking out reverse mortgages.

4.1.3   Measuring Financial Preparedness for Retirement

Financial preparedness varies substantially in Japan, the PRC, and the ROK. It is measured by examining whether older people and households have sufficient financial resources to support their likely spending in their remaining years (Ehrlich and Liu 2024). Figure 4.7

presents available financial resources for retirement held on average by near-old households, within 5 years of statutory retirement age. Expressed in net present value, the resources have four elements: net wealth, estimated intra-family transfers, private pensions, and public pensions. Estimates for multiple years, rural versus urban, are presented for the PRC. Financial preparedness in an economy is expressed as the share of households whose resources exceed expected consumption spending. Anticipated consumption is derived using preretirement consumption in each economy with adjustments to residential rental and medical expenses during retirement.

Retirement financial resources available to households are highest in Japan, followed by the ROK and then the PRC. Japan's retirement resource average was $419,324 in 2011. The figure in the ROK was $245,130 in 2010 and in India $62,818 in 2018. In the PRC, the average was still lower at just $56,801 in 2011 before more than doubling to $129,102 in 2018. A large gap in financial resources persists between urban and rural residents in both the PRC and India. In 2018, the ratio of rural to urban resources was 32% in the PRC and 38% in India.

The share of financially prepared near-old individuals varies by economy. It was 86% in Japan in 2011, 73% in India in 2018, 64% in the PRC in 2018, and 58% in the ROK in 2010.[23] In the PRC, the share declined from 73% in 2011 to 64% in 2018 despite increased financial resources because of higher anticipated spending. The rural–urban preparedness gap in the PRC was wide in 2018, with a very high 82% of urban residents prepared but only 44% of rural residents despite their significantly lower anticipated spending. In India, the urban–rural gap was narrower, at 79% versus 70% in 2018. In all four economies, men are significantly more self-prepared, without relying much on public income sources. In the PRC

and the ROK, college-educated near-old individuals were better self-prepared than those with lower educational attainment, with or without controlling for risky asset holdings. Education was not a factor in Japan, apparently because less-educated Japanese have a lower propensity to consume.

Individuals with more children are more likely to be self-prepared, especially in the PRC and the ROK. This is presumably because children in these economies are more likely to provide financial assistance to their aging parents. Individuals holding stocks and/or investments in real estate are more likely to be self-prepared. Good health improves the likelihood of preparedness, as does being married, which reduces household consumption per capita.

The self-dependency ratio (SDR) is the share of financial resources derived from private sources. The share of private wealth, intra-family transfers, and pensions in all retirement financial resources is much lower in Japan than in India, the PRC, or the ROK. In the ROK, the SDR was constant over the sample period at 85%. This high SDR ratio in the ROK does not reflect a larger wealth share but mostly higher transfer income, providing about 20% of financial resources for old-age support.

The SDR ratio in India and the PRC is higher than in the other two economies. For the whole population, rural and urban, it rose from 84% in 2011 to 88% in 2018, higher for the urban population than for rural. A major contributing factor is the larger share of private pension income, which rose from 40% in 2011 to 45% in 2018.[24] The share of intra-family transfer income in the PRC falls between the shares for Japan and the ROK, but is lower than 0.11 in India in 2018. Transfer income accounts for a larger share of total resources in rural than urban areas in both the PRC and India.

---

[23] The authors estimated consumption preparedness figures for India using household income and household average propensity to consume, there as reported by two World Bank online publications, rather than the Longitudinal Ageing Study in India, for reasons explained on p. 17 of Ehrlich and Liu (2024).

[24] The distinction between private and public pensions is unclear in the PRC because "private" pensions are employer-funded programs, and the state and state-owned enterprises are the main employers.

Figure 4.7: Total Available Household Resources for Retirement, by Economy and Source

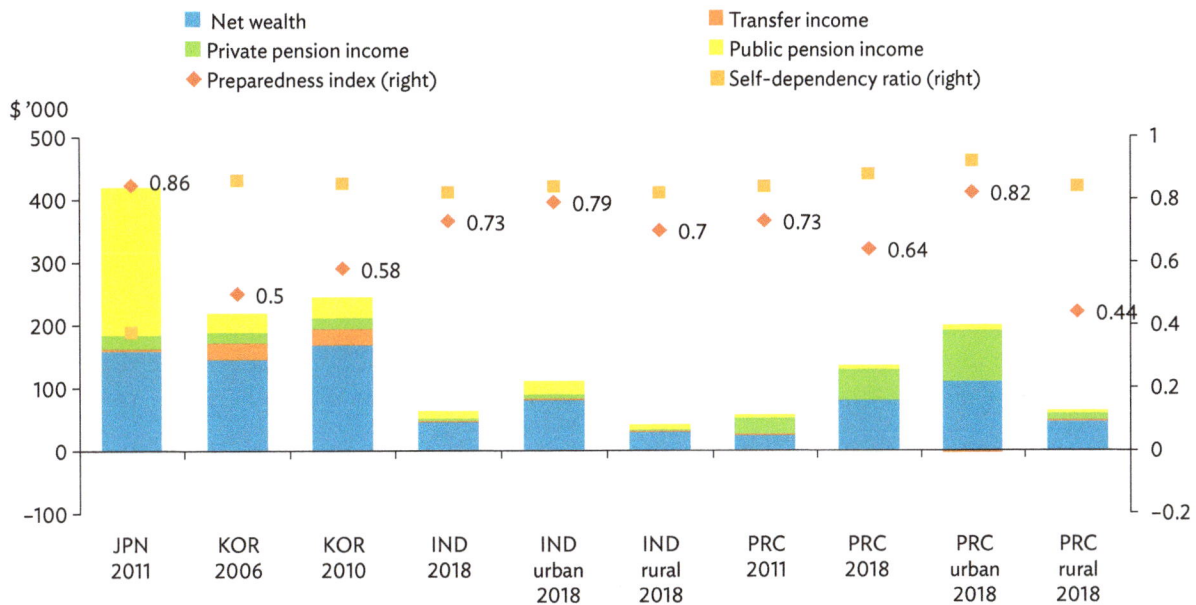

IND = India, JPN = Japan, KOR = Republic of Korea, PRC = People's Republic of China.

Notes: Retirement resources are shown in net present value using 2010 as the base year and exchange rates adjusted for purchasing power parity. Public and private pension definitions follow those of the harmonized data of Gateway to Global Aging Data.

Source: Chapter 1, Box 1.1, Japanese Study of Aging and Retirement, and Ehrlich and Liu (2024).

4.2 Pension Systems in Developing Asia: Current State, Salient Challenges, and Some Key Issues

4.2.1 Overview of Pension Systems in Asia and the Pacific

Older people in the region will struggle to achieve financial security if they continue to depend heavily on private income and wealth.[25] Pension systems are thus set to play a greater role in promoting the economic security of older Asians. However, the task of designing and publicly funding adequate, sustainable, and comprehensive pension systems faces considerable challenges in largely informal economies and labor markets with weak institutional structures for social protection.

Pension system structures are diverse in developing Asia. This is true of both contributory pensions and noncontributory or social pensions (Table 4.1). Regional pension system structures show the following patterns.

While many economies in Asia and the Pacific have noncontributory social pensions, several do not. Those without social pensions are Cambodia, the Federated States of Micronesia, the Lao PDR, the Marshall Islands, Pakistan, Papua New Guinea, Solomon Islands, and Vanuatu. Among those with social pensions, coverage and targeting methods differ.

---

[25]   The following is adapted from an Asian Development Policy Report background paper prepared by Chomik, O'Keefe, and Piggott (2024).

Noncontributory benefits are universal in Georgia, Kazakhstan, Timor-Leste, and some Pacific island economies. In contrast, coverage can be narrowly targeted, as in the Kyrgyz Republic, Malaysia, and Mongolia, or more inclusive with eligibility determined through means testing, as in Azerbaijan, Fiji, the Philippines, and the ROK, or through pension testing, as in Nepal and Thailand. Indonesia and Myanmar restrict eligibility through a very old qualifying age. Armenia, the Kyrgyz Republic, and the Philippines provide a social floor with benefits even for those who participate in contributory programs.

Pension systems for the formal private sector vary significantly. A first group of economies, primarily in East and Southeast Asia, rely on defined benefit programs for the private sector, under which benefits are typically based on salary history and years of service. A second group, largely Commonwealth economies, have defined contribution programs, including provident funds, for private sector formal workers under which contributions are determined as a fixed amount or a percentage of salary, but future benefits are not fixed. Provident funds are not necessarily private but may also be public. A third group in the Caucasus and Central Asia use notional defined contribution systems, which are pay-as-you-go public pension plans with a hypothetical personal account used to calculate individual benefits based on a formula set by the government. A fourth group, notably including the Kyrgyz Republic, the PRC, and Tajikistan, has multi-pillar mandatory systems that combine defined benefits or notional defined contributions with direct-contribution individual accounts.

Some civil service and public sector programs are separate, while others are integrated. Economies in the Pacific and in the Caucasus and Central Asia integrate systems across the public and private sectors. The PRC and Viet Nam are transitioning to integrated systems. Most economies in East, Southeast, and South Asia, however, have separate public sector systems, which are significantly more generous than private ones and, in some cases, do not even require employee contributions.

Structural variation exists as well in some economies that, to expand coverage, have matching voluntary contributory programs for workers in the informal sector. This supplementary approach was initiated in India and Sri Lanka and subsequently taken up by a number of East and Southeast Asian systems but has enjoyed only modest success in expanding coverage.

Table 4.1: Social and Contributory Pension Design in Asia and the Pacific

		Social (Noncontributory)			Contributory			Matching
	Universal	Means Targeted (means tested or proxy means tested)	Advanced Age Targeted (where access is significantly above age 65)	Pension Targeted[a]	Defined Benefit	Defined or Notional Defined Contribution	Civil Separate	Matched Contributions (beyond any tax advantages)
Developing Asia								
Caucasus and Central Asia								
Armenia		■		■		■		
Azerbaijan		■				■		
Georgia	■					■		
Kazakhstan		■			■	■		
Kyrgyz Republic			■	■	■	■		
Tajikistan					■	■		
Uzbekistan		■			■			

continued on next page

Table 4.1 *continued*

	Social (Noncontributory)				Contributory			Matching
	Universal	**Means Targeted** (means tested or proxy means tested)	**Advanced Age Targeted** (where access is significantly above age 65)	**Pension Targeted**[a]	**Defined Benefit**	**Defined or Notional Defined Contribution**	**Civil Separate**	**Matched Contributions** (beyond any tax advantages)
East Asia								
Hong Kong, China				■				
Korea, Republic of		■			■		■	
Mongolia		■			■		■	
PRC				■		■		■
South Asia								
Bangladesh		■			■		■	■
India		■			■	■	■	■
Nepal						■		
Pakistan					■		■	
Sri Lanka		■			■			
Southeast Asia								
Cambodia					■			
Indonesia			■		■		■	
Lao PDR					■			
Malaysia		■				■		
Myanmar		■			■			
Philippines		■			■			
Singapore						■		
Thailand			■		■			
Timor-Leste			■		■			
Viet Nam		■			■			
The Pacific								
Fiji				■		■		
FSM					■	■		
Kiribati	■				■	■		
Marshall Islands					■			
Papua New Guinea						■		
Samoa	■					■		
Solomon Islands						■		■
Tonga			■			■		
Vanuatu						■		
Other economies								
Australia		■				■		
Japan				■	■			
New Zealand	■							

FSM = Federated States of Micronesia, Lao PDR = Lao People's Democratic Republic, PRC = People's Republic of China.

Notes: Data are from latest year available. In Papua New Guinea, social pensions are in only one province. Membership and participation in a contributory pillar excludes civil service.

[a] Benefits for those without a pension or the provision of a contributory floor.

Sources: Allianz (2023); HelpAge International. 2018. Pension Watch Social Pensions Database; ILO. World Social Protection Data Dashboard. OECD. 2022. Pension at Glance, Asia and the Pacific; and Social Security Administration (SSA). SSA Social Security Programs throughout the World: Asia and the Pacific 2018.

4.2.2 Mandated and Voluntary Contributory Pensions

High informality in employment constrains contributory pension system coverage. A contributory program is often the first step for a nascent pension system. However, it remains a challenge for contributory programs to achieve widespread coverage in the region beyond public sector and formal private sector workers (Table 4.2). Many pension systems exclude certain types of workers in the formal sector and all workers in the informal sector, often excluding the self-employed, business owners, and workers employed in smaller enterprises. Some Asian governments have begun addressing regulatory barriers by, for instance, reforming labor and social insurance laws to lower the threshold number of workers for mandatory contributions. How to include the self-employed remains an issue, as is temporary employment for service workers in the gig economy, sometimes in violation of labor laws.

Participation in contributory programs varies but remains generally low. Less than 20% of the working age population participates in a number of economies, notably in South Asia, the Mekong subregion, and the Pacific. Low participation reflects high rates of informal employment and the administrative challenges of observing and taxing the incomes of informal workers (Figure 4.8). Chapter 3 has an extended discussion of informal employment.

To expand coverage, some governments in the region have introduced voluntary programs for workers in the informal sector. Using general revenue to match contributions, governments thus encourage saving for old age. Sri Lanka phased in this approach for farmers and fishers from 1987 to 1990, followed by the ROK in 1995. Other Asian economies that have followed suit are India, Malaysia, the Philippines, Thailand, Viet Nam, and, most recently, Bangladesh. The PRC introduced a hybrid program in 2009 that combines a modest match on contributions ex ante

Table 4.2: Pension Coverage and Adequacy by Economy

	Social Pension					Contributory Pension		
	Coverage		Benefit Adequacy	Access Age (M/F)	Social Pension Spending (% of GDP)	Membership/ Participation (% of working age)	Access Age (M/F)	Contributions (% of wage)
	(% of age eligible)	(% of 60+)	(% of GDP per capita)					
Developing Asia								
Caucasus and Central Asia								
Armenia	0	0	12	65	0.0	27	63	5
Azerbaijan	36	24	11	67/62	0.3	25	61	25
Georgia	100		28	60/55		23	65/60	4
Kazakhstan	100	104	6	63/58	0.7	80	63	19
Kyrgyz Republic			16	63/58		35	58	25
Tajikistan	29	24	12	65/60	0.1	21	58	25
Uzbekistan	0	0	30	60/55	0.0	86	60/55	15
East Asia								
Hong Kong, China	20	14	5	65	0.1	52	65	10
Korea, Republic of	70	40	4	65	0.2	54	62	9
Mongolia	2	1	19	60/55	0.0	47	60/55	25
PRC	62		2	60	0.3	37	60/55	24
South Asia								
Bangladesh	35	32	5	65/62	0.1	2		
India	24		2	60	0.0	15	58	16

continued on next page

Table 4.2 continued

| | Social Pension | | | | | Contributory Pension | | |
| | Coverage | | Benefit Adequacy | | Social Pension Spending | Membership/Participation | | |
	(% of age eligible)	(% of 60+)	(% of GDP per capita)	Access Age (M/F)	(% of GDP)	(% of working age)	Access Age (M/F)	Contributions (% of wage)
Nepal	80	31	31	70	0.7	3	58	20
Pakistan						7	60/55	6
Sri Lanka	33	13	4	70		18	55/50	20
Southeast Asia								
Cambodia						2	60	4
Indonesia	0	0	6	70	0.0	17	65	6
Lao PDR						1	60/55	11
Malaysia	4		11	60	0.05	42	55	24
Myanmar	100	1	7	85	0.0		60	6
Philippines	44		4	60	0.4	35	65	14
Singapore						48	65	37
Thailand	86		4	60	0.4	29	55	7
Timor-Leste	100		15	60	0.5	6		
Viet Nam	28		7	60	0.1	30	62/60	22
Pacific								
Fiji	51	18	6	65	0.1	64	55	18
FSM						33	65	15
Kiribati	93	35	33	67	1.2		50	15
Marshall Islands							61	16
Papua New Guinea	2		8	60	0.0	3	55	12
Samoa	93	65	19	65	0.9	23	55	10
Solomon Islands					0.0	47	50	13
Tonga	100			70		7		10
Vanuatu					0.0	17	55	8
Other economies								
Australia	70	51	28	67	2.6	70	60	12
Japan	3		18	65		85	65	18
New Zealand	99	71	37	65	4.5		65	6

F = female, FSM = Federated States of Micronesia, GDP = gross domestic product, Lao PDR = Lao People's Democratic Republic, M = male, PRC = People's Republic of China.

Notes: Data are latest year available. Traffic-light shading does not indicate value but rather high, middle, and low tertiles in economies or else, for access ages, <60, 60–64, and 65+. In Papua New Guinea, only one province has a social pension. The social pension in the PRC is not a classic social pension but a hybrid that requires modest contributions from employers and employees. Membership and participation in the contributory pillar excludes the civil service.

Sources: Allianz. (2023); Chomik, O'Keefe, and Piggott (2024); HelpAge International. Social Pensions Database, version 1 March 2018; International Labour Organization. World Protection Data Dashboards; International Monetary Fund. World Economic Outlook Databases; OECD. 2023. Pensions at a Glance; United Nations, Department of Economic and Social Affairs, Population Division. 2022. World Population Prospects 2022, Online Edition; World Health Organization. Statistical Information System; World Bank. DataBank; and national sources.

Figure 4.8: Pension Coverage and Informal Employment, by Economy

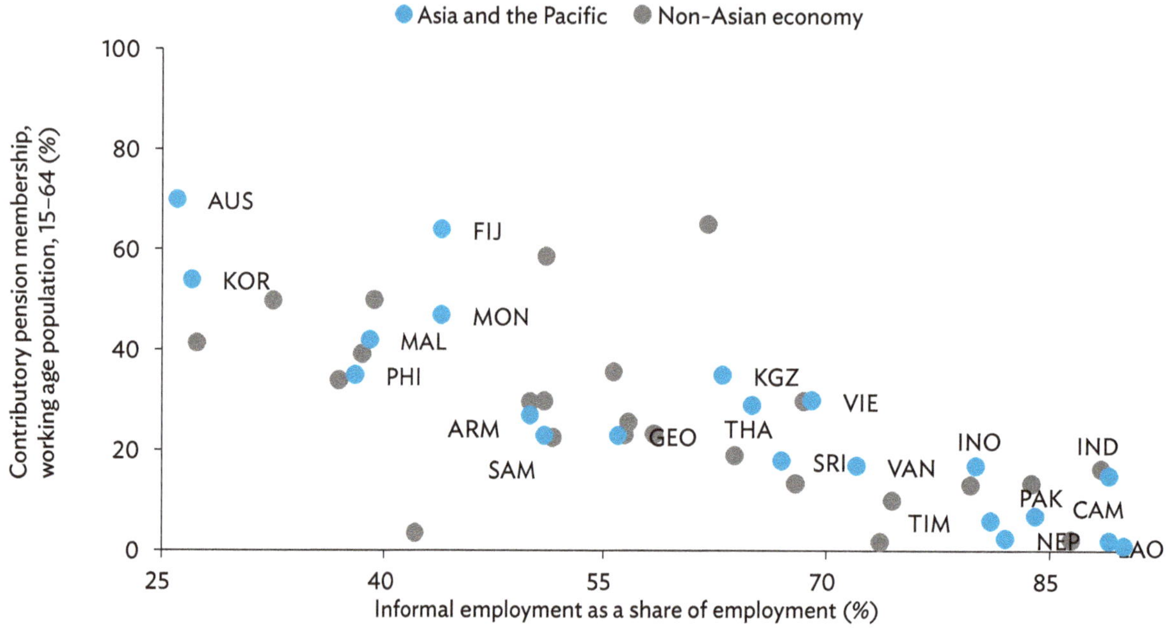

ARM = Armenia, AUS = Australia, CAM = Cambodia, FIJ = Fiji, GEO = Georgia, KGZ = Kyrgyz Republic, IND = India, INO = Indonesia, KOR = Republic of Korea, LAO = Lao People's Democratic Republic, MAL = Malaysia, MON = Mongolia, NEP = Nepal, PAK = Pakistan, PHI = Philippines, SAM = Samoa, SRI = Sri Lanka, THA = Thailand, TIM = Timor-Leste, VAN = Vanuatu, VIE = Viet Nam.

Source: Chomik, O'Keefe, and Piggott (2024).

with the provision of a lifetime basic pension after age 60 or a lump-sum equivalent. Most programs adopt a simple and flexible design to account for modest and irregular contributions (Chomik, O'Keefe, and Piggott 2024). While matching programs can lift voluntary contributions and increase participation, low combined contributions mean that additional funding will be needed as participants reach old age. Coverage expansion has been modest so far, with only 1% of the working age population in Malaysia having joined a matching program, 3% in Viet Nam, and 5% in India. Thailand has enjoyed more success, attracting about 12% of the working age population to matching programs. The most notable successes are the ROK, where participation more than doubled from 1995 to 1999, and the PRC hybrid program, which in 2020 engaged more than 380 million contributors, over 90% of them in rural areas (Wang and Feng 2022).

Other innovations to matching programs exist around the world. They have included bundling retirement savings with other benefits to address the multiple needs of informal workers and overcome myopia about old-age

savings. These include disability, life, and funeral insurance; health and maternity cover; and access to microfinance. Simplified know-your-customer requirements for opening accounts can enhance access, as exemplified by India's Atal Pension Yojana, which uses the Aadhar biometric national identification system. The use of auto-enrollment, auto-deductions, and auto-escalation with opt-outs increases both contributions and membership (Whitehouse 2012). Contribution aggregators and communities such as trade unions, worker associations, co-ops, microfinance institutions, and self-help groups can augment peer incentive effects and the efficiency of program administration. Transaction costs can be reduced through expanded contribution channels, in particular the use of mobile payments, convenience stores, and platforms such as WhatsApp, as used in India.

Defined contribution systems often pay inadequate benefits, and the fiscal sustainability of defined benefit systems is often doubtful. While policies to increase coverage are important, the adequacy of benefits and the fiscal affordability of contributory programs require policy attention. The fiscal sustainability of defined contribution programs is ensured by design, at least in the absence of generous minimum benefit guarantees, but benefit adequacy remains a major challenge. This is commonly because contributions, particularly from women, are low or incomplete (Box 4.2), early withdrawal rules are generous, as in India, Malaysia, and most Pacific island economies; withdrawal ages are low, as in Kiribati, Malaysia, and Sri Lanka; and investment fund returns are sometimes meager, as in several Pacific island economies.

For defined benefit programs, the trade-off is between benefit adequacy and fiscal sustainability. Many regional economies have tended to favor providing adequate benefits, with attendant risks for

fiscal sustainability and a future reversal of pension promises. In the Philippines and Thailand, for example, sustainability concerns are generally that defined benefit contribution rates are low, while in the PRC and Viet Nam concerns are that benefits are too generous, even where contribution rates are significant. As a result, a number of defined benefit programs in the region face serious sustainability challenges in the medium to long run. Sustainability can be enhanced by adjustment mechanisms that automatically change pension parameters or benefits based on the evolution of demographic, economic, or financial indicators (Box 4.3). Notional defined contribution programs pay benefits throughout old age, but the benefit amount is

---

Box 4.3: Automatic Adjustment Mechanisms in Pension Systems

Automatic adjustment mechanisms (AAMs) can enhance the sustainability of pension systems. They have become an increasingly common feature of pension systems in member economies of the Organisation for Economic Co-operation and Development (OECD) but are strikingly absent from pension systems in much of developing Asia. AAMs have been described as "predefined rules that automatically change pension parameters or pension benefits based on the evolution of a demographic, economic, or financial indicator" (OECD 2021). From a system viewpoint, AAMs help pensions remain sustainable as circumstances evolve. From a political perspective, they minimize the political turbulence that can accompany adjustments to pensions. For households, an AAM that indexes pensions according to preset rules makes pension income more predictable, even if benefits are cut. In 2021, two-thirds of OECD economies had at lease one AAM built into their mandatory or quasi-mandatory pension systems.

AAMs can take several forms. (i) A pension system with a notional defined contribution can have inbuilt adjustment mechanisms that respond to shifting demographics, as in Azerbaijan, the Kyrgyz Republic, and Tajikistan, as well as in Italy, Norway, Poland, and Sweden. (ii) Access age can be adjusted automatically directly in line, 1:1, with changes in life expectancy, as in Denmark and Italy, or by some percentage of the increase in life expectancy, as in Finland, the Netherlands, and Portugal. (iii) Benefits can be adjusted automatically in line with life expectancy, demographic ratios, wage bills or gross domestic product (GDP), as in Finland, Greece, Japan, and Portugal. (iv) Balancing mechanisms can ensure

projected financial balance for pensions over the short or long term, relying on a combination of changes to pension benefits, points, or contribution rates, as in Canada, Germany, the Netherlands, Sweden, and the United States (US). (v) Funded defined contribution systems without a minimum benefit guarantee can act as automatic stabilizers, as no fixed promise is made about the pension amount until the point of retirement.

AAMs make pension systems more predictable but have shortcomings. These shortcomings have prompted some OECD members to change or remove them. Like any public policy, they may be reversed or diluted with suspensions under political pressure. Their implementation may be undermined as well by technical design issues or unanticipated developments in indicators, such as divergence between projected and actual life expectancy. An alternative approach to achieving long-term equilibrium in pension systems is to use reserve funds. This approach was initiated in the US social security system and subsequently adopted in over 20 OECD economies, including Japan and the Republic of Korea (ROK), and more recently in the People's Republic of China (PRC). Reserve fund assets in several OECD economies exceed one-quarter of annual GDP. Regional reserves equal about a third of GDP in Japan and 45% of GDP in the ROK but still only 3% of GDP in the PRC (OECD 2021).

Reference

OECD. 2021. *Pensions at a Glance*. Organisation for Economic Co-operation and Development.

Source: Chomik, O'Keefe, and Piggott (2024).

adjusted according to life expectancy at the retirement of each cohort. This ensures fiscal sustainability but may compromise adequacy. Examples are Azerbaijan, the Kyrgyz Republic, and Tajikistan.

4.2.3 Social Pension Programs

Regional economies increasingly supplement contributory programs with noncontributory social pensions. This is in response to low participation in contributory programs and persistently high informality in employment. Social pensions can reach workers in informal sectors. The main challenges to developing Asia's social pension programs are limited coverage in some economies especially for the poor group (Figure 4.4), low benefits that can improve the well-being of older people only modestly, and the risk of fiscal unsustainability as programs are greatly expanded.

Many economies in Asia and the Pacific have introduced social pensions, but coverage and adequacy vary substantially. Coverage ranges from being central to the entire pension system, as in Georgia, to absent or negligible, as in Cambodia, the Lao PDR, Pakistan, Malaysia, and several Pacific island economies. Those that have social pensions have tended to prioritize fiscal sustainability over adequacy. But in general, the region's pension systems are not fiscally sustainable, nor do they provide adequate benefits. Typically, regional social pensions have only narrow coverage, low benefits, or both (Figure 4.9). Only five regional economies pay benefits above the global average of 16% of gross domestic product (GDP) per capita, and only two pay benefits above the Organisation for Economic Co-operation and Development (OECD) average of 22%. Meanwhile, 11 economies in the region pay social pensions to less than half of the population of eligible age—often well less than half.

Figure 4.9: Social Pension Coverage of Older People and Its Adequacy

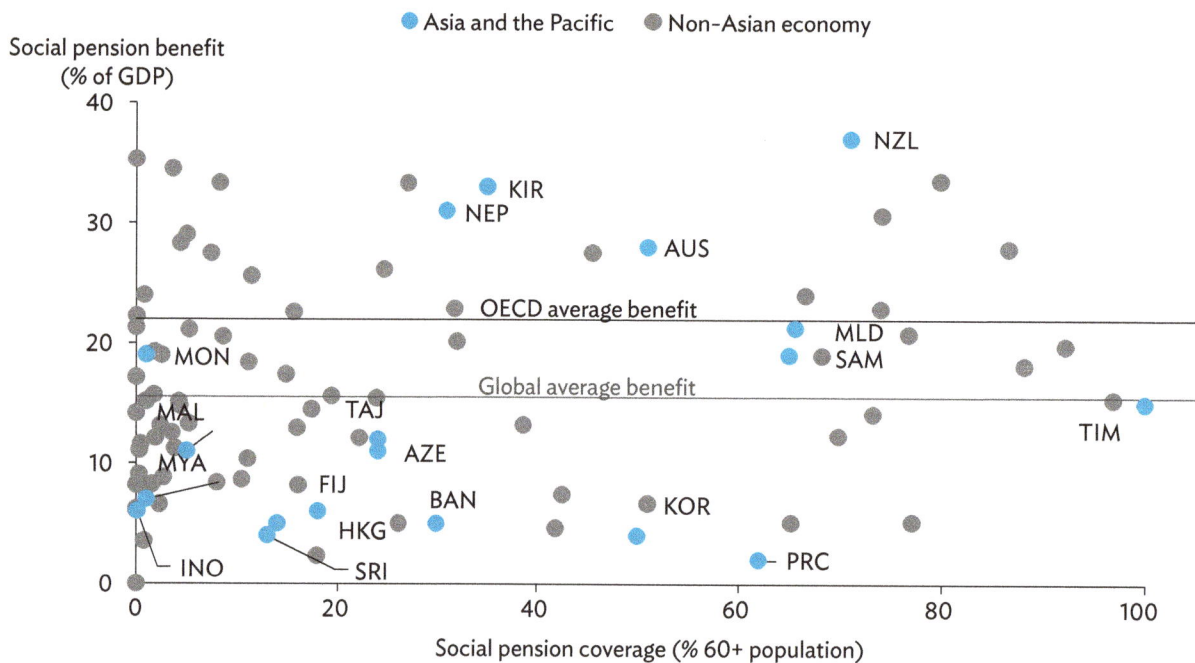

AUS = Australia; AZE = Azerbaijan; BAN = Bangladesh; FIJ = Fiji; GDP = gross domestic product; HKG = Hong Kong, China; INO = Indonesia; KIR = Kiribati; KOR = Republic of Korea; MAL = Malaysia; MLD = Maldives; MON = Mongolia; MYA = Myanmar; NEP = Nepal; NZL = New Zealand; OECD = Organisation for Economic Co-operation and Development; PRC = People's Republic of China; SAM = Samoa; SRI = Sri Lanka; TAJ = Tajikistan; TIM = Timor-Leste.

Notes: Based on data from 2018 or the latest year available. Benefit rates can differ for different groups. For example, Thailand has different monthly rates by age, with those aged 60–69 getting 600 baht (B) plus B100 increments with each decade to a maximum of B1,000 per month at age 90 and older.

Source: Chomik, O'Keefe, and Piggott (2024).

The big advantage of universal coverage over targeting in social pensions is lower administrative cost. As everyone above a certain age is covered by a universal social pension, implementation does not require a lot of administrative capacity. Further, universal coverage is politically popular and avoids work disincentives to qualify for pro-poor targeting. Economies with sufficient administrative capacity, however, may prefer targeting because it channels benefits to those who need them most. Instead of giving identical small benefits to everyone regardless of need, targeting can reach the poorest and most vulnerable and provide them with benefits sufficient for sustenance. Further, targeting may substantially cut fiscal costs. Effective targeting requires sound design.

Targeting mechanisms are important to social pension design. Key concerns for targeting are who the beneficiaries are, to what extent targeting affects incentives and behavior, and how easy the system is to administer. Targeted social pensions should be viewed as important complements to contributory systems. They provide benefits to those most in need, narrowing relative poverty and inequality. Studies have shown that targeting is more efficient than universality and distorts the economy less (Kumru and Piggott 2010; Chomik et al. 2015; Kudrna 2016; Kudrna, Tran, and Woodland 2019, 2022). However, poorly designed targeting and weak administrative capacity risk misidentifying beneficiaries.

A number of economies in developing Asia use means testing in their social pension programs. An alternative is hybrid means testing, which combines verification of easily monitored actual income and imputation of other income. But in many emerging economies, the difficulty of observing informal income, a lack of thorough asset records, and weak administrative capacity challenge comprehensive or even hybrid means testing. To simplify targeting, a number of economies already use pension testing, advanced age targeting, or both (Table 4.1). Pension testing in Thailand, for example, grants social pensions to over 70% of those aged 60 and older, while Myanmar uses a very high age threshold of 85 to restrict eligibility. With advances in digital technology and banking, comprehensive means testing may become more viable in the future.

Social pensions have tangible but modest impacts on the well-being of older people. Low benefits mean that social pensions, even those with substantial reach, tend to improve the well-being of older people only modestly and do little to reduce poverty. In Thailand, for example, social pension benefits are estimated to lift only about 5% of households with older people above the $6.85/day poverty line, lowering the poverty rate from 21% to 16%—assuming universal coverage for people aged 65+ and compared with no program at all (Chomik, O'Keefe, and Piggott 2024). Nevertheless, social pensions do have a tangible impact in some economies (Box 4.4).

4.2.4 How Financialization and Digitalization Can Benefit Pension Systems

Technological innovations will greatly enable Asia's pension systems. Digitization and fintech promise to alleviate the challenges of collecting contributions and delivering pensions in the informal sector, and thus drive inclusion. While these innovations help all age groups, they can be especially beneficial for older Asians. Biometric identification, for example, is now used for pension transactions in Armenia, Cambodia, Indonesia, the Kyrgyz Republic, India, and Pakistan, and is being phased in in the Philippines and Viet Nam. It can substantially simplify know-your-customer requirements for bank and mobile account transactions, making it easier to contribute to and receive pension benefits, especially for unbanked workers in the informal sector. A notable example is the biometric ID in the India Stack, which uses the biometric Aadhaar national ID to link ID, personal authentication, and payments, while protecting data privacy. According to World Bank (2021b), the transition to payment through biometric smart cards has halved internal fraud and leakage in India's pension systems.

Social protection programs are expected to drive financial and digital inclusion. The means will be digital identification and payment mechanisms through financial accounts. Figure 4.10 shows that more than half of adult public transfer recipients in economies across the region typically get government transfers or pensions through an account with a

Box 4.4: Welfare Impacts from Pensions

Evidence is growing that both social and contributory pensions can lift recipients out of poverty. Hybrid pensions for informal workers in the People's Republic of China (PRC), for example, reduce consumption poverty, particularly in poorer rural areas (Zhang, Giles, and Zhao 2014; Zhang, Luo, and Robinson 2020; Zheng, Fang, and Brown 2020). Further improvements to welfare have been observed across multidimensional measures of poverty such as health, household income, and food expenditure (Huang and Zhang 2021; Zhang and Imai 2023). Conversely, studies in Thailand have not found significant poverty impacts from the social pensions (Badiani-Magnusson 2016; Huang and Giles 2017). Contributory pensions also have significant welfare impacts. In Indonesia, the PRC, Thailand, and Viet Nam, contributory pension receipt is associated with considerable poverty reduction and improved well-being in rural and urban areas alike, with a consistently greater impact in rural areas (Chen and Park 2023; Giles and Huang 2016).

Pensions can have significant spillover benefits in emerging economies with many multigenerational households. This effect is not often considered in developed economies. In the PRC, social pensions have improved the care, education, health, and nutrition of children, in particular those left behind by migrant parents, and in Thailand they have improved education and reduced child labor (Zhang, Giles, and Zhao 2014; Zhang, Luo, and Robinson 2020; Zheng, Fang, and Brown 2020).

Source: Asian Development Bank.

References

Badiani-Magnusson, R. 2016. Estimating the Impact of Thailand's Elderly Social Pension on Well-Being. Mimeo. World Bank.

Chen, Z. and A. Park. 2023. Rural Pensions, Intra-Household Bargaining, and Elderly Medical Expenditure in the People's Republic of China. *ADB Economics Working Paper.* No. 693. Asian Development Bank.

Giles, J. and Y. Huang. 2016. Are the Elderly Left Behind in a Time of Rapid Demographic and Economic Change? A Comparative Study of the Poverty and Well-Being East Asia's Elderly. Background Paper for World Bank Regional Report on Aging in East Asia. World Bank.

Huang, W. and C. Zhang. 2021. The Power of Social Pensions: Evidence from China's New Rural Pension Scheme. *American Economic Journal: Applied Economics.* 13(2).

Huang, Y. and J. Giles. 2017. Universal Social Pension and Spousal Labor Supply in Rural Thailand. Mimeo. World Bank.

Zhang, A. and K. S. Imai. 2023. Do Public Pension Programmes Reduce Elderly Poverty in China? *Review of Development Economics.* 28(1).

Zhang C., J. Giles, and Y. Zhao. 2014. A Policy Evaluation of China's New Rural Pension Programme: Income, Poverty, Expenditure, Subjective Well-Being and Labour Supply. *China Economic Quarterly.* 14(1).

Zhang, Z., Y. Luo, and D. Robinson. 2020. Do Social Pensions Help People Living on the Edge? Assessing Determinants of Vulnerability to Food Poverty among the Rural Elderly. *European Journal of Development Research.* 32(1).

Zheng, X., X. Fang, and D. S. Brown. 2020. Social Pensions and Child Health in Rural China. *Journal of Development Studies.* 56(3).

financial institution, into a card, or through a mobile phone. Those lagging in this trend include Armenia, Cambodia, Indonesia, Myanmar, the Philippines, Sri Lanka, and Uzbekistan. Individuals who receive payments into an account are more likely to make payments digitally, as well as to save and borrow.

Another innovation that leverages advances in fintech is consumption-based pensions. These programs enable people to bank micro savings when they complete purchases using digital payment platforms. They are structured in various ways: automated rounding-up of purchase prices, or deductions at a fixed percentage of purchase price or a flat amount. Individual savings derived from such programs are transferred into designated accounts through a payment platform. This approach is being piloted in Mexico, the PRC, and Spain (Hernández-Pacheco, Ramos, and Flores 2022) but has yet to be mainstreamed in Asian pension systems. With growth in digital payments, consumption-based pension programs are expected to gain traction but will need careful assessment.

Figure 4.10: Government Transfer or Pension Recipients Aged 15+ Who Receive Transfers or Pensions into an Account

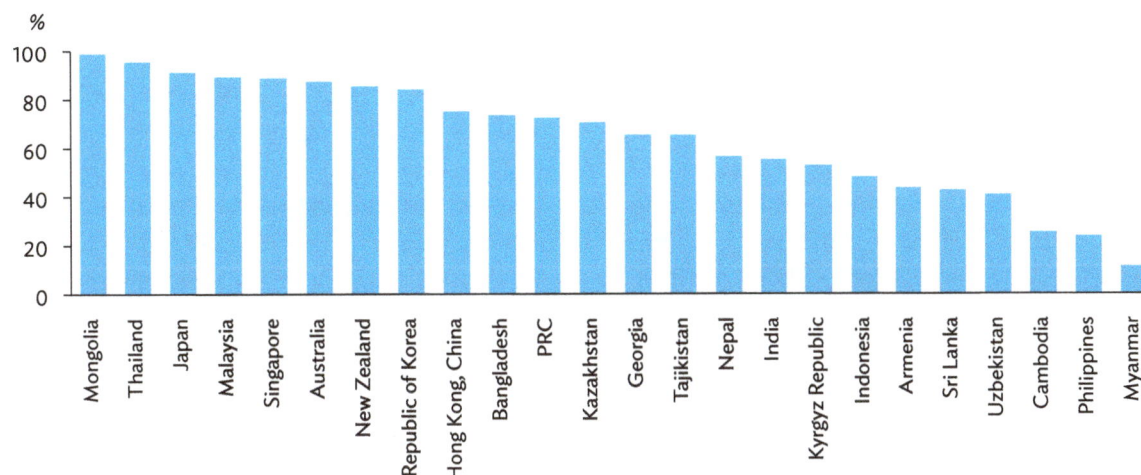

PRC = People's Republic of China.

Note: Among respondents aged 15+ who report personally receiving any transfer or pension from the government in the past year, the figure shows the percentage who received it in a financial institution account, into a card, or through a mobile phone.

Source: World Bank. The Global Findex Database in Chomik, O'Keefe, and J. Piggott (2024).

4.2.5 Pension System Awareness and Accountability

Some Asians may not join contributory pension programs simply for lack of awareness. Lack of information or understanding of pension programs—such as their eligibility criteria, contribution requirements, or long-term advantages—can hamper program expansion (Heckman and Smith 2004). Several Asian governments, notably in India, the Philippines, and Thailand, conduct extensive awareness campaigns and outreach programs to encourage enrollment in pension programs. In a large field experiment in Guangdong Province of the PRC, handing out brochures with personalized benefit information brought a significant increase in pension enrollment, especially among individuals aged 45–55 (Bai et al. 2021). Another information intervention targeting rural migrants garnered an increase by 4 percentage points in participation by young informal workers (Giles et al. 2021).

Willingness to participate in a contributory pension program hinges on trust and accountability. Social security administrators must be accountable and manage programs transparently and predictably. Tanaka et al. (forthcoming) showed that trust in the public service provider plays a crucial role in enhancing contributions to pension programs in Mongolia. Transparency requires that information be available, accurate, essential, and timely to ensure that stakeholders are well informed of the true state of the social security program, and that clear and simple rules, systems, and processes limit discretionary and arbitrary actions by program administration. Predictability means consistent application of the law and its supporting policies, rules, and regulations. For social security programs, the rights and duties of members and beneficiaries must be well defined, protected, and consistently enforced. The imperative of stakeholder participation requires their active education, engagement, and involvement to ensure the protection of their interests. Dynamism is required to ensure ongoing improvement in fund operations.

4.2.6   Financial Literacy and Inclusion for Future Generations of Older People

Financial literacy has important consequences for well-being throughout one's life. Being financially literate means having the financial awareness, knowledge, skills, and positive attitudes and behavior required to make sound financial decisions and ultimately achieve financial well-being (OECD 2020c). It is crucial for retirement security and should be promoted in people who are still young enough to benefit the most (Lusardi and Mitchell 2011).

Financial literacy is deficient in Asia and the Pacific economies. The International Survey of Adult Financial Literacy conducted in 2020 by the OECD and the International Network on Financial Education scored adults for financial literacy, against a perfect 100%, at 63.5% in Indonesia, 59.7% in Malaysia, and 62.1% in the ROK, or close to the 60.5% average score for member economies of the OECD and Asia-Pacific Economic Cooperation (OECD 2021b).[26] Further, while 70.5% of adults in Indonesia and 66.0% in Malaysia reported planning for the long term, far fewer did elsewhere: only 53.5% in Hong Kong, China; 41.1% in the ROK; and 54.0% in Thailand. In the PRC, a large survey of urban households in 2014 found that a sizable percentage of individuals—especially older people, women, and those with low educational attainment—had little financial literacy (Niu, Zhou, and Gan 2020). Klapper, Lusardi, and van Oudheusden (2015) found South Asian economies to have exceptionally low financial literacy scores, with at best a quarter of adults financially literate.

Evidence in the region shows that financial literacy improves retirement planning. Findings from a small set of studies in developing Asia align with existing studies. Results from a survey of urban households in the PRC found that financial literacy is associated with retirement planning that includes determining financial needs in retirement and creating long-term financial plans, and with having private pension insurance. A rural field experiment in the PRC found that explaining compound interest to subjects increased their pension contributions by about 40% (Song 2020). Financial literacy interventions can have a positive impact if they are immersive and introduced at an early age or later at the point of decision (Chomik et al. 2022; Yap et al. 2023).

Financial literacy programs are important to address behavioral biases that favor short-term thinking. To examine attitudes toward financial planning, the 2020 survey by the OECD and the International Network on Financial Education questioned adults on their views toward "living for today" and spending money. Among those surveyed, only 34% in Hong Kong, China; 30% in Malaysia; and 43% in the ROK obtained the minimum target score for an attitude that indicates financial planning (OECD 2021b). Financial literacy programs are important to educate workers on the need for long-term financial planning to ensure income security in old age (Box 4.5).

Key lessons can be drawn from behavioral insights into conducting financial literacy programs. OECD (2019a) found ways to conduct financial education programs that achieve positive outcomes, but no one-size-fits-all approach. It recommends that financial education be focused on content, straightforward, and simple to understand. Financial education programs should be as personalized as possible and go beyond providing only information. Further, programs should teach self-control and mental accounting techniques and enable immediate practice applying the skills learned. Also recommended are digital channels of financial education and approaches that are innovative, entertaining, and easily accessible. Models and frameworks exist that are based on scientific findings, and policymakers can use them to develop their own financial literacy programs.[27] Finally, regulatory support from the government can facilitate private sector initiatives on retirement savings (Box 4.6).

---

[26]   A score is summed across financial knowledge, financial behavior, and financial attitude. Lusardi and Mitchell (2011) found widespread financial illiteracy even in economies with well-developed financial markets.

[27]   The Behavioral Insights Team in the United Kingdom codified four principles—easy, attractive, social, and timely—as EAST to generate and apply behavioral insights. Peru adopted this framework in the design of its two financial education programs: Finanzas en el Cole (Finances in School) and Finanzas para Ti (Finances for You) (OECD 2019a).

Box 4.5: Developing Financial Literacy Programs

Studies conducted in developing Asia highlight the widespread need for financial literacy programs. They should target the people most lacking in financial knowledge—particularly older people, women, and those with low educational attainment—to raise awareness of retirement preparation and provide basic knowledge about saving and retirement planning, including simple interest, compound interest, and risk diversification (OECD 2021). Individuals need to understand inflation and its effect on the value of money over time to encourage budgeting and saving. Financial literacy programs can help people understand which savings and investment products are best suited to their personal situation.

Programs should consider the local contexts. Those intended to foster savings, investment, retirement planning, and pensions should consider national circumstances, including challenges related to national pension systems, investment frameworks, and the overall financial environment (OECD 2022).

Financial literacy programs protect workers and older people from financial scams. Some fraudulent schemes promise high returns with low risk, and others target digital transactions. Since the coronavirus disease (COVID-19) pandemic, several Asian economies have launched digital financial literacy programs to encourage retirement savings with personalized messages, online

retirement income calculators, and interactive apps. In light of the prevalence of fraudulent schemes, governments have initiated campaigns to protect the public from financial and cyber scams. A survey found 23% of adults in Indonesia and 16% in Malaysia have invested in financial products that turned out to be scams (OECD 2021).

Financial literacy programs help individuals understand various financial products and make sound investment decisions. Various financial products can be accessed differently depending on individual situations. An individual can start by regularly setting aside part of his or her income into a regular savings account in a bank. Those without access to a bank may consider saving in a microfinance institution, which are becoming prevalent in rural areas. As income and savings increase, along with financial literacy, one can move into more sophisticated financial products such as equities, bonds, insurance-linked investments, mutual funds, and exchange traded funds.

References

OECD. 2021. *OECD/INFE Report on Financial Literacy and Resilience in APEC Economies*. Organisation for Economic Co-operation and Development.

———. 2022. OECD Legal Instruments. Recommendation of the Council on Financial Literacy. *OECD/LEGAL/0461*. Organisation for Economic Co-operation and Development.

Source: Asian Development Bank.

4.3 Policies for Economically Secure Aging

Low financial preparedness for retirement in developing Asia calls for stronger public support and invigorated pension systems. Great diversity in pension system design exists across Asia and the Pacific in terms of the structure of contributory systems and the roles of noncontributory social programs and mandated and voluntary contributory systems. Social pensions have expanded across the region, but some economies still lack noncontributory social pensions,

and a few lack even a contributory program for private sector workers. Whatever the structure of national systems, they all face challenges, some of them common across the region.

4.3.1 Strengthening Contributory Pension Programs

Coverage under contributory programs remains a major concern. Stubborn informality in employment keeps coverage in Asia and the Pacific low, and this challenge is unlikely to be overcome in most regional economies in the foreseeable future. At the same time,

Box 4.6: Government Regulatory Support Fostering Private Savings Initiatives

Governments can support private sector initiatives to encourage broader retirement and financial planning. Collaboration with private insurers can generate alternative private savings and investment options to supplement public pensions and achieve greater coverage and adequacy. In 2018, the Government of the People's Republic of China, for example, initiated a policy in pilot cities that allowed individuals to defer income taxes by buying private annuity insurance (Fang and Feng 2018).

In pension systems that collect, invest, and manage funds, governments should institute robust financial and legal governance to build trust. Where private pension fund managers are involved, issues can arise with regard to their ability to promote the best interests of the individual accounts they manage. The challenges facing governments tend to be more pronounced in developing economies for lack of regulatory capacity to supervise fund managers, ensure competition among fund managers, or supervise financial institutions (Chomik, O'Keefe, and Piggott 2024). It is critical over the long term to develop an enabling environment for healthy, well-regulated capital markets and strong financial institutions.

Financial and asset regulations must be available to apply when older people experience cognitive impairment or dementia. One solution is to set up adult guardianship, in which a court appoints a person to take care of the affairs of an older person who can no longer manage alone. Guardians can be spouses, adult children, other relatives or friends of the older person, or a government agency appointed to manage personal finances, essential food and housing needs, and health-care requirements. As guardianship is rather a new area, it requires public awareness campaigns, institutional support, and legislation to safeguard against abuse (Tang, Sakurai, and Chong 2023). Aside from guardianship, other arrangements include living trusts, living wills, and power of attorney, which assigns an older person's rights to another person in the event of future incapacity.

References

Chomik, R., P. O'Keefe, and J. Piggott. 2024. *Pensions in Aging Asia: Policy Insights and Priorities.* Asian Development Bank.

Fang, H. and J. Feng. 2018. The Chinese Pension System. *NBER Working Paper.* No. 25088. National Bureau of Economic Research.

Tang, H. W., Y. Sakurai, and Y. Chong. 2023. Aging and the Law in Singapore and Japan: Adult Guardianship and Other Alternatives. *Journal of Aging & Social Policy.*

Source: Asian Development Bank.

regional and global experience suggests significant potential for expanding pension system coverage while preserving fiscal sustainability.

Programs that match workers' contributions can expand contributory pension coverage by incentivizing informal workers to invest voluntarily. While coverage increases to date have not bridged the coverage gap on their own, rich experience in the region can inform the design of such programs. Contribution-matching programs should (i) ensure adequate and sustained matching of contributions; (ii) be flexible to accommodate the low and volatile incomes of workers in the informal sector; (iii) bundle retirement savings with other benefits such as life or funeral insurance and maternity allowances to boost product appeal; (iv) simplify know-your-customer requirements for

bank and mobile money accounts; (v) use automatic enrollment, deductions, and contribution increases; (vi) enlist contribution aggregator communities such as trade unions and microfinance institutions; and (vii) feature expanded contribution channels such as through mobile payments, online platforms, and local merchants.

Defined benefits in contributory programs need close monitoring. Defined benefit systems must be designed in an actuarially fair manner to be sustainable and equitable. Many programs in developing Asia, especially those for public sector workers, are not so designed and thus may not be fiscally sustainable. Challenges posed by contributory programs vary according to their structure and design. Defined contribution pension regimes across Asia and the Pacific tend to be fiscally sustainable but inadequate because of low contributions and generous early withdrawal rules. Many provide only a lump sum at retirement, which often fails to offer financial security in later years. By contrast, most defined benefit programs provide adequate benefits in old age, but many face sustainability challenges with demographic aging. One especially promising policy tool to ensure the sustainability of defined benefit pensions is an automatic adjustment mechanism that indexes pension parameters or benefits to a demographic, economic, or financial variable (Box 4.3).

Women would benefit from a gender lens for pension design. Women work less in the formal sector, earn less, and have more career interruptions even if formally employed—all of which reduce their pension contributions and earnings-determined pensions. Some of the many contributory pension design parameters that could be better designed to address gender issues would (i) improve survivor benefits by making them higher and more accessible; (ii) adjust vesting periods and benefits to take into account career interruptions; (iii) adjust annuity mortality tables to avoid disadvantaging women for having longer life expectancy; and (iv) review and revise gender-differentiated pension access ages to avoid shortening careers, depressing savings, and lengthening retirement.

4.3.2　Toward Effective and Adequate Social Pensions

A priority is to establish effective and adequate social pensions in Asia and the Pacific economies that do not already have them. Where expansion in contributory program coverage is losing the race against demographic change, social pensions can help bridge the coverage gap. When carefully designed, adequate social benefit systems need not be fiscally unsustainable, even as populations age.

Existing social pensions suffer low coverage, low benefits, or both. In nearly every economy in the region that has a social pension, benefits are too low for adequate financial protection. Social pension coverage

of the poor old remains low in some economies, requiring efforts to extend coverage. Boosting social pension payments would substantially reduce the poverty rate for older people. In India, for example, the existing social pension is estimated to lift about 2%–3% above the poverty line of $3.65 per day, lowering the poverty rate for households with older people from 67% to 65%. A simple simulation found that raising the social pension benefit to the global average equal to 16% of GDP per capita would lift as many as 12% of older households above the poverty line, further reducing the poverty rate for older households to 53% (Figure 4.11A).[28] Raising the social pension benefit further to 22% of GDP per capita would reduce the poverty rate to 48%. Raising the universal social pension benefit would, of course, increase fiscal costs. In India, raising it to the global average would cost the equivalent of 1.2% of GDP (Figure 4.11B).

Well-targeted social pensions can be both effective and sustainable. If designed well, such programs can direct funds to those who need them without compromising fiscal sustainability. Two simplified forms of social pension targeting that are already implemented in the region exclude individuals with contributory pensions or set the eligibility age higher than 65. These strategies are administratively straightforward and enable more inclusive targeting to compensate for large contributory coverage gaps. As digital technology advances, so will the potential to improve means testing through online crosschecks.

4.3.3　Innovative Pension Designs and Technological Solutions

Several innovations to pension design and administration can enhance pension program operation and sustainability. Though a standard feature of pension systems in the OECD, formal indexing rules are largely lacking in Asia and the Pacific. This shortcoming threatens pension adequacy and worsens uncertainty for older people. In both contributory and social pensions, rules for indexing benefits are essential to maintain adequacy over time. Equally essential is that clear rules maintain the real value of pensions and appropriately adjust pension eligibility thresholds.

---

[28]　Assuming universal coverage of those aged 65 and over, compared to no program (Chomik, O'Keefe, and Piggott 2024).

Figure 4.11: The Poverty Reduction and Fiscal Costs of Boosting Social Pensions in Selected Economies

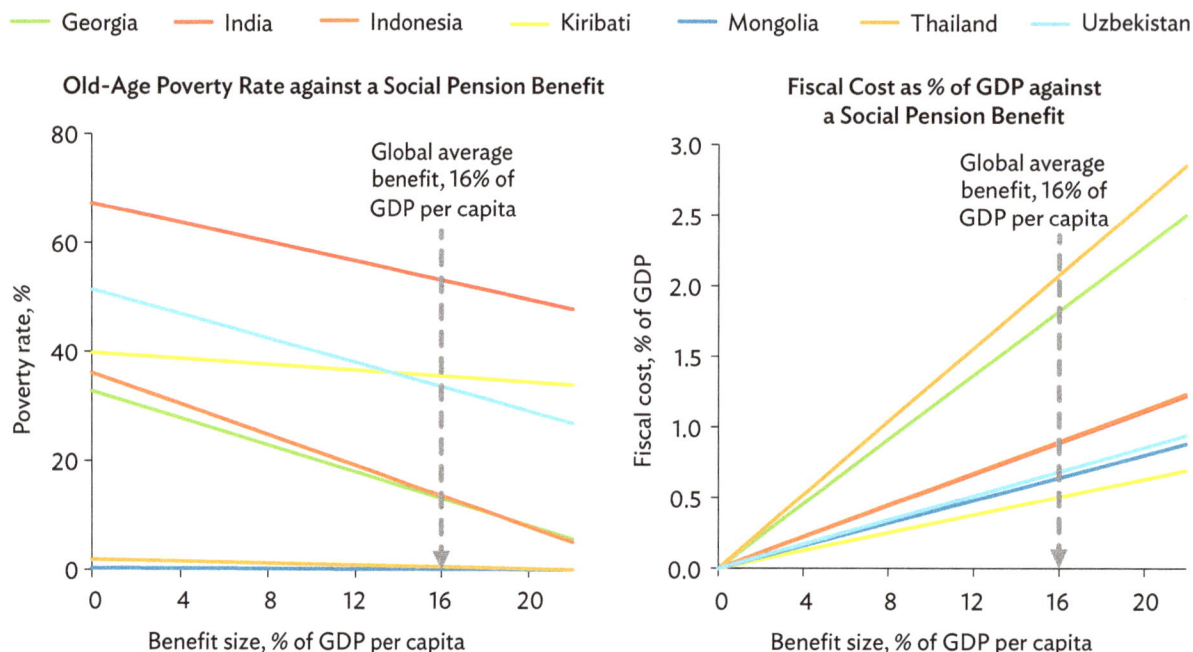

GDP = gross domestic product.

Note: The poverty rate is $3.65 per day at purchasing power parity.

Source: Chomik, O'Keefe, and Piggott (2024).

Digital and financial technologies can improve pension operation. Social programs in developing economies increasingly use digital and biometric identification, digital information dissemination, and digital or mobile payment mechanisms. These technologies need to be mainstreamed in pension collection and payment. Given currently low digital literacy in older people, it is important to either keep the option of traditional transfers open or else impart to older people adequate digital skills and access to internet equipment and connections.

Sound governance can benefit from well-established global guidelines. Promised pension rights must be preserved for long periods, inevitably straining pension governance in any economy. In emerging economies, the governance of pension systems can be further challenged by weak regulatory capacity, shallow capital markets, a lack of competition in fund management, and poorly managed financial institutions. Pension

governance must overcome such difficult challenges. Helpful in this regard are the International Social Security Association (ISSA 2019), International Organization of Pension Supervisors (IOPS 2006), and OECD guidelines (OECD 2016). OECD guidelines include detailed and actionable principles on accountability, transparency, predictability, participation, and engagement in managing pension funds.

4.3.4 Building Financial Literacy in an Aging Society

Enhancing financial literacy in younger workers is critical to prepare them for old age. Older Asians have generally low financial literacy. Financial security in old age requires careful provision for retirement, starting with the development of a savings plan, which financial literacy programs can teach people to do. It is important to formulate financial literacy programs to meet the real needs of participants, especially those with more pronounced financial illiteracy, including low-income groups, women, and people with low educational attainment. Financial literacy interventions can have positive impact if they are immersive and introduced at either an early age or at the point of decision.

Financial literacy programs can foster forward-looking attitudes and behavior in current workers. They should be designed to promote the values of financial prudence and planning to achieve long-term financial goals (OECD 2019b). Financial education should be straightforward, and its content simple to understand and personalized where possible. All-important program delivery may profit by leveraging digital and easily accessible channels, used innovatively to enhance attention, strengthen knowledge retention, and foster behavioral change.

New behavioral insights can help policymakers guide future cohorts of older people to make better financial decisions and become long-term savers. The following tips can help policymakers guide individuals to make optimal financial decisions for and in old age when participating in defined contribution pension schemes: (i) reducing the choice set to relatively few but uniformly high-quality products; (ii) simplifying such necessary information as product disclosure to convey it clearly; (iii) providing nudges for action; (iv) considering the timing of decisions and issuing reminders; (v) coaching decisions; and (vi) providing, in the absence of choice, defaults that are advantageous to individuals, or outsourcing or sharing decisions with financial advisers.

4.4 Conclusion

To sum up, old-age economic security in developing Asia is currently very much a work in progress. Financial preparedness for retirement varies widely across developing Asia and even within economies. A new financial preparedness index based on the adequacy of resources for post-retirement confirms there is ample scope to improve preparedness, especially for informal workers, rural residents, and older women. While family support remains a major source of income for older people across the region, it is likely to play a smaller role in the future. This leaves well-functioning pension systems—with a significant redistributive element to help poor and vulnerable older Asians—as the main viable source of old-age income support in the coming years. However, Asia's pension systems currently offer inadequate coverage and benefits.

Policymakers must act now to strengthen both contributory and social pension systems. In light of inadequate retirement preparedness and the growing role of pensions in old-age income support, policymakers must expand coverage, improve adequacy, and support poor older Asians. Despite being one of the most successful economies in the world, the ROK established a national pension system only in 1988, and it is still maturing. Partly as a result, old-age poverty in the ROK, the highest in the OECD, has emerged as a major social and economic issue. The lesson for the rest of developing Asia is that it is never too soon to establish a sound pension system. Examples of policy priorities include introducing voluntary contributory programs for informal workers and expanding social pension coverage of the older poor. Innovations that can help include the use of digital technology for identification, information dissemination, and payment.

For many rapidly aging populations in the region, stepped-up efforts are needed to promote financial literacy through awareness campaigns. They are also needed to encourage people of all ages to save for retirement. Governments should redouble efforts to create an enabling business environment for private initiatives that support saving and investing for old-age and thus supplement government pension programs. A prerequisite is a clear policy framework and guidance that ensures transparency and safeguards individuals against unwarranted risks.

5 Family, Care, and Social Engagement

Older people spend more time at home and in their community as they gradually retire from work and other responsibilities. In this later stage of life, the quality of family relationships and social engagement becomes increasingly important, exerting a profound influence on life satisfaction, mental health, and overall well-being. Family assumes a critical role in providing financial and emotional support, which becomes especially vital as older people's health, physical functions, and mobility naturally decline over time, necessitating long-term care (LTC).[29]

Family structures, relationships, and support mechanisms remain robust in most parts of developing Asia. This is true despite rapid urbanization through rural-to-urban migration and a gradual decline in traditional multigenerational households in rural areas. The family-based support system for LTC is nevertheless undergoing transition across the region. This shift is influenced by declining fertility, greater longevity, higher opportunity costs for informal care, and more people either childless, divorced, or never married. Older people increasingly prefer independent and autonomous living, and an evolving sociocultural shift is affecting how parents and children perceive their family LTC responsibilities, particularly in light of increasing care needs.

Many older individuals actively engage in paid and volunteer work or participate in social and religious activities. However, deteriorating health and other factors can render social encounters less frequent and leave older people socially isolated and lonely. This emerging social issue gained significant public attention during the pandemic but has so far received little policy consideration.

This chapter sheds light on living arrangements and the social environment for older people. It examines the nature and status of family support, including relationships and caregiving within families, as well as social engagement by older people against the backdrop of societies that are rapidly growing, urbanizing, and aging. Drawing from available microdata sets of aging surveys in the region (Chapter 1, Box 1.1), the chapter begins by exploring family structure and the dynamics of relationships, care, and support. Then it presents patterns of community and social engagement by older people, assessing the extent and nature of social isolation and loneliness. Finally, it examines the role of physical and social infrastructure in promoting the well-being of older people.

5.1 Living Arrangements and Family Relationships

Living arrangements are a key predictor of subjective well-being and mental health in older adults. Both globally and in the region, whether older adults live alone, with a spouse only, with their children, or in another household arrangement can affect their health, social engagement, and isolation (Chapter 1, Box 1.2). As living arrangements around the globe become more varied, shifting from larger multigenerational households to smaller nuclear families, it is crucial to understand the implications of living arrangements for older adults.

---

29 LTC covers both activities of daily living, which are personal care activities such as washing and getting dressed, and instrumental activities of daily living, which are housekeeping tasks like cleaning and shopping. It also covers some types of medical care, including giving medications, caring for wounds, helping with medical equipment, and providing physical therapy.

Solitary living is linked to unfavorable well-being outcomes (Cheung and Kwan 2009). Prior research suggests that the relationship between solitary living and well-being outcomes can vary by gender, socioeconomic status, and social networks. Living alone, for instance, appears to be more detrimental to the psychological well-being of men than women (Jeon et al. 2007). Living alone greatly increased the prevalence of depression in the Republic of Korea (ROK) but was not a significant factor in the People's Republic of China (PRC) or Japan (Ichimura et al. 2017).

Living with family can enhance care and companionship, but the impact on well-being depends on cultural and household dynamics. Living with a spouse significantly benefits older adults' mental well-being, while widowhood is linked to increased depression risk (Bures, Koropeckyj-Cox, and Loree 2009). Living with one's children also boosted psychological health in older parents in Malaysia, Myanmar, Thailand, and Viet Nam (Teerawichitchainan, Pothisiri, and Long 2015; Ichimura et al. 2017; Rodgers et al. 2024). However, the effects vary, as older people burdened

with excessive duties or competing for resources may see their well-being decline (Calvi 2020). In Japan, guilt arising from societal pressures can cause dependent older people to neglect their health (Maruyama 2015), while in Malaysia older males living alone or with a spouse reported feeling less burdensome and thus better (Nakajima et al. 2024). Cultural preferences that, in Viet Nam for example, take a positive view of living with a married son further illustrate the intricate effects of these arrangements on parents' mental health (Teerawichitchainan, Pothisiri, and Long 2015).

The share of older people living in single households increased in many regional economies as the share living with extended families declined. Figure 5.1 shows that, in the Philippines, Thailand, and Viet Nam, the share of older people, defined here as aged 60 or over, living alone has increased in the past 2 decades by 40%–90%, depending on the particular economy. In other regional economies for which recent data are available, increases have been more moderate, but the regional trend toward more solitary living for older people is evident. This trend

Figure 5.1: Change in Living Arrangements for People Aged 60+ in the Past 2 Decades

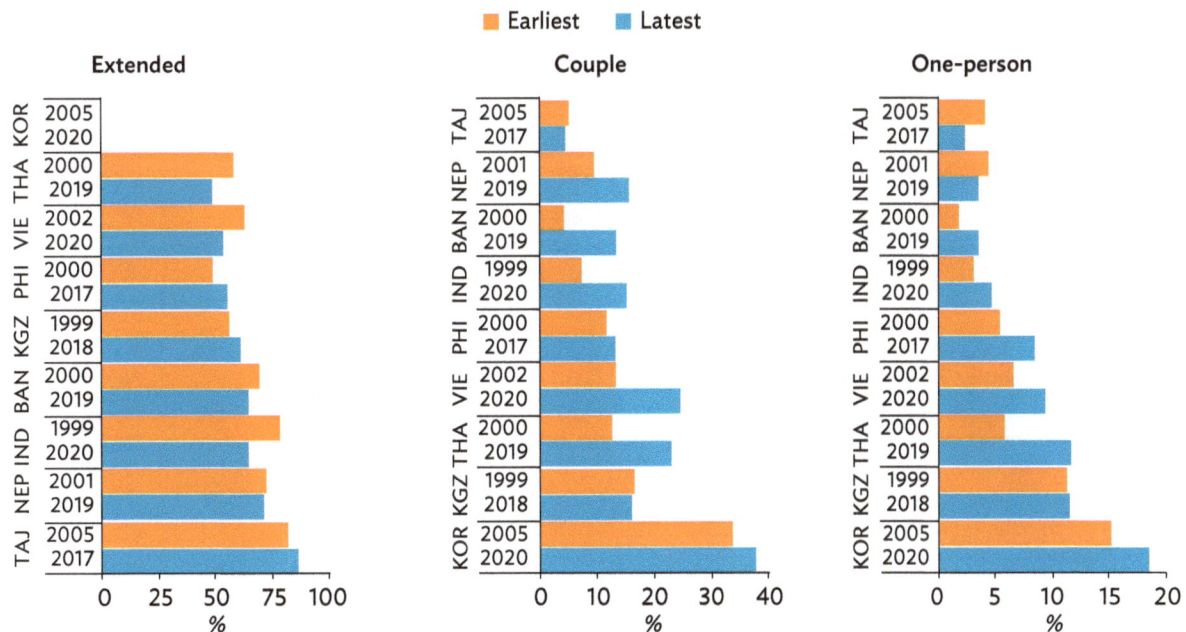

BAN = Bangladesh, IND = India, KOR = Republic of Korea, KGZ = Kyrgyz Republic, NEP = Nepal, PHI = Philippines, TAJ = Tajikistan, THA = Thailand, VIE = Viet Nam.

Note: Earliest available data for India and the Kyrgyz Republic is 1999, Nepal 2001, Viet Nam 2002, and the Republic of Korea and Tajikistan 2005. Latest available data for the Philippines and Tajikistan is 2017; the Kyrgyz Republic 2018; and Bangladesh, Nepal, and Thailand 2019.

Source: United Nations, Department of Economic and Social Affairs, Population Division. Database on the Households and Living Arrangements of Older Persons 2022 (accessed 9 October 2023).

aligns with a global trend toward independent living for older people, as the median share of people living alone increased by 5 percentage points in the past decade to reach 12%.[30] Conversely, the share of older people in extended-family households has declined substantially in Bangladesh, India, Thailand, and Viet Nam, and more moderately in Nepal, even as it increased in the Kyrgyz Republic, the Philippines, and Tajikistan (Figure 5.1).

Projections suggest that the number of solitary households will continue to increase in the coming decades. In Sri Lanka, where such projections have been made, a surge in the share of solitary households is expected, especially for people over 80. The number is projected to quadruple between 2012 and 2060 (Box 5.1). It is therefore urgent to understand the consequences of solitary living for the well-being of older people, given that reduced social support threatens isolation and impedes access to care.

Solitary living arrangements may reflect a preference for autonomous living or indicate a lack of family support. Other factors that influence autonomous living arrangements are income, the ability to save for retirement, public pensions, and health status (Reher and Requena 2018). In developed economies, where public pensions and LTC reduce the need to depend on family members for support, an increase in solitary living of older people is generally considered a preference. In developing economies in Asia and elsewhere, it is worthwhile to consider if the trend toward solitary living reflects a lack of social support and to explore the consequences on well-being.

Box 5.1: Population Aging and Living Arrangements in Sri Lanka

The share of the Sri Lankan population aged 65 and over is expected to exceed 15% by 2040. Living arrangements for older people are expected to evolve in response to demographic change, an expected rise in income, and anticipated shifts in sociocultural values and preferences. Household and living arrangement projections by Zeng et al. (2024) show that the number of older adults aged 65+ and living with a spouse or other person, but not with their child, will triple as a percentage of the whole population from 0.45% in 2012 to 1.46% in 2060 (box table).

In the same period, those living alone are expected to increase from 1.34% to 4.49%. Those aged 80+ and living with a spouse or other person, but not with their child, are projected to record an eightfold increase. The share of those aged 80+ and living alone is projected to rise from 0.16% to 0.94%.

Older Adults by Living Arrangement as a Share of Sri Lanka's Population (%)

	2012	2020	2030	2040	2050	2060
Aged 65+	7.87	10.64	13.70	16.01	18.79	20.61
Aged 65+ and living with a spouse or other person but not with their child	0.45	0.83	1.09	1.24	1.38	1.46
Aged 65+ living alone	1.50	2.20	2.79	3.29	4.00	4.49
Aged 80+	1.34	1.68	2.62	3.92	5.06	6.37
Aged 80+ and living with a spouse or other person but not with their child	0.07	0.16	0.26	0.38	0.47	0.56
Aged 80+ living alone	0.16	0.21	0.31	0.49	0.68	0.94

Source: Zeng et al. (2024).

Source: Asian Development Bank using data and estimates from Zeng et al. (2024).

---

[30]   United Nations, Department of Economic and Social Affairs, Population Division. Database on the Households and Living Arrangements of Older Persons 2022 (accessed 9 October 2023).

Many older people who live alone report having their children nearby, so living alone does not necessarily mean aging alone. On average in the sample of economies presented here, 98% of older people have children, and 40% of those parents live with their children (Figure 5.2). Across economies for which data are available, the share of parents whose children live within 30 minutes travel is 50%–70%. Substantial differences exist across economies. In the PRC and the ROK, the share of older people living without their children nearby is high at over 45%, but it is much lower at 13%–16% in Indonesia, the Philippines, and Viet Nam. When considering one-person households, while 55% of older people live alone, only 10% do not live with their children nearby. The determinants of whether adult children live close to their aging parents are complex. In settings where intergenerational support is more prevalent, physical proximity may be greater. At the same time, young people may have to migrate away from their birthplace for economic reasons, often leaving their parents behind.

Solitary older households are far more likely to be headed by females, many of them widows. Older women live alone more than men do in the economies selected for presentation in this section (Figure 5.3, panel A). This is also true globally (see footnote 30). This gender difference reflects more widowhood for women than men, as women tend to marry younger than men and live longer, and older widows in the region seldom remarry. As a result, some economies have very high widowhood rates for older women: 55% in Indonesia, 54% in the Philippines, and 52% in India.

The distribution of solitary households skews toward both ends of the wealth distribution, but differently for men and women. Older men living alone tend to be concentrated in wealthier quintiles, while women living alone are more evenly distributed or, as in the Philippines, the PRC, and Viet Nam, concentrated in poorer quintiles (Figure 5.3, panel B). This demonstrates that, while some older people choose independent living and can afford it, other older people living alone, particularly women, are vulnerable. Many of these women are widows and live alone because they lack social support, not by choice. They may therefore face higher risk of social isolation and loneliness, which may require special policy attention (Esteve et al. 2020, Schaan 2013).

Figure 5.2: Older People's Proximity to Their Children

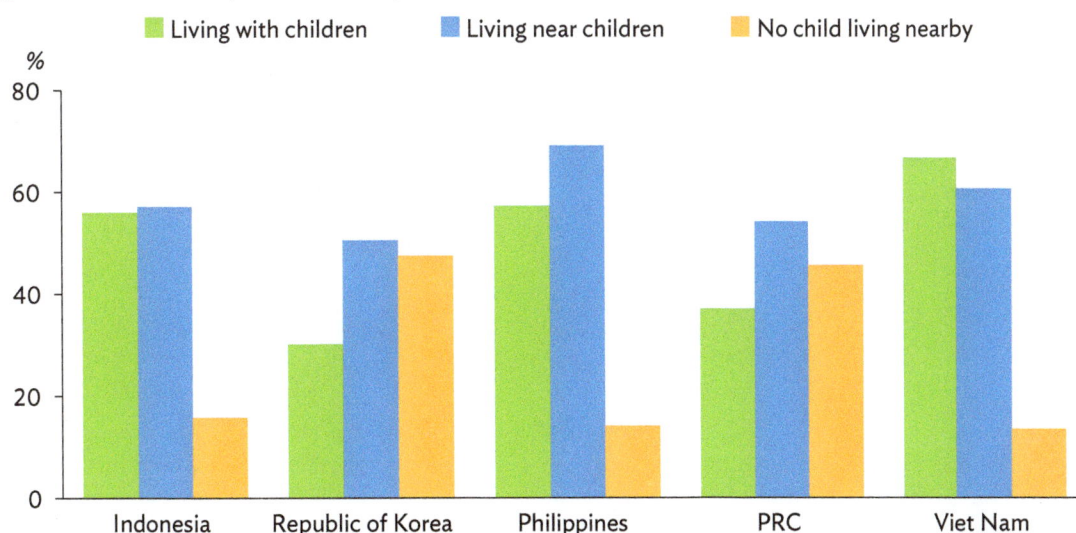

PRC = People's Republic of China.

Notes: Figure shows share of households headed by older people (one or more older persons) by proximity of their children. Living near children is defined as having at least one child within about 30 minutes travel time. Survey years are 2018, 2019, and 2023.

Source: Chapter 1, Box 1.1.

Figure 5.3: Living Arrangements of Older People

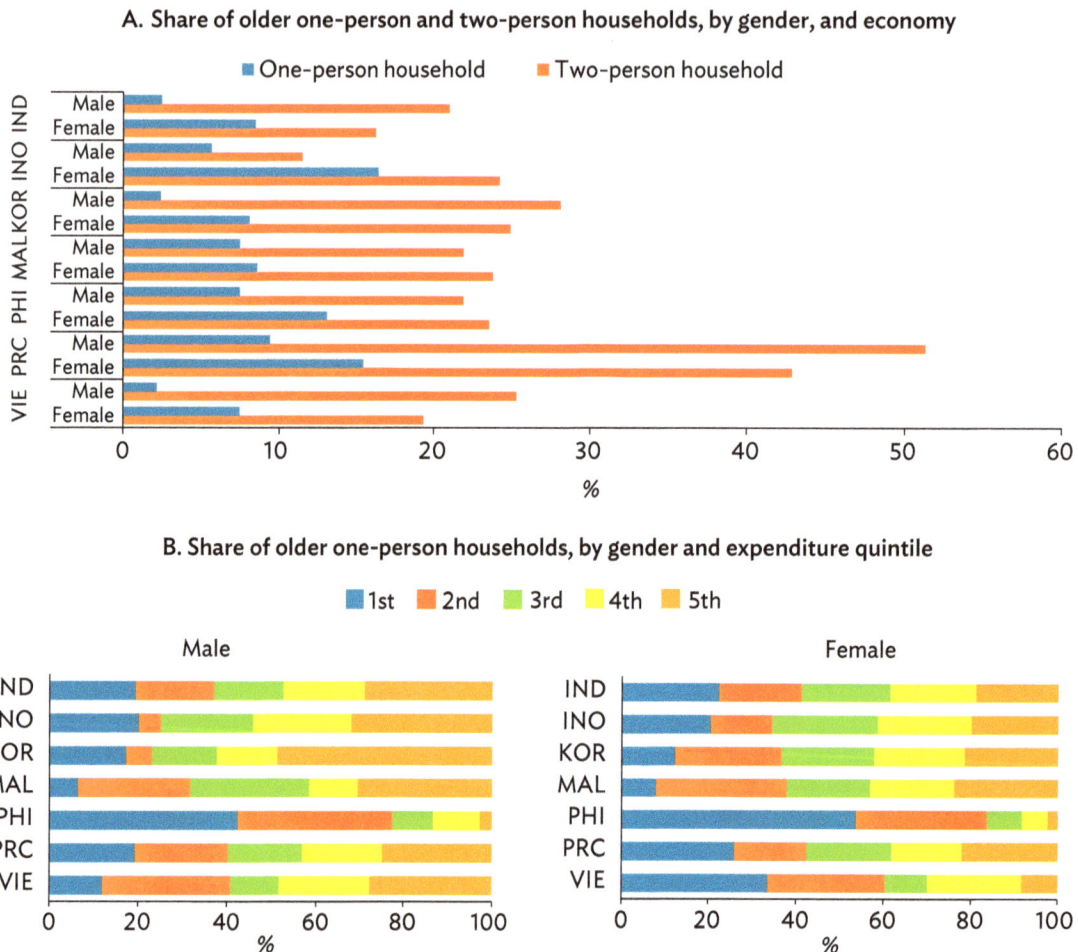

A. Share of older one-person and two-person households, by gender, and economy

B. Share of older one-person households, by gender and expenditure quintile

IND = India, INO = Indonesia, KOR = Republic of Korea, MAL = Malaysia, PHI = Philippines, PRC = People's Republic of China, VIE = Viet Nam.

Notes: Considers older people aged 60 and above. Quintiles are numbered from the poorest (1st) to the wealthiest (5th). Survey years are 2017–2019, 2021, and 2023.

Source: Chapter 1, Box 1.1.

5.2 Family and Informal Care

Increasing care needs and changing family structures can leave gaps in the care provision for older people. As populations age, more people need more support to accomplish daily activities such as bathing, dressing, cooking, and housecleaning. This type of support with some types of medical care is called long-term care (LTC).[1] LTC is mostly informal in emerging regional economies and likely to become hard to supply as fertility rates decline, families consequently become smaller, more homemakers work outside of the home, and traditional cultural beliefs and practices change regarding care for parents (ADB 2022a). Without intervention, a gap in LTC demand and supply is likely to mean that the care needs of more older people will be unmet. The following paragraphs explore how family structure and care for older people interact and how policy could better support informal carers.

Family members are the primary providers of LTC for their older relatives. Virtually all LTC for older people in India, the PRC, and Viet Nam is provided informally by family members (Figure 5.4). This is generally true in most emerging economies in the region (ADB 2022a). However, differences exist among economies in the share of older people receiving LTC, ranging from about 11% in Viet Nam and India to 28% in the PRC. This partly reflects differences in the composition of people over 60 and of their care needs. It also reflects differences in unmet care needs.

Informal carers are often adult children, predominantly women. Responsibility to care for older people tends to fall to their children. Recent surveys in Viet Nam found that daughters and daughters-in-law provided most of the care (ADB 2020b). Surveys in Thailand and Mongolia had similar findings (ADB 2020a and 2020b). The same holds in wealthier members of the Organisation for Economic Co-operation and Development (OECD), in which three out of five informal carers are women (OECD 2023).

Older people are often caregivers themselves. Carers are often older people themselves, caring for a spouse or other family member (Box 5.2). Older carers are at high risk of injury from performing caregiving tasks and vulnerable to psychological strain (Arriagada 2020). As these concerns are neither well understood nor well defined, it is essential to address the risk of caregiver neglect and monitor their health (Jull 2010).

Change notwithstanding, cultural norms still obligate adult children to provide LTC to their parents. In most economies, the majority of people agree that adult children should care for their parents (Figure 5.5). However, the broad agreement on cultural norms masks substantial differences across economies. The share of people who agree that adult children have a duty to provide LTC for their parents tends to decline as the population ages, as seen in Japan, where only a minority agree. In Bangladesh, Kazakhstan, Myanmar, and Tajikistan, an overwhelming majority either agree or strongly agree with the statement, and only a very small fraction disagree. In Indonesia, the Philippines, Pakistan, and Viet Nam, the majority still agree with the norm, but the percentage strongly agreeing is somewhat lower. In economies that are aging rapidly—notably Hong Kong, China; Singapore; Taipei,China; and the ROK—a much smaller share strongly agree, and many disagree.

Figure 5.4: Share of Older People Receiving Support for Activities of Daily Living, by Provider

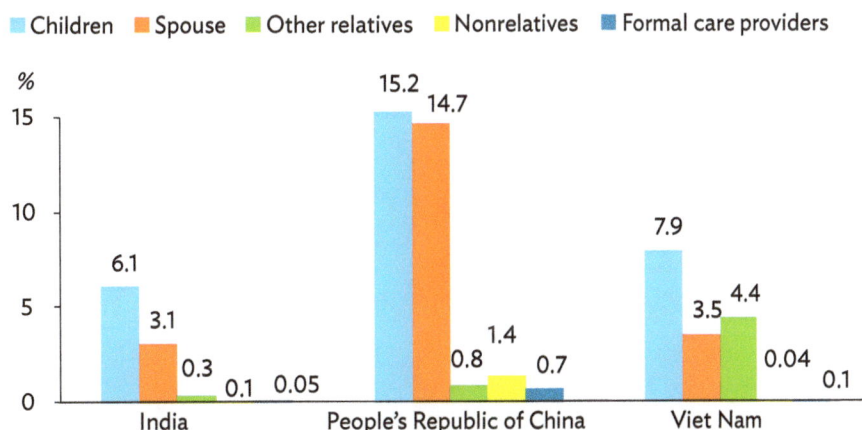

Note: Caregivers assisting in any activity of daily living: dressing, bathing, eating, getting in and out of bed, and using the toilet. Survey years are 2017–2019.

Source: Chapter 1, Box 1.1.

The social norm of filial care is less popular among younger people in many economies. Figure 5.5 shows not only neutrality but also disagreement with this social and cultural norm. How quickly Asia shifts away from it will determine when gaps in LTC for older people arise. In Japan, for instance, the shift away from the norm occurred quickly (Ogawa and Retherford 1993). Research using a repeated cross-sectional newspaper opinion survey demonstrated a sudden shift in opinion toward less acceptance of the norm of filial care from 1986 to 1990. The shift was attributed to popular rejection of government efforts at the time to pass the care obligation back to families. Homogeneity in Japanese society may have facilitated a rapid transition, and other societies that are less homogenous may not shift as quickly.

Box 5.2: The Older Person as a Net Provider of Care

Family-based informal care and support can be reciprocal, as older people contribute to informal care. Often, an older person is not only a care consumer but also a caregiver and may remain a net provider until very old age.

Unpaid care work (UCW) is a large part of all work and is done mostly by women. Women work more unpaid hours than paid in all economies surveyed, particularly as they age (box figure 1).

1. Average Paid and Unpaid Worktime, by Gender

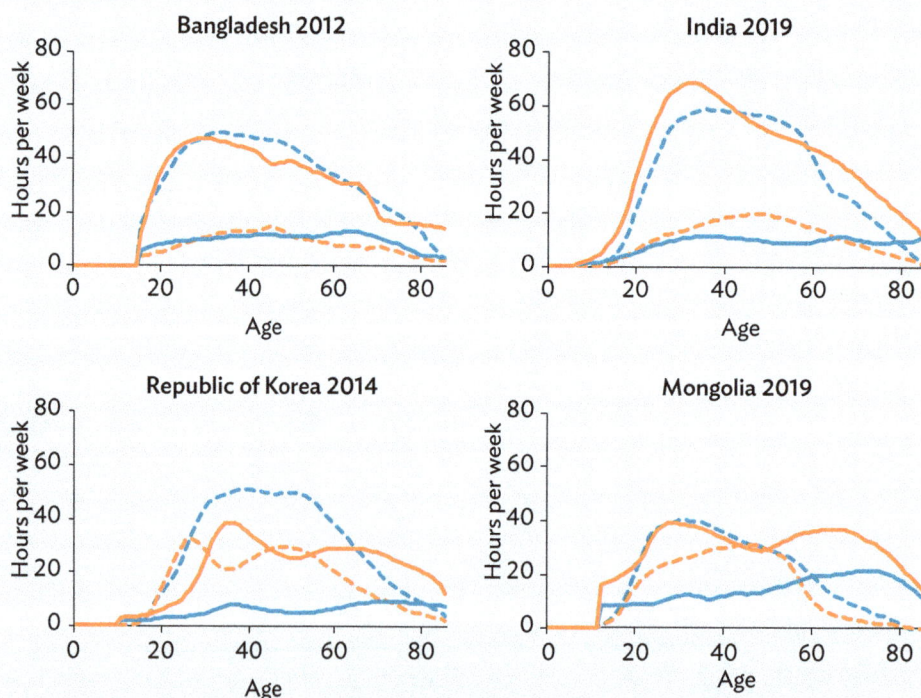

continued on next page

Box 5.2 *continued*

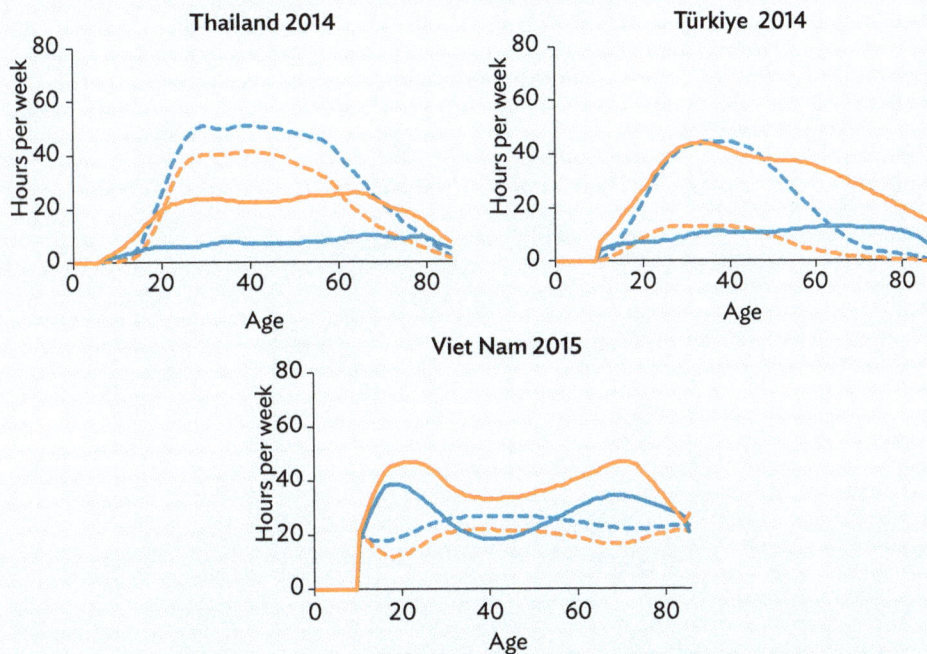

Thailand 2014

Türkiye 2014

Viet Nam 2015

Note: Unpaid care includes unpaid time spent on housework, care for children and adults, and community service.
Source: Donehower (2024).

Gender differences vary, however, by economy. In Bangladesh, men and women very closely mirror each other in terms of work hours by age but with paid and unpaid work flipped. In Viet Nam, the genders look more similar in terms of their work lives as they age.

Older women are net providers of UCW in terms of time transfers, even into very old age (box figure 2). This is true in all economies studied, and men are net recipients. While most men and women both provide and receive UCW, this generalization holds on balance. It is a clear trend in all economies studied that women provide much more UCW than they receive throughout life. They start to receive as much UCW as they provide only from about their 80th birthday, on average, and in India, Mongolia, and Viet Nam even the oldest women are only small net receivers. This finding suggests that aging

economies in the region may not be headed for an imminent care crisis. Rather, the care needs for growing cohorts of older people are only gradually rising, and because older women continue to provide care into old age, older people in these economies are not massive net consumers of care.

Older people become net beneficiaries of UCW, often provided by other older people. There will be a continuing need for formal care and support for families that provide informal care, but this may come from older people themselves, especially women, and possibly to a greater extent as life expectancy lengthens. It is important to support older women's provision of care and ensure that it is meaningful, rewarding work instead of an endless, exhausting burden that leaves them vulnerable to later struggles with poor health and social vulnerability.

continued on next page

Box 5.2 *continued*

2. Transfers of Unpaid Care, by Age and by Gender

Men ——   Women ——

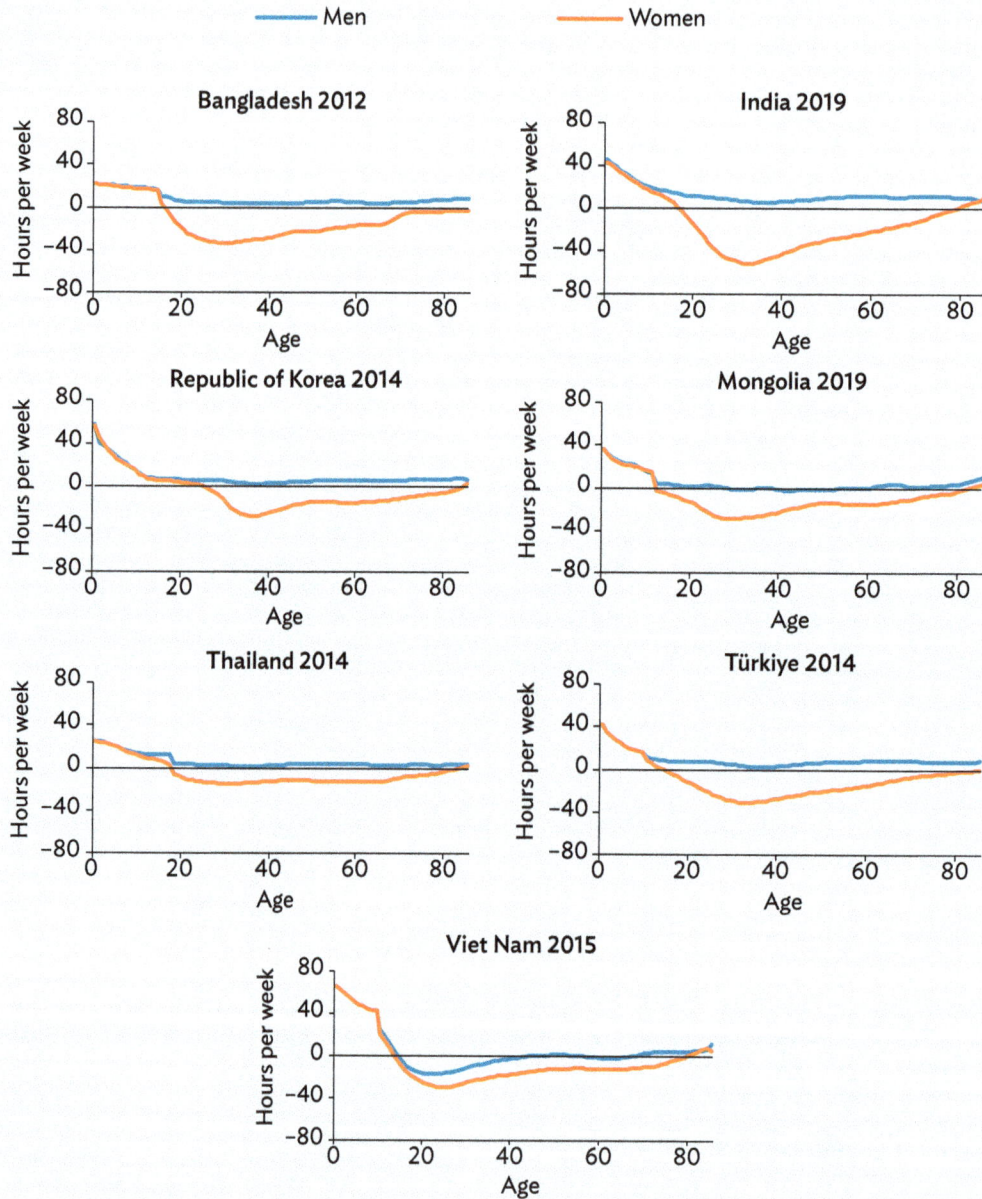

Bangladesh 2012

India 2019

Republic of Korea 2014

Mongolia 2019

Thailand 2014

Türkiye 2014

Viet Nam 2015

Note: Lines show the net transfers of unpaid care, calculated as the difference between the unpaid care provided and received. More receipt than provision of care generates surplus hours, more provision than receipt deficit hours.

Source: Donehower (2024).

Source: Donehower, G. 2024 *Mapping the Unpaid Care Economy in the Asia-Pacific Region.* Asian Development Bank.

Figure 5.5: Perspectives on Whether Adult Children Have a Duty to Provide Long-Term Care for Their Parents

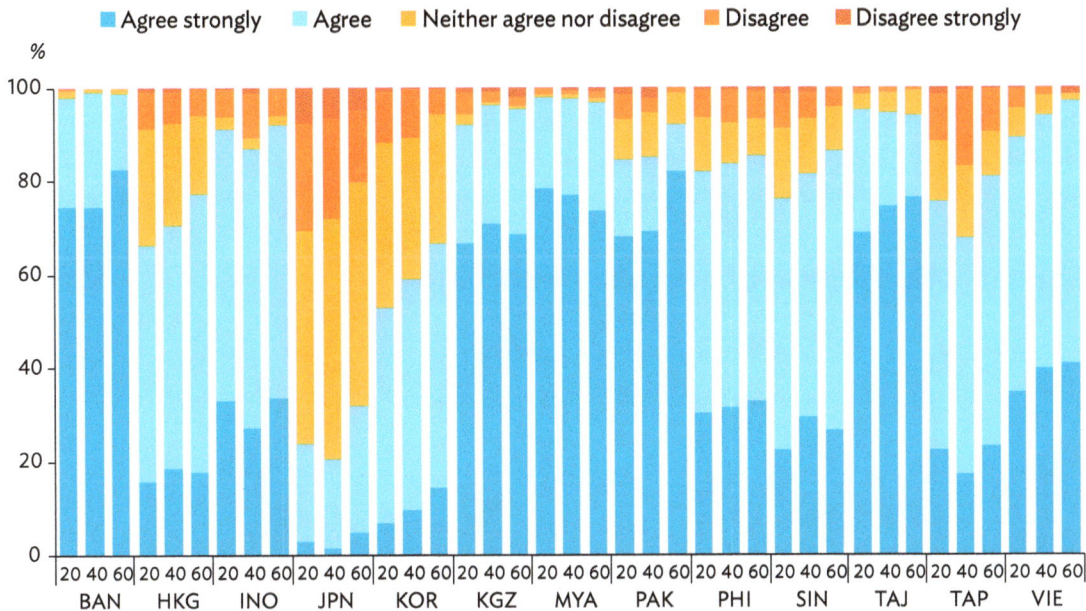

BAN = Bangladesh; HKG = Hong Kong, China; INO = Indonesia; JPN = Japan; KOR = Republic of Korea; KGZ = Kyrgyz Republic; MYA = Myanmar; PAK = Pakistan; PHI = Philippines; SIN = Singapore; TAJ = Tajikistan; TAP = Taipei,China; VIE = Viet Nam.

Note: The values on the x-axis indicate age groups where 20 = 20–39 years old, 40 = 40–59 years, and 60 = 60–79.

Source: World Values Survey. World Values Survey Database. Wave 7, 2017–2021.

The LTC needs of many older adults are unmet. Considering the care requirements for older adults with impairments that affect at least one activity of daily living (ADL), it is estimated that 43% of these needs are unmet on average in India, the PRC, and Viet Nam (Figure 5.6A). However, unmet care needs are difficult to measure. Figure 5.6 considers the share of people reporting ADL limitations but receiving no care in the past month. As shown in the figure, the share of unmet needs varies substantially depending on the number of ADLs. It can be as high as 80% for people with one ADL limitation, as seen in Viet Nam. The average unmet care needs are 8% on average when considering older people with three or more ADL limitations. More generally, not everyone with ADL limitations requires care. This depends on the extent and the context regarding, importantly, the housing situation and access to assistive technology and devices. Large differences between economies persist and correlate with the share of care received (Figure 5.4) but also with differences in ADL incidence (Chapter 2).

The needs of older women and poorer households are less likely to be met. To shed more light on who is most affected by unmet care needs, Figure 5.6B and Figure 5.6C decompose care gaps by gender and income quintile. Across economies, women suffer larger care gaps than men. This and the observation that most women are net providers of care until late in life highlights that caregiving has a strong gender component (see Box 5.2). Poorer households also suffer greater care gaps. This disparity is pronounced in the PRC and Viet Nam, where the care gaps that poorer seniors endure narrow as income increases. By contrast, care gaps are fairly equally distributed across income in India, suggesting that multiple factors are at play in explaining these differences.

Without policy intervention, the burden of LTC is bound to increase, jeopardizing older people's well-being. Helping older adults with daily tasks can prevent accidents, enhance nutrition, and improve health management—and informal care in particular promotes emotional well-being by reducing depression risks and increasing satisfaction (Wang and Yang 2021). This can lead to reduced use of formal health-care services, including hospital admissions and professional home health care, which can save a lot of money. However, smaller families can impose caregiving obligations on fewer people even though older people are very often caregivers themselves.

The opportunity costs of caregiving can become profound as caregivers sacrifice personal time, career progress, and often financial stability. Moreover, informal caregiving can exacerbate gender disparity, as women predominate in shouldering these responsibilities.

Figure 5.6: Share of Older People with Unmet Long-Term Care Needs

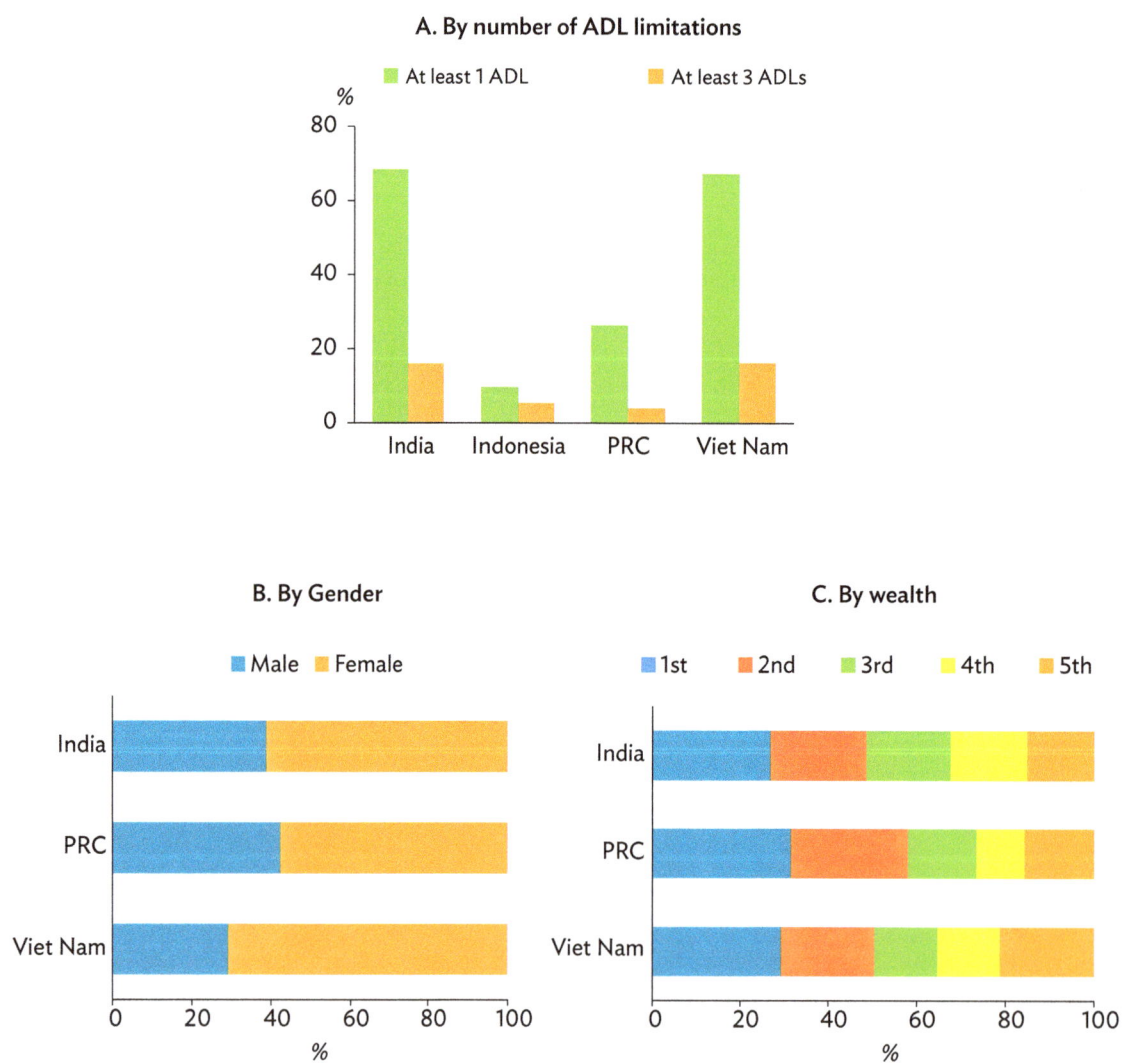

A. By number of ADL limitations

B. By Gender

C. By wealth

ADL = activity of daily living, LTC = long-term care, PRC = People's Republic of China.

Notes: Panel A shows percentages of people aged 60+ who reported receiving no care in the past month despite impairment affecting at least one ADL or at least three ADLs. Panels B and C consider people aged 60+ who received no care despite impairment affecting at least three ADLs. Quintiles are numbered from poorest (1st) to wealthiest (5th). Survey years are 2017–2019.

Source: Chapter 1, Box 1.1.

People are increasingly willing to receive and pay for formal home care. In line with a cultural shift away from expecting children to provide informal care, current and future cohorts of older people express interest in receiving support from professionals in their own homes (Figure 5.7A). In Indonesia, Malaysia, and Viet Nam, 43%–58% of the people aged 80+ are willing to receive home care. This share is larger among younger cohorts, suggesting that willingness to use professional home care is on the increase. While the majority are willing to receive home care, a smaller share are willing to pay for it (Figure 5.7B). In the same three economies, only 22%–35% of people 80+ are willing to pay for home care—but, again, the younger cohorts are substantially more willing. This mismatch between the willingness to receive home care and the willingness to pay for it reflects several factors. To some extent, it suggests the difficulty of obtaining information on willingness to pay and the need for more accurate assessment to inform policy decisions. It also reflects a cross-generational subsidy, in that older adults benefit from informal caregiving while younger people bear most of the burden, which can be lightened by paying for formal care.

Strong social stigma is still attached to institutional care. Unlike for home care, a large majority of older and younger people are unwilling to receive or pay for professional care in an institution. This reflects a strong desire to age in place, surrounded by familiar people and environments, as well as a stigma persistently attached to LTC institutions.

5.2.1 Supporting Informal Caregivers and Fostering the Care Economy

Low- and middle-income economies in the region offer few formal care services in the home, communities, or institutions (ADB 2022a). As longevity and elevated comorbidity in older persons heighten LTC needs, relying mostly on informal caregiving leaves large and rapidly widening care gaps in the region. Fostering the care economy and supporting informal caregivers is essential to improve well-being in an aging society. As care needs multiply and become more complex, informal caregivers will be challenged to acquire specialized knowledge and skills.

Figure 5.7: Willingness to Receive and Pay for Home Care, by Age Group and Economy

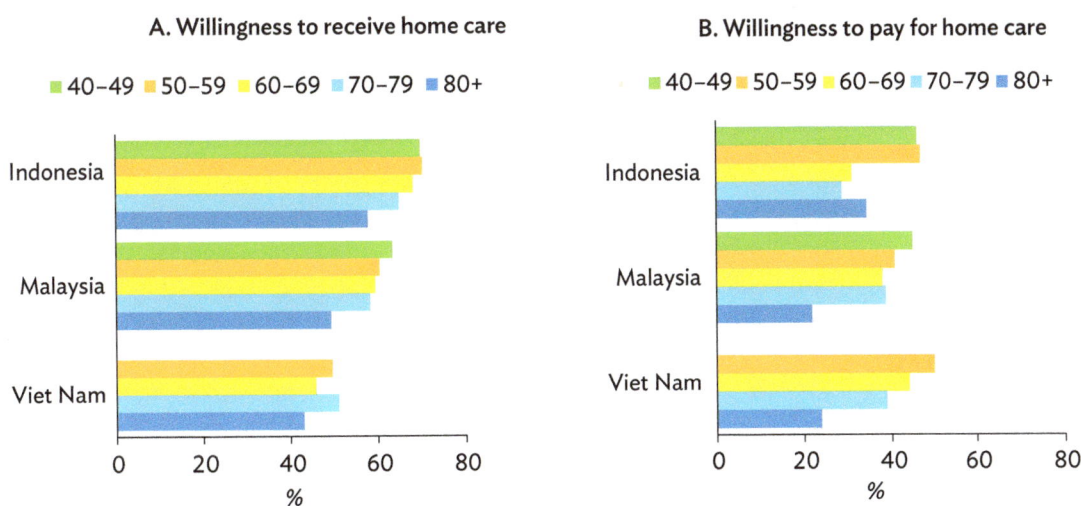

Notes: Willingness to receive home care is estimated using answers to the question, "Will you be willing to receive home-based long-term care service provided by a professional?" Willingness to pay for home care is estimated using answers to the question, "Are you willing to pay for home-care service?" Survey years are 2019, 2021, and 2023.

Source: Chapter 1, Box 1.1.

It is essential to understand older people's needs and preferences for care. Preferences for LTC depend on factors such as individual health needs, national old-age care policies, health-care infrastructure, societal values and traditions, and demographic differences within older adult populations (Hou, Sharma, and Zhao 2023). Consultative processes that ensure a strong voice for older people in decision-making and engage older adults as actors in their own care will be fundamental to developing person-centered care systems.

As the family is still the central social unit for caregiving, supporting informal caregivers remains a priority. In many regional economies, tradition still requires that grown children assume responsibility for aging parents, though less stringently than in the past. The role of informal caregivers can be very challenging and, without adequate support, can put carers at risk of poverty, ill-health, and social isolation (Box 5.3).

Community interventions cost-effectively support informal caregivers with information, counseling, and training. Such interventions are common in economies in the region, often implemented through local bodies and nongovernment organizations (Hinton et al. 2019). Most of them are effective, but community efforts alone offer only fragmented geographic coverage with wide disparities in the quality of care. Viet Nam offers a positive example, as training and emotional support for informal caregivers are included in national policy and integrated into older people's associations across Viet Nam (ADB 2022b). This ensures that initiatives that originally were grassroots efforts become widely adopted.

Informal caregivers should be granted respite care. Respite care, which provides caregivers a break from their regular duties, is one of the most important ways to support informal caregivers (COFACE Families Europe 2017). Yet, respite care is rarely provided in regional economies, perhaps because professional caregivers are in short supply.

A vital need is to invest in developing caregiver and other specialist human resources. In developing Asia, informal caregivers themselves present an opportunity to expand the supply of professional caregivers. By recognizing prior caregiving experience and offering additional training, regulators could provide to informal caregivers professional certification that would allow them to work formally for other families. This system could provide a first step up the career ladder from unpaid caring into a spectrum of paid work in the health-care industry (ADB 2023b). Through the New Integrated Aged Care Project in Tonga, ADB facilitates training for informal caregivers and pathways to formalize their competencies. Evaluation of this project will help fill current knowledge gaps about how best to promote such formalization pathways.

Facilitated by regional cooperation and labor market integration, caregiver migration can help sustain Asian societies as they age. While some economies have opened their doors to migrant caregivers, their work qualifications and experience vary greatly, as do working conditions (Asato 2021). This situation calls for simplified, transparent migration channels and better regulation to prevent exploitation by brokers and ensure ethical recruitment practices. An ongoing challenge is to balance domestic needs for health-care workers with the opportunities offered by deployment overseas. The aim is regional coordination that optimizes human resources allocation, provides necessary training and skills, and upholds workers' rights.

5.2.2 Developing Formal Long-Term Care Systems

LTC system development needs a strong emphasis on services offered in the home and the community. As described above, living arrangements for older adults are becoming more diverse in the region, and social values toward filial care are evolving. In addition, the data show that people in India, Indonesia, and the PRC who juggle paid work and caregiving range from 68% to 88% of the workforce, and that caregivers are more likely than others to struggle to thrive at work (Thom et al. 2023). Recognizing this, more governments in developing Asia now acknowledge the need to address the growing and diverse demand for LTC and have introduced policies and programs to formalize it (ADB 2022a). Efforts continue to encourage a market response that provides care and

Box 5.3: Caring for Caregivers

The strain of providing long-term care, often underappreciated, may adversely affect the health of caregivers. Studies have linked full-time caregiving to increased musculoskeletal disorders, deteriorating mental health, and alcohol abuse (Macneil et al. 2010; Rospenda 2010; Yiengprugsawan et al. 2017). While some caregivers reported that their role earned them social status, increased their self-esteem, and improved family ties, many require social support and respite to meet their caring responsibilities sustainably (Brouwer et al. 2005).

Family caregivers pay opportunity costs for which there is typically no formal accounting. Informal family caregivers are likely to be female and disadvantaged financially by out-of-pocket expenses and, if they leave formal employment, loss of income, career opportunities, and other benefits. They often have difficulty returning to formal employment.

Self-assessment tools exist to measure and improve awareness of the burden on family caregivers. Commonly used in Asia, the Zarit caregiver burden interview covers caregivers' physical health, psychological and spiritual well-being, personal and social life, and labor force participation and finances. (Chan et al. 2023; Zarit, Reever, and Bach-Peterson 1980).

The tool is underpinned by its questions about relationships between caregivers, care recipients, and other household members and the nature of the caregiving provided, illuminating the need for formal and informal support.

References

Brouwer, W. M. F., N. J. A. van Excel, B. van den Berg, G. A.M. van den Bos, and M. A. Koopmanschap. 2005. Process Utility from Providing Informal Care: The Benefit of Caring. *Health Policy*. 74(1).

Chan, C-Y., J. G. De Roza, G. T. Young Ding, H. L. Koh, and E. S. Lee. 2023. Psychosocial Factors and Caregiver Burden among Primary Family Caregivers of Frail Older Adults with Multimorbidity. *BMC Primary Care*.

Macneil, G., J. I. Kosberg, D. W. Durkin, W. K. Dooley, J. Decoster, and G. M. Williamson. 2010. Caregiver Mental Health and Potentially Harmful Caregiving Behavior: The Central Role of Caregiver Anger. *Gerontologist*. 50.

Rospenda K. M., L. M. Minich, L. A. Milner, and J. A. Richman. 2010. Caregiver Burden and Alcohol Use in a Community Sample. *Journal of Addictive Diseases*. 29.

Yiengprugsawan V., D. Hoy, R. Buchbinder, C. Bain, S. A. Seubsman, and A. C. Sleigh. 2017. Low Back Pain and Limitations of Daily Living in Asia: Longitudinal Findings in the Thai Cohort Study. *BMC Musculoskelet Disorders*. 18(1).

Zarit, S., K. Reever, and J. Bach-Peterson. 1980. Relatives of The Impaired Elderly: Correlates of Feelings of Burden. *Gerontologist* 20(6).

Conceptual Framework for Health and Social Impacts of Caregiving by Gender

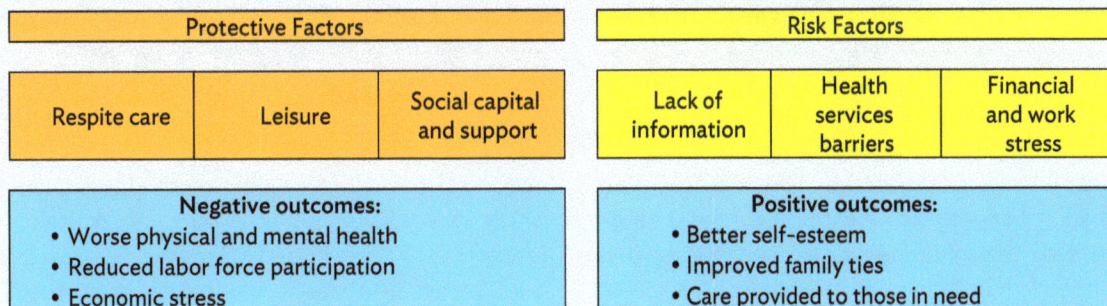

Protective Factors				Risk Factors		
Respite care	Leisure	Social capital and support		Lack of information	Health services barriers	Financial and work stress
Negative outcomes: • Worse physical and mental health • Reduced labor force participation • Economic stress				**Positive outcomes:** • Better self-esteem • Improved family ties • Care provided to those in need		

Source: Asian Development Bank.

to foster this care economy by establishing standards for quality assurance and an accreditation system for care services, as well as providing public financial incentives. Certainly, the private sector needs to play a larger role in developing the care economy.

Aging in place with care at home and in the community is preferred over residential care. Some regional governments encourage aging in place in the community, in line with people's preferences. In Singapore, for instance, the government provides integrated home- and day-care packages for a flexible, needs-oriented combination of care services in centers and at home for seniors. When combined with support for family and other informal caregivers in the form of care guidance, respite care, financial support, training and empowerment, and workplace support, these packages better enable seniors to age well in the community (UN 2021). Developing residential care services is still important, however, as some older people have medical needs that make it necessary, or else they simply prefer it.

Developing care systems for older adults requires integrated service delivery. It is essential to integrate actors and systems across health care, social care, support for family and other informal caregivers, and social protection. Most governments in the region coordinate these disparate sectors, but in most economies they are still grassroots initiatives rather than fully fledged coordination bodies and systems (UN 2021). Governments can develop LTC strategies that lay out the key stakeholders and possibly assign a coordinating body. In Japan, for instance, an LTC insurance scheme serves as the main body ensuring coordination between home medical care and long-term care so that older people who need both can continue to live at home until the end of their lives (OECD 2021a). In Thailand, the Long-Term Care Program offers a continuum of community-based care services overseen by subdistrict administrations. The National Health Security Office ensures program coordination by supervising local administrations ad coordinating inputs from three ministries: Public Health, Social Development and Human Security, and Education and Interior (ADB 2020a).

LTC financing systems need to be better designed and expanded. In most economies, LTC services are financed out of pocket.[31] Governments need to raise adequate funds to deliver services, pool financial risk, provide clarity of coverage, and offer incentives to drive efficiency (ADB 2022a). Earning public support and trust, particularly for instruments such as LTC insurance, requires sustained public contributions to ensure system sustainability.

5.3 Isolation, Loneliness, and Social Engagement

Social isolation and loneliness are widespread among older people in most regions of the world. Until recently, however, little attention has been paid to their isolation and its consequences for public health. The coronavirus disease (COVID-19) pandemic further heightened social isolation and loneliness for older adults (Wu 2020). This brought isolation into public discourse in high-income economies, but it is far from being a problem solely for rich economies. Isolation is also a pressing issue in poor economies in the region, though little is known about its extent or consequences.

Loneliness and social isolation can seriously undermine older adults' physical and mental health. These afflictions have been associated with higher mortality rates and lower life satisfaction and well-being (WHO 2021b; NAP 2020). Most people who report frequently feeling lonely also experience depression, which can accelerate the progression of dementia (Steffens 2017). The impact of loneliness on depression is of particular concern, particularly given the lack of treatment for people with depression in low- and middle-income economies, where only 2%–3% receive professional services (Banerjee et al. 2022).

Isolation and loneliness affect over 16% of older people on average in some regional economies (Figure 5.8). The share of those who feel lonely often, defined as at least 3 days per week, has increased very rapidly along with aging in India, Malaysia, the PRC, and the ROK. In Indonesia, the Philippines, Thailand, and Viet Nam, loneliness is substantially less prevalent across all age groups, and its age gradient is much less pronounced, as older people do not report feeling more lonely than younger cohorts.

5.3.1 Family Interaction, Social Activities, and Loneliness

Loneliness strongly correlates with health, income, and marital status. Figure 5.9 sheds light on the characteristics and context of people who report feeling lonely regularly in India, Indonesia, Malaysia, the PRC, and the ROK. Demographic characteristics such as gender, education, geographic location, and even age appear to be only moderately associated with frequent loneliness. Instead, loneliness appears to be strongly associated with not being married, having an ADL limitation, and, to a lesser extent, not having a pension or not living with one's child. As seen above, widowhood increases with age, as do ADL limitations, which partly explains the increased share of people feeling lonely as they age. Older people face a heightened risk of experiencing loneliness than individuals in other age groups because of life events such as widowhood, declining health and mobility, diminished social connection, and inadequate socioeconomic resources (Fakoya, McCorry, and Donnelly 2020; Kemperman et al. 2019).

While being married and living with one's child are associated with less loneliness, living alone does not always mean aging alone. Most older people who do not live with their children still meet them frequently. From 77% to 81% of older individuals in the economies analyzed reported maintaining frequent contact, daily or weekly, with at least one of their children (Figure 5.10). This is partly because older people who live near their children report meeting them about as often as those who actually live with them. For those who do not live near their children, meetings are less frequent, but the share of people meeting their children only yearly or never remains low. In fact, older parents report being very satisfied with their relationships with their children across economies and regardless of living arrangements.

Figure 5.8: The Share of People Who Report Feeling Lonely Frequently, by Age Group and Economy

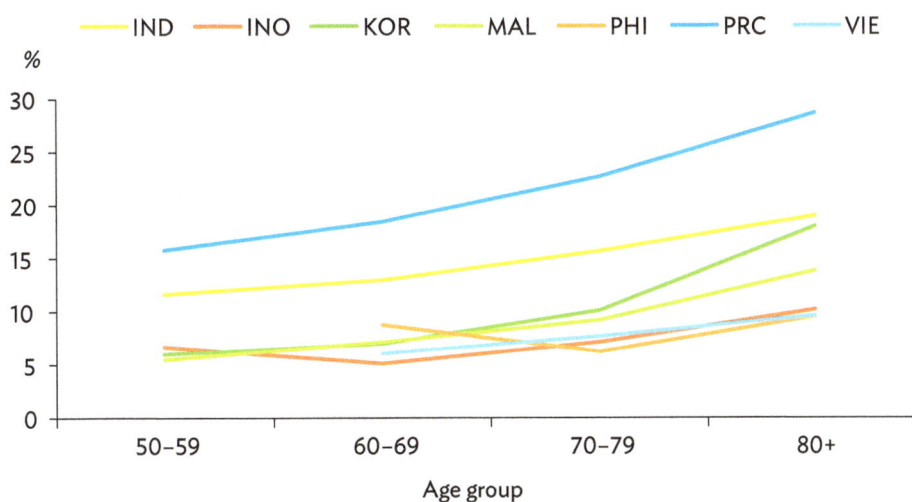

IND = India, INO = Indonesia, KOR = Republic of Korea, MAL = Malaysia, PHI = Philippines, PRC = People's Republic of China, VIE = Viet Nam.

Note: Frequent loneliness is defined as feeling lonely 3 days per week or more. Survey years are 2017, 2018, 2020, 2022, and 2023.

Source: Chapter 1, Box 1.1.

Figure 5.9: Characteristics and Contexts of People Who Report Feeling Lonely Frequently

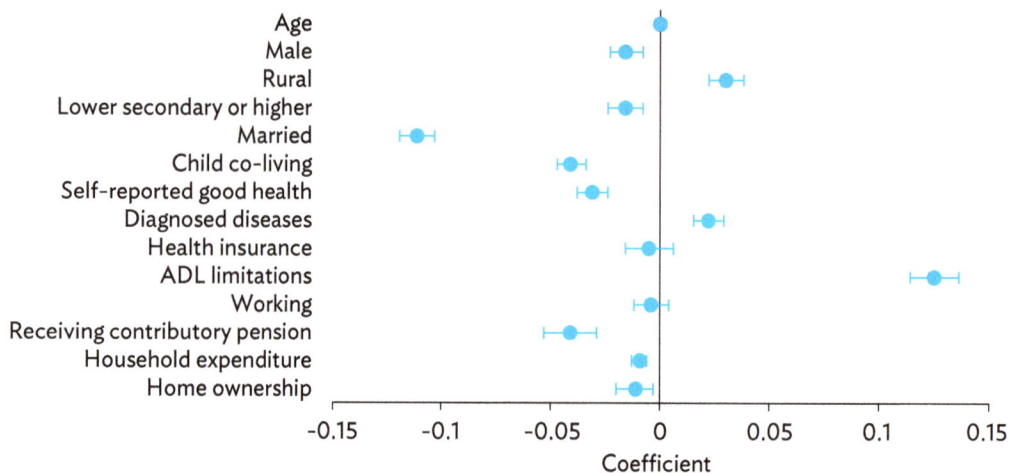

ADL = activity of daily living.

Notes: The binary dependent variable captures whether respondents reported feeling lonely frequently (three times or more per week, sample mean: 0.15, standard deviation: 0.36). Regression includes an interaction term between working and pension, which is insignificant. Household expenditure is presented as the log of expenditure per household member, estimated using ordinary least squares. Harmonized sampling weights applied. Sample includes India, Indonesia, Malaysia, the People's Republic of China, and the Republic of Korea. N = 47,713.

Source: Kikkawa et al. (2024b).

Figure 5.10: Older People's Frequency of Meetings with Children, by Economy

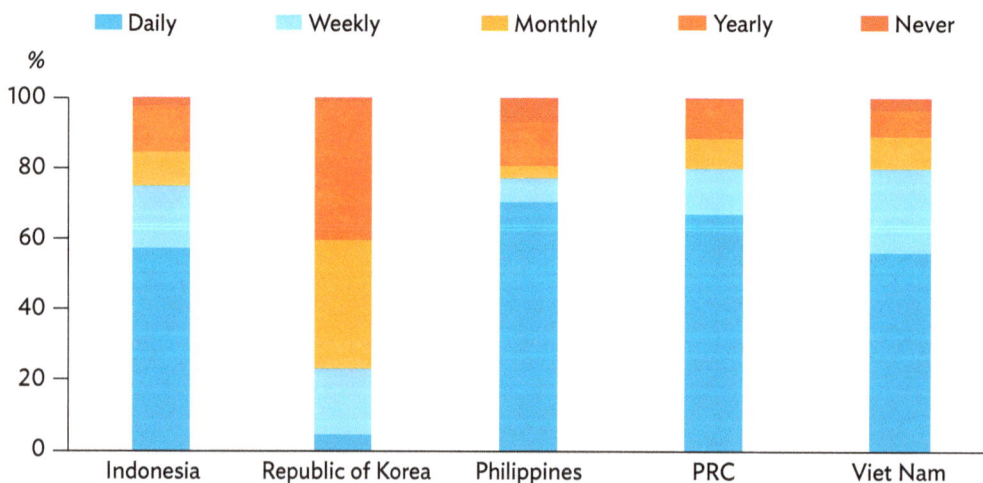

PRC = People's Republic of China.

Notes: Frequency of meeting with children is reported only for people 60+ who do not live with their children. Survey years are 2018, 2019, and 2023.

Source: Chapter 1, Box 1.1.

As family contact goes digital, connectivity and connection become an issue for older people who lack digital skills. In the ROK, for instance, physical contact with children is not as frequent as in some economies, with interaction occurring more frequently over the phone and in digital spaces (Figure 5.11). Generally, however, virtual contact is not as frequent as physical contact and is notably low among the older old, likely reflecting their lower digital skills and literacy, ownership of equipment, and internet access. Indeed, there is a strong age gradient in the use of mobile phones and the internet, which declines dramatically by age in most economies. Ensuring that older people have the necessary digital skills and access to the internet will be increasingly important to maintain their social connection.

Maintaining frequent social connection outside the household later in life benefits health, well-being, and cognition (Townsend, Chen, and Wuthrich 2021). Several meta-analyses link social participation globally with better social and emotional well-being (Mikkelsen et al. 2019), continued cognitive function into older

age (Kelly et al. 2017), and the overall quality of life (Levasseur, Desrosiers, and St-Cyr Tribble 2008). A study in the PRC showed that good social cohesion can mitigate the negative effects of widowhood on well-being in older age and can generate better outcomes than living with an adult child (Huang, Liu, and Bo 2020). A recent study using data from Japan identified social participation, either interaction with friends or participation in social activities, as crucial to enhancing happiness in older people (Ide et al. 2022; Nakagomi et al. 2023).

Many older people remain engaged with their community through social or religious activities. Social engagement varies across economies (Figure 5.12A). In Indonesia, half of people of all ages report social engagements at least weekly, but fewer than 5% do in the Philippines. This may be because social engagement in the Philippines is largely religious, as close to 60% of Filipino respondents report engagement in religious activities at least once a week (Figure 5.12B).

Figure 5.11: Share of Older People Who Report Frequent Interaction with Their Children, by Age Group, Type of Interaction, and Economy

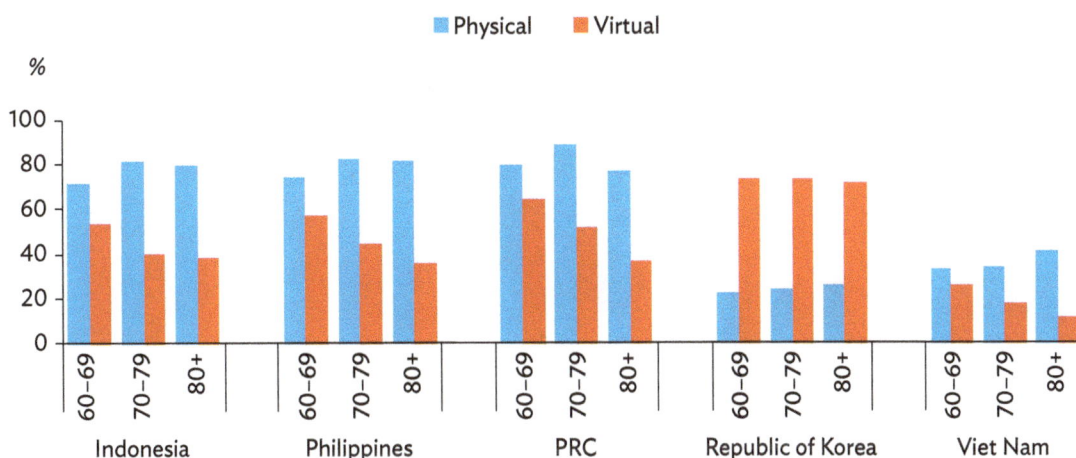

PRC = People's Republic of China.

Notes: Considers people aged 60+. Frequent interaction is daily or weekly contact, in person for physical, or by e-mail, phone call, or text messaging for virtual. Survey years are 2018, 2019, and 2023.

Source: Chapter 1, Box 1.1.

Maintaining a strong social engagement into old age is easier for those who were more socially engaged in their younger years. Two interesting patterns arise when looking at social engagement across age groups. People who engage in social activities daily or weekly continue to do so as they age (Figure 5.12A). In the ROK, for example, this share increases even as people age, possibly because they have more free time. However, those who engage in social activities only irregularly, once a month or less, often become less socially engaged as they age. This may reflect underlying factors that influenced people's social availability when young, such as health and mobility, but also indicates the importance of facilitating good social engagement in the young to sustain this social skill better in old age.

Those who exhibit lower participation in all economies are generally less educated, older, women, or rural residents (Figure 5.13). Factors inhibiting social activity and engagement include lack of time because of work or family obligations, poor health, and difficult transport or access. Addressing some of these hindrances can enhance life satisfaction and mental well-being. Life shocks such as deteriorating health or physical mobility, or the loss of a spouse, can make sustained social engagement a major challenge, as can physical access constrained by lack of public transport or roads that are safe to walk.

Globally, one older person in six experiences abuse in the home and community (WHO 2022). This share is higher in Asia and the Pacific, reaching one in five (Yon et al. 2017). Abuse can take various forms: psychological, physical, sexual, financial, and through neglect. Factors affecting the risk of violence vary by economy and region, but the risk is generally higher for older individuals with poor physical or mental health or low cognitive function, and among those financially dependent on others for aged care. The prevalence of violence against older people is exacerbated by widespread violence against women in the region.[32] Notably, older widows are at high risk of violence and abuse.

Figure 5.12: Reported Frequency of Social and Religious Activity among Older People, by Age Group and Economy

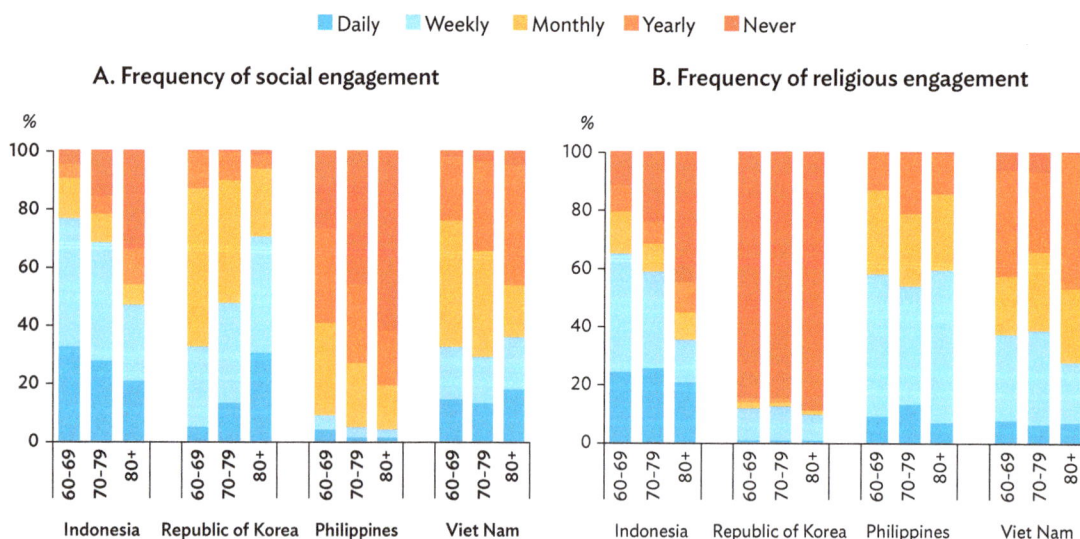

Note: Social engagement is defined as a gathering of individuals for a hobby, exercise, or chatting. Religious activity includes participation in religious groups or movements. Survey years are 2018, 2019, and 2023.

Source: Chapter 1, Box 1.1.

---

[32] UN Women. Facts and Figures: Ending Violence against Women and Girls.

Figure 5.13: Determinants of Social or Religious Engagement

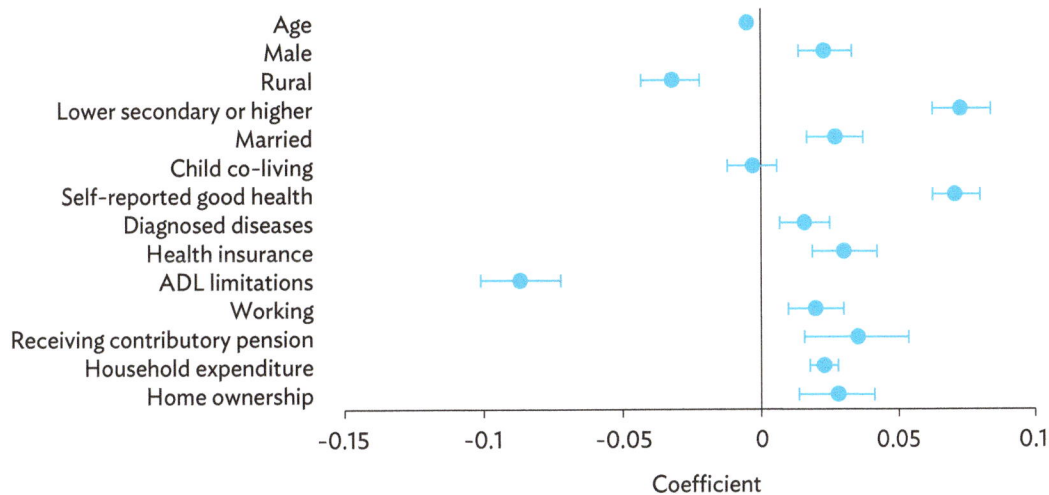

ADL = activity of daily living.

Note: The binary dependent variable captures whether respondents reported engaging in social and/or religious activities at least once a month (sample mean: 0.61). Regression includes an interaction term between working and pension, which is insignificant, and estimated using ordinary least squares. Harmonized sampling weights applied. Sample includes data from India, Indonesia, Malaysia, the Republic of Korea, and Viet Nam. N = 41,670.

Source: Kikkawa et al. (2024b).

The neglect or abuse of an older person at home is often triggered by an excessive care burden placed on a caregiver. Evidence from Japan highlights that major contributing factors to neglect and abuse include care fatigue at 25% and disability and morbidity in caregivers at 18%, with physical abuse more prevalent than mental abuse. Notably, 40% of violators were sons (Government of Japan, Ministry of Health, Labour and Welfare 2021). Addressing violence against older people requires not only general awareness but also a thorough examination of the well-being of carers and of the environment in which care is provided (Box 5.3).

Reducing Barriers to Social Connection for Older Adults

Fighting loneliness and isolation requires that older adults have good social connections in the family or the community. As people age, their social connections often deteriorate as their family disperses, loved ones are lost, and their income, mobility, and health decline. Maintaining good social engagement in old age requires strong social connections forged early on and that barriers to maintaining such connections are overcome.

Those at risk of social isolation can be identified by partnering with the health-care sector. Community health and social workers can be trained to identify vulnerable people, conduct needs assessments, and direct older people to appropriate community initiatives to promote their social engagement.

Communities need a range of social initiatives to engage older individuals. A growing number of economies in the region have a range of multifaceted programs to promote social activity and reduce older people's isolation. Some promising programs have been replicated elsewhere. Many community programs are implemented by existing government programs, such as the activities of community health workers and volunteers of nongovernment organizations, religious groups, and groups organized by older people themselves. The following summarizes aspects to these initiatives that appear to be most beneficial toward promoting social engagement in older adults.

- **Establishing dedicated physical spaces for older people through clubs and associations.** The Ibasho Project in Japan, Nepal, and the Philippines is a unique, community-driven initiative to promote social engagement and empower older people by creating through a bottom–up approach common physical space in the community. Project ability to build social capital has been profound, though nuanced by the existing social fabric in each locale (Aida et al. 2023). In the Philippines, Ibasho has strengthened existing relationships among community members, and in Nepal it has fostered new connections. These various outcomes underscore that community projects should adapt to the respective social and infrastructure context.

- **Promoting volunteer activities.** In Japan, clubs for older people organize regular activities to promote health, recruit volunteers for civic activities, and conduct outreach with visits to solitary and otherwise vulnerable households of older people (Someya and Hayashida 2022). The government provides regular subsidies to these groups because clubs and volunteer groups for older people need regular budgetary support. Irregular public or private funds are insufficient to ensure their sustained ability to pursue social activities that enrich people's lives by promoting connectedness, social purpose, and well-being.

- **Intergenerational connections.** Programs can promote intergenerational social contact by supporting lifelong learning programs and facilitating intellectual and/or physical activities for older adults such as reading, art, and singing. Such interventions aim to promote active aging by improving social connection and slowing cognitive deterioration, and they generally succeed. In Viet Nam, intergenerational self-help clubs have buoyed the health and well-being of an aging population (Pardoel et al. 2023). In Singapore, creative and social activities or performances led by high-school students in senior day care centers generated in participating seniors more active engagement in society (Leong 2020).

- **Developing age-friendly neighborhoods and communities.** Such communities adapt their services and physical infrastructure to be more inclusive and receptive to the needs of their aging populations and thus improve their quality of life. Initiatives can promote co-housing for older adults, as does the Borin Housing Project in Seoul, ROK. Housing has senior-friendly features like barrier-free construction and personal safety elements, and the project promotes a sense of community by having residents share common areas like living rooms and kitchens, while respecting individual needs by providing private bedrooms and baths. Conflict-resolution workshops and community-building events have been essential to foster better management of shared spaces by the residents themselves. However, the program has faced challenges, notably in resource allocation and the seniors' growing dependence on external assistance.

Demographic shift is prompting goverments in the region to invest in age-friendly cities by removing barriers to social connectivity for older adults. The convergence of urbanization and aging populations has brought "urban aging," heralded as an example of successful human development (Plouffe and Kalache 2010). This raises a fundamental question for urban planners, whether to adopt an integrated or segregated planning strategy (van Hoof, Marston, and Kazak 2021). The Age-Friendly Cities model of the World Health Organization (WHO) lists eight domains requiring action to address the challenges of older people living in cities: outdoor spaces, public transportation, housing, social participation, respect and social inclusion, civic participation and employment, communication and information, and community support and health services.[33] The development of age-friendly cities in

---

[33]   The concept of age-friendly cities and communities evolved from initiatives pursued by WHO in the early 2000s that advocated active aging. Its Global Age-Friendly Cities Project, launched in 2006, had focus groups in 33 cities in 22 economies identify how to render urban environments more age-friendly. This project defined an age-friendly city as one that encourages active aging by optimizing opportunities for health, participation, and security (WHO 2007). By 2021, the Global Network of Age-Friendly Cities and Communities had grown to include over 1,100 cities and communities.

Asia faces challenges from high population density, rapid urbanization, and cultural diversity, but these features also offer opportunity for innovation and tailored approaches. Further, the use of technology in advanced Asian cities presents novel solutions to improve the lives of older adults. Singapore, Tokyo, and Seoul are exemplars of comprehensive, city-wide approaches to creating age-friendly environments. They collectively showcase a diverse yet unified approach to creating urban environments that cater to the needs of their aging populations:

- **Singapore.** A multifaceted strategy includes initiatives such as the Action Plan for Successful Ageing and the Building and Construction Authority's Universal Design Guidelines (Government of Singapore, Ministry of Health 2016). These initiatives collectively address health, housing, transport, and social inclusion.
- **Tokyo.** Grappling with the challenges of a super-aged society, Japan has launched several age-friendly programs, most notably the 10-Year Plan for an Age-Friendly City, which emphasizes integrated care systems in communities (Tokyo Metropolitan Government 2018).
- **Seoul.** The ROK capital has embraced age-friendliness through projects like the Senior Welfare Center Program and the No Step Bus Program, underscoring its commitment to respecting and actively involving older people in urban life (Seoul Metropolitan Government 2019).

Services that keep older people mobile should be of acceptable quality, affordable, accessible, available, and adaptable (Bokolo 2023). Mobility is necessary for accessing various activities and services, and it promotes healthy aging and a high quality of life by facilitating physical movement. Inequality in mobility can hinder the participation of seniors in social activities, especially as their ability to drive is curtailed by vision impairment, dementia, and cognitive decline. Older people, particularly women and the oldest old, favor flexible transport services such as demand-responsive transport and community transport, yet often lack awareness of them (Coutinho et al. 2020).

The silver digital divide needs to be addressed to maintain social connections. Digital technology and cyberspace offer great potential as alternative or complementary tools and locales for fostering social engagement. They can be particularly beneficial for older people with restricted mobility. Digital literacy and skills, equipment, and internet access are a prerequisite, but out of reach for many older people, particularly the poor group and those with little education. Opportunity exists to promote the adaptation of technology to make it user-friendly for older people (ADB 2019). Inclusiveness must be ensured by offering offline options or using more traditional modes of information dissemination, such as community outreach, radio, and newspapers.

Implementing solutions to promote social engagement requires the participation of older people themselves. This report presents some promising solutions to promote social engagement through individual, communal, and infrastructure interventions. These comprehensive approaches can be planned and implemented with the participation of older people themselves, along with other generations, to stir and deepen socialization among neighbors and community members across generations.

5.4 Conclusion

In Asia, the rapid evolution of family structures and the growing trend of older adults living alone are revealing significant challenges, particularly for women. These demographic shifts put women at a disadvantage and confront them with large unmet LTC needs when they are alone and economically vulnerable. Additionally, women often find themselves the core providers of informal care, compromising their professional trajectories and personal well-being well into their later years. These risks to older women's well-being are compounded by loneliness, social isolation, and a heightened risk of abuse. Predominantly widows, they face reduced social interaction and deeply entrenched cultural norms that further isolate them and render them susceptible to exploitation. Alarmingly, by some estimates, one in three older women in the region experiences abuse in her home, neighborhood, or community.

To safeguard the well-being of older adults, particularly women, it is imperative to address their unmet care needs and combat isolation. This need is urgent, as care demands are expected to rise in parallel with population aging. As the formal care infrastructure is still nascent and the pressure on informal caregivers is increasing, proactive measures are essential. These include implementing cost-effective community care programs, leveraging migration to mitigate a deficit in care workers, and bolstering family support by disseminating information and providing respite care. Additionally, mitigating older adults' isolation necessitates dismantling barriers to social engagement. Strategies to achieve this entail bridging the digital divide that often isolates older adults, fostering age-friendly urban environments, and encouraging social participation in communities.

6 Living Well and Aging Well

As Developing Asia ages, it needs to step up efforts to help people age well. Economic and social progress in the region has sharply reduced poverty, tangibly improved the quality of life, and significantly extended longevity. Yet the well-being of current and future cohorts of older people in the region is at risk from multiple threats. Yawning inequality separates older Asians across all four dimensions of well-being: health, productive work, economic security, and social engagement. A key policy agenda across the region is to help Asians age well. Comprehensive aging policies can ensure a healthy and productive older population offering a large silver dividend and other economic and social contributions.

A lifelong, life-cycle, population-wide approach is needed to meet the aging challenge. This three-pronged strategy can help the region raise the well-being of its older citizens. A lifelong approach encourages continuous investment in human capital throughout people's lives. Well-being in old age can be enhanced by individuals' lifetime investment in their own health, education, skills, financial preparedness for retirement, and family and social ties. A life-cycle approach provides intervention in accordance with age-specific needs. And population-wide outreach targets people of all ages.

There are plenty of policy options for governments in the region to promote well-being in old age. Access to quality health care is crucial for healthy aging. Making good progress toward universal health coverage is a top priority. The health-care system should strive to meet older people's diverse health-care needs using an integrated approach that can sustain physical and mental health and functional ability, while adopting efficiency-enhancing innovation and reform that prevents financial stress to the health system. Reducing the risk of noncommunicable diseases in all age groups by promoting healthy lifestyles and offering cost-effective preventative health measures such as regular check-ups is a crucial step toward achieving healthy aging. The mental health of older people, particularly older women, is at risk and multifaceted actions are needed at clinical, social, and community levels to address the root causes. Behavioral insights and health technologies can offer a range of low-cost and personalized preventative and curative health interventions.

Diverse circumstances of formal and informal older workers call for tailored policies. No one-size-fits-all approach can address the needs of the two groups, which have different work and retirement patterns. Economies need to make a concerted effort to improve working conditions and strengthen labor protection for informal workers. Older workers in the formal sector will benefit from more flexible career pathways and transitions from work to retirement. Outdated statutory retirement ages should be extended. Lifelong learning introduced early in working life enhances productivity and employability. Improved job matching effectively creates new job opportunities, as do incentives for employers to hire and retain older workers.

There is a great need to enhance economic security in old age by expanding pension coverage. For contributory pensions, top policy priorities include expanding coverage in the formal sector, introducing voluntary programs for informal workers and women, and improving benefit adequacy for lower-income contributors through redistribution within contributory schemes. Meanwhile, social pension coverage for poor people must be expanded to provide greater security to informal workers. Better targeting with fewer gaps is key to strengthening social pensions. Furthermore, pension systems can be made more efficient and effective by adopting innovative administrative tools. Beyond expanding public pension programs, governments can do more to raise financial literacy, which enables better retirement planning.

Old-age care can be improved by transitioning from informal caregiving by families to a mixed care model. Governments must partner with the private sector and community organizations to strengthen market and community inputs into care systems. This transition will entail investing in service delivery, fostering the care economy, and offering incentives to drive efficiency. The main challenge, especially in rural areas, is to ensure that the bolstered services are both affordable and sustainable. Against a backdrop of shifting living arrangement for older people, local communities and organizations should play a greater role in helping older people age well. Greater effort is needed to remove physical barriers to social connectivity by developing age-friendly communities and cities, investing in public transport, and addressing digital divides that exclude older adults.

The four dimensions of well-being in old age are closely interconnected. Physical and mental health, work capacity, economic security, and social engagement mutually reinforce each other. Boosting one dimension can weaken another, however, as when generous pensions strengthen economic security but disincentivize work. Among the four dimensions of well-being, health stands out because it facilitates the other three. Governments must strive to design and implement well-aligned and coordinated policies to maximize policy synergy while mitigating policy discord. The private sector has an important role to play in creating age-friendly jobs, offering suitable financial products for retirement, and developing the care economy.

Promoting well-being in old age has fiscal costs, but countermeasures can help contain them. Expanding health-care and long-term care services will entail substantial fiscal costs, as will improving pension coverage and adequacy. Experience in advanced economies shows that expanded fiscal space is indispensable. Tax resource mobilization can be augmented by deploying greater fiscal effort toward generating more revenues. Public and private

investment in human capital—notably preventative and curative health care, and lifelong education—can generate big silver dividends as healthier and better educated older Asians become more productive and require less healthcare and long-term care. Retirement savings can be a significant new source of capital for productive investment that generates more economic growth and tax revenue.

Governments can do more to empower all Asians to plan and prepare for old age. They can disseminate information and raise awareness that helps workers of all ages set realistic expectations about future retirement needs, taking into account that future policies may change the retirement age and pension terms. They can also support initiatives that help firms and workers develop career plans and retirement paths in anticipation of longer working lives as well as the banning of discrimination against older workers.

Policies must be monitored and periodically updated given rapidly changing demographics and characteristics of older Asians. They must take into consideration changes in epidemiology, societal and family structures, social norms, and expectations for later years. Policies must also pay due attention to heterogeneity among older individuals in terms of gender, formal versus informal work, socioeconomic status, retirement expectations, and access to social support. The profile of older Asians changes over time, which needs to be monitored so that policy can be periodically updated to reflect these changes.

A priority is to pay special attention to the gender dimension of aging and to address the increased vulnerability of older women while meeting the unmet needs of all women to age well. Policymakers must act to reduce institutional and cultural barriers that limit women's opportunities to prepare for their old age and invest in their well-being. Governments can offer voluntary contributory pension schemes for all workers, including women, and improve the adequacy of benefits. Family caregivers, including older caregivers, must be supported through community-based initiatives. Greater efforts are needed, particularly in some of the rapidly aging economies, to increase the public provision of long-term care by building the care workforce and promoting the care economy.

One big challenge for policymakers in the region is to fill a sizable knowledge gap about aging. While there is a large and growing body of research on some aging issues, knowledge gaps persist on the dimensions of well-being of older people, as well as the characteristics and policies associated with vulnerability. The knowledge gap tends to be larger in economies with a younger demographic profile. Learning from the experiences of older economies, such as Japan and the Republic of Korea, could provide valuable lessons for other younger but rapidly aging economies. A high-priority need is to develop individual or household datasets on aging to improve policymakers' ability to assess current conditions for older people. At the same time, randomized control trials and other innovative research approaches are important tools to evaluate the benefits, effectiveness, and costs of different policy options and interventions, and to provide policymakers with useful insights on behavior and decision-making.

Early investment is key for Asia to harness its silver dividend. Future generations of older people will live healthier and longer lives and be more educated. To leverage their full potential to the benefit of their own well-being and the broader society, the time is now for Asian governments to take action to improve all four dimensions of well-being in old age. If they do this, people throughout Asia and the Pacific can aspire to live well and age well.

Background Papers

Albert, J. R. G., A. Martinez Jr., A. Kikkawa, D. Park, J. A. N. Bulan, I. Sebastian-Samaniego, G. Estrada, and M. A. Umali. 2024. *An Examination of Poverty Among Elderly in Asia and the Pacific.* Asian Development Bank.

Chen, Z. and A. Park. 2024. Understanding the Health Capacity to Work among Older Persons in Rural and Urban Areas in the People's Republic of China. *Asian Development Review.* 41(1).

Chomik, R., P. O'Keefe, and J. Piggott. 2024. *Pensions in Aging Asia: Policy Insights and Priorities.* Asian Development Bank.

Donehower, G. 2024. *Mapping the Unpaid Care Economy in the Asia-Pacific Region.* Asian Development Bank.

Ehrlich, I. and Z. Liu. 2024. *Analyzing the Sources of Households Old-Age Self-Dependency and Overall Financial Wellness in Four Major Asian Countries and the US.* Asian Development Bank.

Giang, L. T., A. Kikkawa, and D. Park. 2024. Health Capacity to Work among Older Adults in Viet Nam. *Asian Development Review.* 41(1).

Kikkawa, A., M. Pelli, L. Reiners, and D. Rhein. 2024a. *The Determinants of Well-Being of Older Persons: A Comparative Study across Developing Asia.* Asian Development Bank.

Kikkawa, A., and R. Gaspar. 2022. Trends and Characteristics of Labor Force Participation Among Older Persons in Developing Asia: Literature Review and Cross-Country Assessment. *Journal of Population Ageing.* 16.

Kikkawa A., T. Oshio, Y. Sawada. S. Shimizutani, N. Ogawa, A. Park and T. Sonobe. 2024b. Health Capacity to Work among Older Persons in Asia: Key Findings from a Regional Comparative Study. *Asian Development Review.* 41(1).

Kowal, P., Nawi. Ng, and T. Hoang. 2024. *Universal Health Coverage and Ageing in Developing Asia.* Asian Development Bank.

Lee, S-H., C-K. Park, H. K. Kim, and D. Park. 2024. Health Capacity to Work at Older Ages in the Republic of Korea. *Asian Development Review.* 41(1).

Lee, S-H. and D. Park. 2024. *Well-Being of Older Asians: An Overview.* Asian Development Bank.

Mansor, N., H. Awang, and D. Park. 2024. Health Capacity to Work among Older Malaysians. *Asian Development Review.* 41(1).

Mason, A., D. Park, and G. Estrada. 2024. *Funding Developing Asia's Old Age Needs: Challenges and Opportunities.* Asian Development Bank.

Nakajima N., A. Kikkawa, N. Mansor, and H. Awang. 2024. *Subjective Well-Being of Older Persons in Malaysia.* Asian Development Bank.

Oshio, T., S. Shimizutani, and A. Kikkawa. 2024. Health Capacity to Work among Older Japanese Persons. *Asian Development Review.* 41(1).

Rodgers, Y. V., J. E. Zveglich, K. Ali, and H. Xue. 2024. *The Role of Family Support in Elderly Well-Being: Evidence from Malaysia and Viet Nam.* Asian Development Bank.

Suriastini, N. W., I. Y. Wijayanti, and D. Oktarina. 2024. Older People's Capacity to Work in Indonesia. *Asian Development Review*. 41(1).

Zeng, Y., W. Zhenglian, M. Guo, and L. Dissanayake. 2024. *Analyses and Projections of Family Households, Living Arrangements and Home-based Care Needs for Disabled Older Adults in Sri Lanka, 2012–2060.* Asian Development Bank.

Zhao, J., C. K. Law, J. Piggott, and V. S. Yiengprugsawan. 2024. Health Capacity to Work among Older People in Thailand. *Asian Development Review*. 41(1).

References

ADB. 2019. *Asian Economic Integration Report 2019/2020: Demographic Change, Productivity, and the Role of Technology*. Asian Development Bank.

——. 2020a. *Lessons from Thailand's National Community-based Long-term Care Program for Older Persons*. Asian Development Bank.

——. 2020b. *Country Diagnostic Study on Long-Term Care in Mongolia*. Asian Development Bank.

——. 2022a. *The Road to Better Long-Term Care in Asia and the Pacific: Building Systems of Care and Support for Older Persons*. Asian Development Bank.

——. 2022b. Long-Term Care for Older People in Viet Nam: The Current Scenario, and Next Steps toward a Healthy, Aging Population. *ADB Briefs* 218. Asian Development Bank.

——. 2023a. *Key Indicators for Asia and the Pacific*. Asian Development Bank.

——. 2023b. Proceed with Care: Meeting the Human Resources Needs for Health and Aged Care in Asia and the Pacific. *ADB Briefs* 285. Asian Development Bank.

ADB and SWRC. 2023. *Malaysia Ageing and Retirement Survey Wave 2 (2021–2022): Survey Report*. Asian Development Bank and Social Wellbeing Research Centre.

Agarwal, A. K., K. J. Waddell, D. S. Small, C. Evans, T. O. Harrington, R. Djaraher, A. L. Oon, and M. S. Patel. 2021. Effect of Gamification with and without Financial Incentives to Increase Physical Activity among Veterans Classified as Having Obesity or Overweight: A Randomized Clinical Trial. *JAMA Network Open*. 4(7).

Aida T., E. Kiyota, Y. Tanaka, and Y. Sawada. 2023. Building Social Capital with Elders' Leadership through a Community Hub "Ibasho" in the Philippines and Nepal. *Scientific Reports*. 13.

Albanese, A. and B. Cockx. 2019. Permanent Wage Cost Subsidies for Older Workers: An Effective Tool for Employment Retention and Postponing Early Retirement? *Labour Economics*. 58.

Allen, J., F. Alpass, A. Szabó, and C. Stephens. 2023. Impact of Flexible Work Arrangements on Key Challenges to Work Engagement among Older Workers. *Work, Aging and Retirement*. 7(4).

Alzua, M. L., N. Cantet, A. C. Dammert, and D. Olajide. 2020. *Mental Health Effects of an Old Age Pension: Experimental Evidence for Ekiti State in Nigeria*. Conference Paper prepared for the Agricultural and Applied Economics Association Conferences 2020 Annual Meeting. Kansas, MO. 26–28 July.

Anriquez, G. and L. Stloukal. 2008. Rural Population Change in Developing Countries: Lessons for Policy Making. *European View*. 7(2).

Arriagada, P. 2020. Insights on Canadian Society: The Experiences and Needs of Older Caregivers in Canada. Statistics Canada.

Asato, W. 2021. Care Workers Migration in Ageing Asia. In Komazawa, O. and Y. Saito, eds. *Coping with Rapid Population Ageing in Asia.* Economic Research Institute for ASEAN and East Asia.

Awaliyah, S., Suhariningsih, A. R. Budiono, R. Safa'at. 2017. Law Review on Age Discrimination for Job Seekers in Indonesia. *Journal of Law, Policy and Globalization.* 63.

Bai, C-E., W. Chi, T. X. Liu, C. Tang, and J. Xu. 2021. Boosting Pension Enrollment and Household Consumption by Example: A Field Experiment on Information Provision. *Journal of Development Economics.* 150.

Bando, R., S. Galiani, and P. Gertler. 2020. The Effects of Noncontributory Pensions on Material and Subjective Well-Being. *Economic Development and Cultural Change.* 68(4).

Banerjee, A., E. Duflo, E. Grela, M. McKelway, F. Schilbach, G. Sharma, and G. Vaidyanathan. 2022. Depression and Loneliness among the Elderly Poor. *NBER Working Paper.* 30330. National Bureau for Economic Research (NBER).

Benjamins, M. R., R. A. Humer, I. W. Eberstein, and C. B. Nam. 2004. Self-Reported Health and Adult Mortality Risk: An Analysis of Cause Specific Mortality. *Social Science and Medicine.* 58.

Bertoni, M. and G. Brunello. 2021. Does a Higher Retirement Age Reduce Youth Employment? *Economic Policy.* 36(106).

Bhat, B., J. de Quidt, J. Haushofer, V. H. Patel, G. Rao, F. Schilbach, and P-L. P. Vautrey. 2022. The Long-Run Effects of Psychotherapy on Depression, Beliefs, and Economic Outcomes. *NBER Working Paper.* 30011. National Bureau for Economic Research (NBER).

Boeri, T., P. Garibaldi, and E. R. Moen. 2022. In Medio Stat Victus: Labor Demand Effects of an Increase in the Retirement Age. *Journal of Population Economics.* 35.

Bokolo, A. J. 2023. Inclusive and Safe Mobility Needs of Senior Citizens: Implications for Age-Friendly Cities and Communities. *Urban Science.* 7(4).

Boockmann, B., T. Zwick, A. Ammermüller, and M. Maier. 2012. Do Hiring Subsidies Reduce Unemployment among Older Workers? Evidence from Natural Experiments. *Journal of the European Economic Association.* 10(4).

Börsch-Supan A. and C. Coile, eds. 2021. *Social Security and Retirement Programs around the World: Reforms and Retirement Incentives.* National Bureau for Economic Research (NBER).

Brandão, D. J., L. F. Fontenelle, S. A. da Silva, P. R. Menezes, and M. Pastor-Valero. 2019. Depression and Excess Mortality in the Elderly Living in Low- and Middle-Income Countries: Systematic Review and Meta-analysis. *International Journal of Geriatric Psychiatry.* 34.

Brown, C., R. Calvi, and J. Penglase. 2021. Sharing the Pie: An Analysis of Undernutrition and Individual Consumption in Bangladesh. *Journal of Public Economics.* 200.

Bures, R. M., T. Koropeckyj-Cox, and M. Loree. 2009. Childlessness, Parenthood, and Depressive Symptoms among Middle-Aged and Older Adults. *Journal of Family Issues.* 30(5).

Burn I., D. Firoozi, D. Ladd, and D. Neumark. 2023. Stereotypes of Older Workers and Perceived Ageism in Job Ads: Evidence from an Experiment. *Journal of Pension Economics and Finance.* 22(4).

Cai, S., A. Park, and W. Yip. 2021. Time Well Spent Versus a Life Considered: Changing Subjective Well-Being in China. *Oxford Economic Papers.* 73(3).

Calvi, R. 2020. Why Are Older Women Missing in India? The Age Profile of Bargaining Power and Poverty. *Journal of Political Economy.* 128(7).

CEDEFOP. 2012. *Working and Ageing: The Benefits of Investing in an Ageing Workforce.* European Centre for the Development of Vocational Training.

Charness, N., and S. J. Czaja. 2006. Older Worker Training: What We Know and Don't Know. *ERIC.* ED530333. American Association of Retired Persons.

Chauhan, S., S. Srivastava, P. Kumar, and R. Patel. 2022. Decomposing Urban–Rural Differences in Multimorbidity among Older Adults in India: A Study Based on LASI Data. *BMC Public Health.* 22.

Chen C., G. G. Liu, Y. Sun, D. Gu, H. Zhang, H. Yang, L. Lu, Y. Zhao, and Y. Yao. 2020. Association Between Household Fuel Use and Sleep Quality in the Oldest Old. Evidence From A Propensity Score Matched Case Control Study in Hainan, China. *Environmental Research.* 191.

Chen, X., J. Giles, Y. Yao, W. Yip, Q. Meng, L. Berkman, H. Chen, et al. 2022. The Path to Healthy Aging in China: A Peking University–Lancet Commission. *The Lancet.* 400(10367).

Chen, Z., R. Peto, M. Zhou, A. Iona, M. Smith, L. Yang, Y. Guo. et al. 2015. Contrasting Male and Female Trends in Tobacco-Attributed Mortality in China: Evidence from Successive Nationwide Prospective Cohort Studies. *The Lancet.* 386(10002).

Cheung, C. K. and A. Y. H. Kwan. 2009. The Erosion of Filial Piety by Modernisation in Chinese Cities. *Ageing & Society.* 29(2).

Chomik, R., G. Yan, K. Anstey, and H. Bateman. 2022. Financial Decision Making for and in Old Age. *CEPAR Research Brief.* Australian Research Council, Centre of Excellence in Population Ageing Research (CEPAR).

Chomik, R., J. Piggott, A. Woodland, G. Kudrna, and C. Kumru. 2015. Means Testing Social Security: Modelling and Policy Analysis. *CEPAR Working Paper.* 2015/35. Australian Research Council, Centre of Excellence in Population Ageing Research (CEPAR).

Clark, W. A. V., D. Yi, and Y. Huang. 2019. Subjective Well-Being in China's Changing Society. *Proceedings of the National Academy of Sciences of the United States of America.* 116(34).

COFACE Families Europe. 2017. *Who Cares? Study on the Challenges and Needs of Family Carers in Europe.*

Coutinho, F. M, N. van Oort, Z. Christoforou, M. J. Alonso-González, O. Cats, and S. Hoogendoorn. 2020. Impacts of Replacing a Fixed Public Transport Line by a Demand Responsive Transport System: Case Study of a Rural Area in Amsterdam. *Research in Transportation Economics.* 83.

Cutler, D. M., E. Meara, and S. Richards-Shubik. 2013. *Health and Work Capacity of Older Adults: Estimates and Implications for Social Security Policy.* Social Science Research Network.

Deaton, A. 2008. Income, Health, and Well-Being around the World: Evidence from the Gallup World Poll. *Journal of Economic Perspectives.* 22(2).

Deaton, A. and C. Paxson. 1994. Intertemporal Choice and Inequality. *Journal of Political Economy* 102(3).

———. 1995. Measuring Poverty among the Elderly. *NBER Working Paper.* No. 5296. National Bureau for Economic Research (NBER).

———. 1997. *Poverty among Children and the Elderly in Developing Countries*. Research Program in Development Studies, Princeton University.

DeLuca, L., T. Toro-Ramos, A. Michaelides, E. Seng, and C. Swencionis. 2020. Relationship between Age and Weight Loss in Noom: Quasi-Experimental Study. *Journal of Medical Internet Research Diabetes*. 5(2).

Dent, E., O. R. L. Wright, J. Woo, and E. O. Hoogendijk. 2023. Malnutrition in Older Adults. *The Lancet*. 401(10380).

De Neve, J-E., G. Ward, F. De Keulenaer, B. Van Landeghem, G. Kavetsos, and M. Norton. 2018. The Asymmetric Experience of Positive and Negative Economic Growth: Global Evidence Using Subjective Well-Being Data. *Review of Economics and Statistics*. 100(2).

de Walque, D., A. Chukwuma, N. Ayivi-Guedehoussou, and M. Koshkakaryan. 2022. Invitations, Incentives, and Conditions: A Randomized Evaluation of Demand-Side Interventions for Health Screenings. *Social Science & Medicine*. 296.

Dias, A., F. Azariah, S. J. Anderson, M. Sequeira, A. Cohen, J. Q. Morse, P. Cuijpers, V. Patel, and C. F. Reynolds III. 2019. Effect of a Lay Counselor Intervention on Prevention of Major Depression in Older Adults Living in 25 Low- and Middle-Income Countries: A Randomized Clinical Trial. *JAMA Psychiatry*. 76(1).

Diener, E. D., R. A. Emmons, R. J. Larsen, and S. Griffin. 1985. The Satisfaction with Life Scale. *Journal of Personality Assessment*. 49(1).

Easterlin, R. A. 2006. Life Cycle Happiness and Its Sources: Intersections of Psychology, Economics, and Demography. *Journal of Economic Psychology*. 27(4).

Erwin, W., A. Leyva, A. Beaman, and P. M. Davidson. 2017. Health Impact of Climate Change in Older People: An Integrative Review and Implications for Nursing. *Journal of Nursing Scholarship*. 49(6).

Esteve, A., D. S. Reher, R. Treviño, P. Zueras, and A. Turu. 2020. Living Alone over the Life Course: Cross-National Variations on an Emerging Issue. *Population and Development Review*. 46.

Fakoya, O. A., N. K. McCorry, and M. Donnelly. 2020. Loneliness and Social Isolation Interventions for Older Adults: A Scoping Review of Reviews. *BMC Public Health*. 20.

Fang, H., X. Qiu, and Y. Zhang. 2022. "Growing Pains" in China's Social Security System.

Fonseca R., A. Kapteyn, J. Lee, G. Zamarro, and K. Feeney. 2013. Financial and Subjective Well-Being of Older Europeans. In Borsch-Supan A., M. Brandt, H. Litwin, and G. Weber, eds. *Active Ageing and Solidarity between Generations in Europe: First Results from SHARE after the Economic Crisis*. De Gruyter.

———. 2014. A Longitudinal Study of Well-Being of Older Europeans: Does Retirement Matter? *Journal of Population Ageing*. 7(1).

Freire, T. 2018. Wage Subsidies and the Labor Supply of Older People: Evidence from Singapore's Workfare Income Supplement Scheme. *Singapore Economic Review*. 63(05).

Frimmel, W., R. Winter-Ebmer, M. Schnalzenberger, and T. Horvath. 2018. Seniority Wages and the Roles of Firm in Retirement. *Journal of Public Economics*. 168(2).

Fritz, M. 2022. Temperature and Non-communicable Diseases: Evidence from Indonesia's Primary Health Care System. *Health Economics*. 31(11).

Giang, L. 2024. Heterogeneity in Activities of Daily Living among the Vietnamese Older Persons in 2019 and 2022: A Latent Class Analysis. *Working draft*.

Giles, J., X. Meng, S. Xue, and G. Zhao. 2021. Can information influence the social insurance participation decision of China's rural migrants? *Journal of Development Economics*. 150.

GBD 2019 Universal Health Coverage Collaborators. 2020. Measuring universal health coverage based on an index of effective coverage of health services in 204 countries and territories, 1990–2019: a systematic analysis for the Global Burden of Disease Study 2019. *The Lancet*. 396(10258).

Global Wellness Institute. 2018. *Global Wellness Economy Monitor 2018*.

Government of Japan, Ministry of Health, Labour and Welfare. 2021. *Survey Concerning the Prevention of Elder Abuse, Support for the Caregivers of the Elderly*.

Government of Singapore. SkillsFuture.

Government of Singapore, Ministry of Health. 2016. *Action Plan for Successful Ageing*.

Grossman, M. 1972. On the Concept of Health Capital and the Demand for Health. *Journal of Political Economy*. 80.

Gruber, J. and D. A. Wise, eds. 2010. *Social Security Programs and Retirement around the World: The Relationship to Youth Employment*. University of Chicago Press.

Guillemyn, I. and J. Horemans. 2023. Age-Related Differences in Job Search Behavior: Do Older Jobseekers Need a Larger Social Network? *Work, Aging and Retirement*. waad003.

Guriev, S. and N. Melnikov. 2018. Happiness Convergence in Transition Countries. *Journal of Comparative Economics*. 46(3).

Halperin, R. O., J. M. Gaziano, and H. D. Sesso. 2008. Smoking and the Risk of Incident Hypertension in Middle-Aged and Older Men. *American Journal of Hypertension*. 21(2).

Harper, S. 2023. The Implications of Climate Change for the Health of Older Adults. *Population Ageing*. 16.

Headey, B., E. Holmstrom, and A. Wearing. 1985. Models of Well-Being and Ill-Being. *Social Indicators Research*. 17(3).

Heckman, J. J. and J. A. Smith. 2004. The Determinants of Participation in a Social Program: Evidence from a Prototypical Job Training Program. *Journal of Labor Economics*. 22(2).

Helliwell, J., R. Layard, J. D. Sachs, J-E. De Neve, L. B. Aknin, and S. Wang, eds. 2023. *World Happiness Report*. Gallup, the Oxford Wellbeing Research Centre, and the United Nations Sustainable Development Solutions Network.

Hernández-Pacheco, A., A. M. Ramos, and R. C. Flores. 2022. Saving for Retirement through Consumption: An Application for Portugal. *ASFF Research Prize Submission*. Lisbon: Autoridade de Supervisão de Seguros e Fundos de Pensões.

Hinton, L., D. Tran, T. Nguyen, J. Ho, and L. Gitlin. 2019. Interventions to Support Family Caregivers of People Living with Dementia in High, Middle and Low-income Countries in Asia: A Scoping Review. *BMJ Global Health*. 4(6).

Hossain Z., M. Khanam, and A. Razzaque Sarker. 2023. Out-of-Pocket Expenditure Among Patients With Diabetes in Bangladesh: A Nation-Wide Population-Based Study. *Health Policy Open*. 13(5).

Hou, X., J. Sharma, and F. Zhao. 2023. *Silver Opportunity: Building Integrated Services for Older Adults around Primary Health Care*. World Bank.

Hu, X, X. Sun, Y. Li, Y. Gu, M. Huang, J. Wei, X. Zhen, S. Gu, and H. Dong. 2019. Potential Gains in Health-Adjusted Life Expectancy from Reducing Four Main Non-communicable Diseases among Chinese Elderly. *BMC Geriatrics*. 19(1).

Huang, B., P. J. Morgan, and N. Yoshino, eds. 2019. *Demystifying Rising Inequality in Asia*. Asian Development Bank Institute.

Huang, X., J. Liu, and A. Bo. 2020. Living Arrangements and Quality of Life among Older Adults in China: Does Social Cohesion Matter? *Aging & Mental Health.* 24(12).

Huppert, F. A. 2009. Psychological Well-Being: Evidence Regarding its Causes and Consequences. Applied Psychology: Health and Well-Being. *Applied Psychology* 1(2).

Huttunen, K., J. Pirttilä, and R. Uusitalo. 2013. The Employment Effects of Low-Wage Subsidies. *Journal of Public Economics.* 97.

Ichimura, H., X. Lei, C. Lee, J. Lee, A. Park, and Y. Sawada. 2017. Wellbeing of the Elderly in East Asia: China, Korea, and Japan. *RIETI Discussion Paper Series.* 17-E-029. Research Institute of Economy, Trade and Industry (RIETI).

Ide, K., S. Jeong, T. Tsuji, R. Watanabe, Y. Miyaguni, H. Nakamura, M. Kimura, and K. Kondo. 2022. Suggesting Indicators of Age-Friendly City: Social Participation and Happiness, An Ecological Study from the JAGES. *International Journal of Environmental Research and Public Health.* 19.

IOPS. 2006. *Principles of Private Pension Supervision.* Organisation for Economic Co-operation and Development.

ISSA. 2019. *Good Governance Guidelines for Social Security Institutions.* International Social Security Association.

Jansen, A., M. Höchner, H. Schulze, and M. Zölch. 2019. Does Workplace Flexibility Help to Retain Older Workers in Their Career Jobs up to and beyond Retirement Age? A Qualitative Study in the Knowledge-Intensive Sector in Switzerland. *Die Unternehmung.* 73(3).

Jeet G., J. S. Thakur, S. Prinja, and M. Singh. 2017. Community Health Workers for Non-communicable Diseases Prevention and Control in Developing Countries: Evidence and Implications. *PLoS One.* 12(7).

Jeon, G. S., S. N. Jang, S. J. Rhee, I. Kawachi, and S. I. Cho. 2007. Gender Differences in Correlates of Mental Health among Elderly Koreans. *The Journals of Gerontology Series B: Psychological Sciences and Social Sciences.* 62(5).

Jha, P. and R. Peto. 2014. Global Effects of Smoking, of Quitting, and of Taxing Tobacco. *New England Journal of Medicine.* 370(1).

Jiang, M., G. Yang, L. Fang, J. Wan, Y. Yang, and Y. Wang. 2018. Factors Associated with Healthcare Utilization among Community-Dwelling Elderly in Shanghai, China. *PLoS ONE.* 13(12).

Jull, J. 2010. Seniors Caring for Seniors: Examining the Literature on Injuries and Contributing Factors Affecting the Health and Well-Being of Older Adult Caregivers. Canada Association of Occupational Therapists.

Kahneman, D. and A. B. Krueger. 2006. Developments in the Measurement of Subjective Well-Being. *Journal of Economic Perspectives.* 20(1).

Kalemli-Ozcan, S. and D. N. Weil. 2010. Mortality Change, the Uncertainty Effect, and Retirement. *Journal of Economic Growth.* 15(1).

Kalwij, A., A. Kapteyn, and K. de Vos. 2010. Retirement of Older Workers and Employment of the Young. *De Economist.* 158.

Kaselitz, E, G. K. Rana, and M. Heisler. 2017. Public Policies and Interventions for Diabetes in Latin America: a Scoping Review. *Current Diabetes Reports.* 17(8).

Kelly, M. E., H. Duff, S. Kelly, J. E. McHugh Power, S. Brennan, B. A. Lawlor, and D. G. Loughrey. 2017. The Impact of Social Activities, Social Networks, Social Support and Social Relationships on the Cognitive Functioning of Healthy Older Adults: A Systematic Review. *Systematic Reviews.* 6(1).

Kemperman, A., P. van den Berg, M. Weijs-Perrée, and K. Uijtdewillegen. 2019. Loneliness of Older Adults: Social Network and the Living Environment. *International Journal of Environmental Research and Public Health.* 16(3).

Kim, K. and H. Mitra. 2022. Dynamics of Health and Labor Income in Korea. *Journal of Economics of Ageing.* 21.

Kim, S. H., B. Cho, C. W. Won, Y. H. Hong, and K. Y. Son. 2017. Self-reported health status as a predictor of functional decline in a community-dwelling elderly population: Nationwide longitudinal survey in Korea. *Geriatric Gerontology International.* 17(6).

Klapper, L., A. Lusardi, and P. Van Oudheusden. 2015. *Financial Literacy around the World.* World Bank.

Kondo, A. 2016. Effects of Increased Elderly Employment on Other Workers' Employment and Elderly's Earnings in Japan. *IZA Journal Labor Policy.* 5(2).

Kowal, P., B. Corso, K. Anindya, F. C. D. Andrade, T. L. Giang, M. T. C. Gutierrez, W. Pothisiri et al. 2023. Prevalence of Unmet Health Care Need in Older Adults in 83 Countries: Measuring Progress towards Universal Health Coverage in the Context of Global Population Ageing. *Population Health Metrics.* 21.

Kudrna, G. 2016. Economy-Wide Effects of Means-Tested Pensions: The Case of Australia. *Journal of the Economics of Ageing.* 7.

Kudrna, G., C. Tran, and A. Woodland. 2019. Facing Demographic Challenges: Pension Cuts or Tax Hikes? *Macroeconomic Dynamics.* 23(2).

———. 2022. Sustainable and Equitable Pensions with Means Testing in Aging Economies. *European Economic Review.* 141.

Kudrna, G., T. Le, and J. Piggott. 2020. Review Report on Demographics, Labour Force and Older People in Indonesia. *CEPAR Working Paper.* 2020/27. Australian Research Council, Centre of Excellence in Population Ageing Research (CEPAR).

Kumru, C. S. and J. Piggott. 2010. Should Public Retirement Pensions Be Means-Tested. *DEGIT Conference Papers* No. 049. Dynamics, Economic Growth, and International Trade. (DEGIT)

Kwak, D. W. and J-W. Lee. 2024. Impact of Retirement and Re-employment on the Life Satisfaction of Older Adults in Korea. *CAMA Working Paper* 14/2024. Crawford School of Public Policy, Australian National University.

Lai, W., S. Li, Y. Li, and X. Tian. 2022. Air Pollution and Cognitive Functions: Evidence from Straw Burning in China. *American Journal of Agricultural Economics.* 104(1).

Lee, J-W, J-S. Han, and E. Song. 2019. The Effects and Challenges of Vocational Training in Korea. *International Journal of Training Research* 17 (Supplementary 1).

Lee, J-W., D. W. Kwak, and E. Song. 2022. Can Older Workers Stay Productive? The Role of ICT Skills and Training. *Journal of Asian Economics.* 79.

Lee, S-H., J. Kim, and D. Park. 2017. Demographic Change and Fiscal Sustainability in Asia. *Social Indicators Research.* 134.

Leong, K. S. 2020. *Older Adults' Perspective of an Intergenerational Programme at Senior Day Care Centre: A Descriptive Qualitative Study.* National University of Singapore.

Levasseur, M., J. Desrosiers, and D. St-Cyr Tribble. 2008. Do Quality of Life, Participation and Environment of Older Adults Differ according to Level of Activity? *Health Quality Life Outcomes.* 6(30).

Levine, S., E. Malone, A. Lekiachvili, and P. Briss. 2019. Health Care Industry Insights: Why the Use of Preventive Services Is Still Low. *Preventing Chronic Disease.* 16.

Leyva, E., A. Beaman, and P. Davidson. 2017. Health Impact of Climate Change in Older People: An Integrative Review and Implications for Nursing. *Journal of Nursing Scholarship.* 49.

Li, J., Y. Yao, W. Xie, B. Wang, T. Guan, Y. Han, H. Wang, T. Zhu, and T. Xue. 2021. Association of Long-Term Exposure to PM2.5 with Blood Lipids in the Chinese Population: Findings from a Longitudinal Quasi-experiment. *Environment International.* 151.

Li X, X. Feng, X. Sun, N. Hou, F. Han, and Y. Liu. 2022. Global, Regional, and National Burden of Alzheimer's Disease and Other Dementias, 1990-2019. *Front in Aging Neuroscience.* 14.

Liu Y., X. Chen, and Z. Yan. 2020. Depression in the House: The Effects of Household Air Pollution from Solid Fuel Use among the Middle Aged and Older Population in China. *Science of the Total Environment.* 703.

Lusardi, A., and O. S. Mitchell. 2011. Financial Literacy around the World: An Overview. *Journal of Pension Economics & Finance.* 10(4).

MAFF. 2021. *The Statistical Yearbook of MAFF.* Government of Japan, Ministry of Agriculture, Forestry and Fisheries (MAFF).

Marmamula, S., T. R. Kumbham, S. B. Modepalli, N. R. Barrenkala, R. Yellapragada, and R. Shidhaye. 2021. Depression Combined Visual and Hearing Impairment (Dual Sensory Impairment): A Hidden Multi-morbidity among the Elderly in Residential Care in India. *Scientific Reports.* 11.

Marques, S., J. Mariano, J. Mendonça, W. De Tavernier, M. Hess, L. Naegele, F. Peixeiro, and D. Martins. 2020. Determinants of Ageism against Older Adults: A Systematic Review. *International Journal of Environmental Research and Public Health.* 17(7).

Maruyama, S. 2015. The Effect of Coresidence on Parental Health in Japan. *Journal of Japanese and International Economies.* 35.

Mayor, S. 2016. Quitting Smoking Reduces Mortality at Any Age, Study of Over 70s Finds. *BMJ.* 355.

Mikkelsen, A. S. B., S. Petersen, A. C. Dragsted, and M. Kristiansen. 2019. Social Interventions Targeting Social Relations among Older People at Nursing Homes: A Qualitative Synthesized Systematic Review. *The Journal of Health Care Organization, Provision, and Financing.* 56.

Milligan, K. and D. A. Wise. 2011. Social Security and Retirement around the World: Historical Trends in Mortality and Health, Employment, and Disability Insurance Participation and Reforms—Introduction and Summary. *NBER Working Paper.* 16719. National Bureau for Economic Research (NBER).

———. 2015. Health and Work at Older Ages: Using Mortality to Assess the Capacity to Work across Countries. *Journal of Population Ageing.* 8(1-2).

Mitra S., Q. Gao, W. Chen, and Y. Zhang. 2020. Health, Work, and Income among Middle-Aged and Older Adults: A Panel Analysis for China. *The Journal of Economics of Ageing.* 17.

Mori K., K. Odagami, M. Inagaki, K. Moriya, H. Fujiwara, and H. Eguchi. 2024. Work Engagement among Older Workers: A Systematic Review. *Journal of Occupational Health.* 66(1).

Mossey, J. N. and E. Shapiro. 1982. Self-Reported Health: A Predictor of Mortality among the Elderly. *American Journal of Public Health.* 72.

Munnell, A. H. and A. Y. Wu. 2012. Will Delayed Retirement by the Baby Boomers Lead to Higher Unemployment Among Younger Workers? *CRR Working Paper.* 2012-22. Center for Retirement Research at Boston College.

Murray, C. J. L., A. Y. Aravkin, P. Zheng, C. Abbafati, K. M. Abbas, M. Abbasi-Kangevari, F. Abd-Allah, et al. 2020. Global burden of 87 risk factors in 204 countries and territories, 1990–2019: a systematic analysis for the Global Burden of Disease Study 2019. *The Lancet.* 396(10258).

Nakagomi, A., T. Tsuji, M. Saito, K. Ide, K. Kondo, and K. Shiba. 2023. Social Isolation and Subsequent Health and Well-being in Older Adults: A Longitudinal Outcome-wide Analysis. *Social Science & Medicine.* 327.

NAP. 2020. *Social Isolation and Loneliness in Older Adults: Opportunities for the Health Care System.* National Academies of Sciences, Engineering, and Medic and National Academies Press.

Niu, G., Y. Zhou, and H. Gan. 2020. Financial Literacy and Retirement Preparation in China. *Pacific-Basic Finance Journal.* 59.

Notthoff, N. and L. L. Carstensen. 2014. Positive Messaging Promotes Walking in Older Adults. *Psychology and Aging.* 29(2).

OECD. 2011. *How's Life? Measuring Well-Being.* Organisation for Economic Co-operation and Development.

———. 2013. *OECD Employment Outlook 2013.* Organisation for Economic Co-operation and Development.

———. 2016. *OECD Core Principles of Private Pension Fund Regulation.* Organisation for Economic Co-operation and Development.

———. 2018a. *Working Better with Age: Korea. Ageing and Employment Policies.* Organisation for Economic Co-operation and Development.

———. 2018b. *Working Better with Age: Japan. Ageing and Employment Policies.* Organisation for Economic Co-operation and Development.

———. 2019a. *Smarter Financial Education: Key Lessons from Behavioural Insights for Financial Literacy Initiatives.* Organisation for Economic Co-operation and Development.

———. 2019b. *Working Better with Age.* Organisation for Economic Co-operation and Development.

———. 2020a. *A Large Potential for the Future. Promoting an Age-Inclusive Workforce: Living, Learning and Earning Longer.* Organisation for Economic Co-operation and Development.

———. 2020b. *How's Life? 2020 Measuring Well-Being.* Organisation for Economic Co-operation and Development.

———. 2020c. *OECD Recommendation on Financial Literacy.* Organisation for Economic Co-operation and Development.

———. 2021a. Health for the People, by the People: Building People-Centered Health Systems. *OECD Health Policy Studies.* Organisation for Economic Co-operation and Development.

———. 2021b. *OECD/INFE Report on Financial Literacy and Resilience in APEC Economies.* Organisation for Economic Co-operation and Development.

———. 2023. *Health at a Glance 2023: OECD Indicators.* Organisation for Economic Co-operation and Development.

Ogawa, N. and R. D. Retherford. 1993. Care of the Elderly in Japan: Changing Norms and Expectations. *Journal of Marriage and the Family.* 55(3).

Ohtake, F. and M. Saito. 1998. Population Aging and Consumption Inequality in Japan. *Review of Income and Wealth.* 44(3).

Oshio, T., E. Usui, and S. Shimizutani. 2020. Labor Force Participation of the Elderly in Japan. In Coile C., K. Milligan, and D. A. Wise, eds. *Social Security Programs and Retirement around the World: Working Longer.* University of Chicago Press.

Pardoel, Z., S. A. Reijneveld, R. Lensink, M. Postma, T. B. Thuy, N. C. Viet, L. N. T. Phuong, J. A. R. Koot, and J. J. A. Landsman. 2023. The Implementation of Community-Based Programs in Vietnam Is Promising in Promoting Health. *Frontiers in Public Health.* 11.

Park, D., P. Quising, G. Bodeker, M. Helble, I. Qureshi, and S. Tian, eds. 2021. *Wellness for a Healthy Asia.* Asian Development Bank.

Patel, V., B. Weobong, H. A. Weiss, A. Anand, B. Bhat, B. Katti, S. Dimidjian, R. Araya, et al. 2017. The Healthy Activity Program (HAP), a Lay Counsellor-Delivered Brief Psychological Treatment for Severe Depression, in Primary Care in India: A Randomised Controlled Trial. *The Lancet.* 389 (10065).

Paudel, J. 2021. *Plight of the Elderly: Senior Citizen Allowances and Gender Disparities in Economic and Behavioral Outcomes.* Boise State University.

Picchio, M., and J. C. van Ours. 2013. Retaining through Training Even for Older Workers. *Economics of Education Review.* 32(1).

Plouffe, L. and A. Kalache. 2010. Towards Global Age-Friendly Cities: Determining Urban Features that Promote Active Aging. *Journal of Urban Health.* 87(5).

Rahaman, M., P. Chouhan, A. Roy, M. J. Rana, and K. C. Das 2022. Examining the Predictors of Healthcare Facility Choice for Outpatient Care among Older Adults in India Using Andersen's Revised Healthcare Utilization Framework Model. *BMC Geriatrics.* 22.

Reher, D. and M. Requena. 2018. Living Alone in Later Life: A Global Perspective. *Population and Development Review.* 44(3).

Reinwarth, A. C., F. S. Wicke, N. Hettich, M. Ernst, D. Otten, E. Brähler, P. S. Wild, et al. 2023. Self-Rated Physical Health Predicts Mortality in Aging Persons Beyond Objective Health Risks. *Scientific Reports.* 13.

Ridley, M., G. Rao, F. Schilbach, and V. Patel. 2020. Poverty, Depression, and Anxiety: Causal Evidence and Mechanisms. *Science.* 370(6522).

Saha, A., B. Mandal, T. Muhammad, and W. Ali. 2024. Decomposing the Rural–Urban Differences in Depression among Multimorbid Older Patients in India: Evidence From a Cross-Sectional Study. *BMC Psychiatry.* 24(1).

Schaan, B. 2013. Widowhood and Depression among Older Europeans—The Role of Gender, Caregiving, Marital Quality, and Regional Context. *Journals of Gerontology Series B: Psychological Sciences and Social Sciences.* 68(3).

Seoul Metropolitan Government. 2019. *Seoul's Age-Friendly City Project.*

Shoghik, H., M. Montalva-Talledo, V. Sonia, T. Remick, C. Rodriguez-Castelan, and K. Stamm. 2022. Global Job Quality: Evidence from Wage Employment across Developing Countries. *Policy Research Working Paper.* WPS 10134. World Bank.

Someya Y., and C. T. Hayashida. 2022. The Past, Present and Future Direction of Government-Supported Active Aging Initiatives in Japan: A Work in Progress. *Social Sciences.* 11(2).

Song, C. 2020. Financial Illiteracy and Pension Contributions: A Field Experiment on Compound Interest in China. *Review of Financial Studies.* 33(2).

Sorensen, R. J. D., R. M. Barber, D. M. Pigott, A. Carter, C. N. Spencer, S. M. Ostroff, R. C. Reiner, Jr., et al. 2022. Variation in the Covid-19 Infection–Fatality Ratio by Age, Time, and Geography During the Pre-Vaccine Era: A Systematic Analysis. *The Lancet.* 399(10334).

Srisompun, O., T. Charoenrat, and N. Thipayanet. 2014. *Final Report on the Project of Production and Marketing Structures of Thai Jasmine Rice.* Khonkaen: Thailand Research Fund.

Steffens, D. C. 2017. Late-Life Depression and the Prodromes of Dementia. *JAMA Psychiatry*. 74(7).

Sun, S., J. Chen, M. Johannesson, P. Kind, and K. Burström. 2016. Subjective Well-Being and Its Association with Subjective Health Status, Age, Sex, Region, and Socio-economic Characteristics in a Chinese Population Study. *Journal of Happiness Studies*. 17.

Szanton, S. L., R. J. Thorpe, C. Boyd, E. K. Tanner, B. Leff, E. Agree, Q-L. Xue, et al. 2011. Community Aging in Place, Advancing Better Living for Elders: a Bio-Behavioral-Environmental Intervention to Improve Function and Health-Related Quality of Life in Disabled Older Adults. *Journal of the American Geriatrics Society*. 59(12).

Tanaka, T., J. Yamasaki, Y. Sawada, and K. Dovchinsuren. Forthcoming. Barriers to Saving for Retirement: Evidence from a Public Pension Program in Mongolia. *Journal of Political Economy: Microeconomics*.

Teerawichitchainan, B., W. Pothisiri, and G. T. Long. 2015. How Do Living Arrangements and Intergenerational Support Matter for Psychological Health of Elderly Parents? Evidence from Myanmar, Vietnam, and Thailand. *Social Science & Medicine*. 136.

Thom, S., P. Aggarwal, G. May, J. McDonnell, and C. Price. 2023. As Asia-Pacific Ages, a Caregiver Crisis Looms. *Article*. 18 July. Boston Consulting Group.

Thornicroft, G., S. Chatterji, S. Evans-Lacko, M. Gruber, N. Sampson, S. Aguilar-Gaxiola, A. Al-Hamzawi, et al. 2017. Undertreatment of People with Major Depressive Disorder in 21 Countries. *British Journal of Psychiatry: The Journal of Mental Science*. 210(2).

Tokyo Metropolitan Government. 2018. *10-Year Plan for an Age-Friendly City*.

Townsend, B. G., J. T.-H. Chen, and V. M. Wuthrich. 2021. Barriers and Facilitators to Social Participation in Older Adults: A Systematic Literature Review. *Clinical Gerontologist*. 44(4).

UN. 2021. *Voluntary National Survey on the Implementation of the Madrid International Plan of Action on Ageing (MIPAA) in Asia and the Pacific*. United Nations.

UNESCAP. 2022a. *Asia-Pacific Report on Population Ageing 2022*. United Nations Economic and Social Commission for Asia and the Pacific.

———. 2022b. COVID-19 and Older Persons in the Asia-Pacific Region: The Health, Social and Economic Impacts of a Global Pandemic. *Policy Paper*. United Nations Economic and Social Commission for Asia and the Pacific.

———. Dashboard of National Policies on Aging. United Nations Economic and Social Commission for Asia and the Pacific.

UN Women. Facts and Figures: Ending Violence against Women and Girls.

van Hoof, J., H. R. Marston, and J. K. Kazak. 2021. Ten Questions Concerning Age-Friendly Cities and Communities and the Built Environment. *Building and Environment*. 199.

van Rijn, R. M., S. J. W. Robroek, S. Brouwe, and A. Burdorf. 2014. Influence of Poor Health on Exit from Paid Employment: A Systematic Review. *Occupational and Environmental Medicine*. 71.

Vipin, A., V. Satish, S. E. Saffari, W. Koh, L. Lim, E. Silva, M. M. Nyu, et al. 2021. Dementia in Southeast Asia: Influence of Onset-Type, Education, and Cerebrovascular Disease. *Alzheimer's Research & Therapy*. 13.

Wang, D. and J. Feng. 2022. China's Pension Reform: Progress, Challenges, and Prospects. *Mimeo*. World Bank Beijing Office.

Wang, Y. and W. Yang. 2021. Does Receiving Informal Care Lead to Better Health Outcomes? Evidence From China Longitudinal Healthy Longevity Survey. *Sage Journals.* 44(7-8).

Watkins, D., S. Ahmed, and S. Pickersgill. 2024. Priority Setting for NCD Control and Health System Investments, in Unlocking the Power of Healthy Longevity: Compendium of Research for the Healthy Longevity Initiatives. World Bank.

Whitehouse, E. 2012. Policies to Encourage Private Pension Savings: Evidence from OECD Countries. In Hinz, R., R. Holzmann, D. Tuesta, and N. Takayama, eds. *Matching Contributions for Pensions: A Review of International Experience.* World Bank.

WHO. 1948. *Constitution.* World Health Organization.

———. 2007. *Global Age-Friendly Cities: A Guide.* World Health Organization.

———. 2017. *Global strategy and action plan on ageing and health.* World Health Organization.

———. 2021a. *Global Report on Ageism.* World Health Organization.

———. 2021b. *Social Isolation and Loneliness.* World Health Organization.

———. 2022. *Abuse of Older People.* World Health Organization.

———. 2023. Mental health of older adults. *Newsroom.* 20 October. World Health Organization.

World Bank. 2015. *World Bank East Asia and Pacific Regional Report: Live Long and Prosper: Aging in East Asia and Pacific.*

———. 2021a. *Aging and the Labor Market in Thailand.*

———. 2021b. The Global Findex Database: Financial Inclusion, Digital Payments, and Resilience in the Age of COVID-19.

Wu, B. 2020. Social Isolation and Loneliness among Older Adults in the Context of COVID-19: A Global Challenge. *Global Health Research and Policy.* 5(1).

Yang J. J., D. Yu, W. Wen, X-O. Shu, E. Saito, S. Rahman, P. C. Gupta, et al. 2019. Tobacco Smoking and Mortality in Asia: A Pooled Meta-analysis. *JAMA Network Open.* 2 (3).

Yang Y. 2006. How Does Functional Disability Affect Depressive Symptoms in Late Life? The Role of Perceived Social Support and Psychological Resources. *Journal of Health Social Behavior.* 47(4).

Yao, Y., X. Lv, C. Qiu, J. Li, X. Wu, H. Zhang, D. Yue, et al. 2022. The Effect of China's Clean Air Act on Cognitive Function in Older Adults: A Population-Based, Quasi-experimental Study. *The Lancet Healthy Longevity.* 3(2).

Yap, B., N. Chong, D. R. Krishnan, N. N. A. Hazis, and C. Ng. 2023. Encouraging Retirement Savings in Malaysia: A Behavioural Perspective. *Staff Discussion Paper.* Securities Commission Malaysia.

Ye, X., D. Zhu, S. Chen, X. Shi, R. Gong, J. Wang, H. Zuo, and P. He. 2022. Effects of Providing Free Hearing Aids on Multiple Health Outcomes among Middle-Aged and Older Adults with Hearing Loss in Rural China: A Randomized Controlled Trial. *BMC Medicine.* 20(124).

Yon, Y., C. Mikton, Z. D. Gassoumis, and K. H. Wilber. 2017. Elder Abuse Prevalence in Community Settings: A Systematic Review and Meta-Analysis. *The Lancet.* 5.

Yu, X., X. Lei, and M. Wang. 2019. Temperature Effects on Mortality and Household Adaptation: Evidence from China. *Journal of Environmental Economics and Management.* 96.

Zhou Y-F., X-Y. Song, A. Pan, and W-P. Koh. 2023. Nutrition and Healthy Ageing in Asia: A Systematic Review. *Nutrients.*15(14).

Projected Impact of Population Aging on Asia's Future Growth

Population aging is one of the biggest structural challenges facing developing Asia. The region has grown faster than the rest of the world for decades. One factor contributing to its remarkable economic success has been a demographic dividend from a youthful population. More recently, though, the region's population has started to age. An immediate question is how the changing demographic landscape will affect regional economic growth in the future. More than 10 years ago, Park and Shin (2012) projected the impact of demographic transition on economic growth in 12 major economies in developing Asia in 2011–2020 and 2021–2030. The time has come to update age structures in these economies and check the validity of earlier forecasts. Equally important is to extend the forecast horizon. Park and Shin (2023) thus projected the impact of demographic changes on growth in the 12 economies in 2021–2030, 2031–2040, and 2041–2050.

Population aging affects economic growth through a smaller working age population and a number of other channels (Lee and Hong 2012; Lee and Shin 2021). The projection uses the latest data to estimate, as in Park and Shin (2012), the impact of two key demographic variables—old-age dependency ratio and youth dependency ratio—on four key determinants of economic growth: labor hours per capita, total factor productivity growth, physical capital accumulation, and human capital accumulation.

Two significant changes from the Park and Shin (2012) analysis improved the accuracy of the projections. First, the previous study used labor force participation as the first determinant, but the 2023 follow-up study used labor hours, defined as hours worked divided by the whole population, which provided a more accurate measure of labor input. Second, whereas the previous study simply borrowed estimates made in Lee and Francisco (2012), the follow-up study estimated the impact of demographic variables on the fourth determinant, human capital accumulation.

Based on the new estimates, projections are done on the effect of dependency ratios on the determinants of growth in the next 3 decades. Separate projections were done for labor hours per capita and human capital accumulation. However, for the determination of total factor productivity and physical capital accumulation, Park and Shin (2012) followed Lee and Hong (2012) by combining a third equation of savings rate determination and taking a simultaneous-equation approach to jointly estimate the three equations. This approach generated estimates of the impact of the two demographic variables on total factor productivity growth as well as their direct and indirect impacts on physical capital. The indirect impact is the effect of the two demographic variables on physical capital accumulation through a change in the savings rate. Summing up the projected impacts of the two demographic variables on the four determinants of growth, including both direct and indirect impacts on capital accumulation, yields the projected impact on gross domestic product (GDP) growth per capita.

From empirical results, projections about the impact of demographic change on future GDP growth per capita are drawn up for 12 Asian economies. The annex table reports projections for 2031–2040. Please refer to Park and Shin (2023) for projections for 2021–2030 and 2041–2050, as well as for a comprehensive description of methodology. Demographic change affects growth through four channels: (i) labor hours per capita, (ii) total factor productivity, (iii) capital accumulation, and (iv) human capital. The third channel is further divided into direct and indirect impacts through the savings rate.

Consider as an example the Republic of Korea. Combining the impact of the four channels, the collective impact of the change in the youth dependency ratio reduces GDP growth per capita by 0.11 percentage points. The impact of the change in the old-age dependency ratio is to reduce GDP growth per capita by 0.32 percentage points. Overall, demographic change reduces GDP growth per capita by 0.43 percentage points in 2020–2030. Repeating the same exercise for the other 11 economies estimates the impact of demographic change on their GDP growth per capita.

Overall, economies in the region with older populations, such as the Republic of Korea, are projected to see a sizable demographic correction. In economies in the middle of the demographic transition, such as the People's Republic of China and Viet Nam, a small demographic dividend or otherwise will turn into a tangible correction. Finally, younger economies such as India and Indonesia will continue to enjoy sizable dividends, albeit dwindling ones. Overall, the analysis resoundingly confirms the conventional wisdom that the demographic tailwinds that helped propel developing Asia's past economic growth will turn into demographic headwinds in the coming decades. The analysis also yields quantitative estimates that point to the significant impact of demographic change on the region's future growth. However, promoting the well-being of older Asians, in particular their health, can significantly increase their capacity to work. This additional work capacity can contribute tangibly to regional economic growth.

References

Lee, J.-W. and R. Francisco. 2012. Human Capital Accumulation in Emerging Asia, 1970–2030. *Japan & the World Economy.* 24(2).

Lee, J.-W. and K. Hong. 2012. Economic Growth in Asia: Determinants and Prospects. *Japan & the World Economy.* 24(2).

Lee, H.-H. and K. Shin. 2021. Decomposing Effects of Population Aging on Economic Growth in OECD Countries. *Asian Economic Papers.* 20(3).

Park, D. and K. Shin. 2012. Impact of Population Aging on Asia's Future Growth. In Park D., S.-H. Lee, and A. Mason, eds. *Aging, Economic Growth, and Old-Age Security in Asia. Edward Elgar Publishing* and Asian Development Bank.

———. 2023. Impact of Population Aging on Asia's Future Economic Growth, 2021–50. *Asian Development Review.* 40(1).

Annex Table: The Projected Impact of Aging on Economic Growth of 12 Asian Economies, 2031–2040

	Variable (dependency ratio)	Labor Force/ Population	Human Capital	Total Factor Productivity	Physical Capital/Labor Hours		Total
					Indirect, through Savings	Direct	
Hong Kong, China	Youth	0.050	0.009	0.005	0.004	−0.003	0.066
	Old age	−0.103	0.009	−0.053	−0.089	0.045	−0.191
India	Youth	0.164	0.030	0.018	0.014	−0.008	0.219
	Old age	−0.028	0.002	−0.015	−0.024	0.012	−0.053
Indonesia	Youth	0.129	0.021	0.014	0.013	−0.007	0.170
	Old age	−0.049	0.004	−0.025	−0.047	0.024	−0.094
Malaysia	Youth	0.219	0.031	0.024	0.024	−0.014	0.284
	Old age	−0.038	0.002	−0.020	−0.042	0.021	−0.076
Pakistan	Youth	0.398	0.084	0.044	0.029	−0.017	0.538
	Old age	−0.012	0.001	−0.006	−0.008	0.004	−0.021
People's Republic of China	Youth	0.020	0.004	0.002	0.002	−0.001	0.027
	Old age	−0.118	0.011	−0.061	−0.088	0.044	−0.211
Philippines	Youth	0.174	0.031	0.019	0.016	−0.009	0.231
	Old age	−0.027	0.002	−0.014	−0.024	0.012	−0.050
Republic of Korea	Youth	−0.080	−0.015	−0.009	−0.007	0.004	−0.106
	Old age	−0.174	0.015	−0.089	−0.151	0.076	−0.323
Singapore	Youth	0.035	0.005	0.004	0.004	−0.002	0.046
	Old age	−0.124	0.009	−0.064	−0.125	0.063	−0.241
Taipei,China	Youth	−0.035	−0.008	−0.004	−0.002	0.001	−0.048
	Old age	−0.113	0.012	−0.058	−0.071	0.036	−0.195
Thailand	Youth	0.020	0.004	0.002	0.001	−0.001	0.027
	Old age	−0.118	0.012	−0.061	−0.077	0.039	−0.204
Viet Nam	Youth	0.209	0.044	0.023	0.015	−0.009	0.282
	Old age	−0.061	0.006	−0.031	−0.045	0.022	−0.109

Source: Park and Shin (2023).